Case Study Research

Case Study Research

What, Why and How?

Peter G. Swanborn

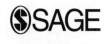

Los Angeles | London | New Delhi
Singapore | Washington DC

First published 2010
Reprinted 2010

SAGE Publications Ltd
1 Oliver's Yard
55 City Road
London EC1Y 1SP

SAGE Publications Inc.
2455 Teller Road
Thousand Oaks, California 91320

SAGE Publications India Pvt Ltd
B 1/I 1 Mohan Cooperative Industrial Area
Mathura Road, New Delhi 110 044
India

SAGE Publications Asia-Pacific Pte Ltd
33 Pekin Street #02-01
Far East Square
Singapore 048763

Library of Congress Control Number: 2009935548

British Library Cataloguing in Publication data

A catalogue record for this book is available from
the British Library

ISBN 978-1-84920-611-2
ISBN 978-1-84920-612-9 (pbk)

Typeset by C&M Digitals (P) Ltd, Chennai, India
Printed in the UK by the MPG Books Group
Printed on paper from sustainable resources

Mixed Sources
Product group from well-managed
forests and other controlled sources
www.fsc.org Cert no. SA-COC-1565
© 1996 Forest Stewardship Council

Contents

Preface

What is a case study? How should cases be selected? How do case study results compare to those of a survey? Is case study methodology fundamentally different from the methodology of more extensive methods? What, in fact, is a case? These are questions with which many social researchers, certainly those in the fields of applied research, are confronted.

The ideas in the present book are largely based on experience with case studies in sociology and educational research. Case study methodology constitutes a difficult and confusing field because many research traditions use the same expression, 'case study'.[1] The majority of publications are restricted to one of those traditions, and a world of difference exists, for instance, between case studies in traditional anthropology and, say, Yin's work, which focuses on changes in organisations.

In this book, case study methodology is posited in a general methodological framework. This may help researchers from different backgrounds in their understanding of case study research. It is not a book of recipes for data collection. For suggestions in this respect, the reader can use many handbooks, depending on the kind of research (s)he has in mind. I have tried to keep the text itself as concise as possible. Links to relevant literature are mentioned in footnotes. Some frequently cited sources are also commented upon in the footnotes, and a few historical debates are briefly summarised. The boxes in the chapters serve a double purpose: sometimes they contain an example; sometimes they contain a not-necessary-but-useful elaboration of the main text.

This is not a handbook on 'qualitative methods'. A case study usually contains qualitative as well as quantitative elements, and many other subjects may be arranged under the flag of 'qualitative methods', such as in-depth interviewing, qualitative content analysis of texts, films, photographs, videotapes and emails, narrative analysis, conversation analysis, unstructured observation and most historical methods.

This book may be used in many methodology courses, but it concentrates on the graduate level. It will also be useful in Master's courses that put a strong emphasis on quantitative research, especially those courses where nowadays, unfortunately, computerised analysis of survey data files seems to be the core content of methodology education. The text is also meant to offer a helping hand for PhD students and researchers in the field who wish to make a responsible choice between research strategies.

---

[1] To get picture, try 'Googling' with the term 'case studies' or even 'case studies, social sciences'!

It can be supplemented by e-learning, such as downloaded (summaries of) recent case studies selected according to the specific discipline of interest, such as education, health or business. Used in this way, the book offers a ready-to-use set of questions with which to examine a selected case study. Finally, the book makes the case for a more extensive use of case studies, and in doing so concurs with developments in actual social research.

If we sketch out the phases of a social research project in terms of the well-known sequence of deciding the research question, design, data collection, data analysis and communicating results in a report, Chapters 2 and 3 and in part also Chapters 4 and 5, may be categorised under the 'design' heading. This already illustrates that design features are central in this book.

In Chapter 2 we tackle the 'when to do a case study?' question. As the answer to this question is highly dependent on the research question, ample space is devoted to the topic of phrasing the research question(s). Clarity in this respect is a necessity for the success of a research project.

In Chapter 3, we address the second important problem – which cases to select. The choice of these cases has to be justified, of course, in order to validly answer the research question.

The phase of data collection is discussed in Chapter 4, where the usefulness of theoretical ideas to guide the selection of concepts and variables is emphasised.

Chapter 5 examines several approaches for enriching the information, that is, increasing the number of 'degrees of freedom', contained in the data. The most important approaches deal with extending the number of observation points in time, and working with sub-units within the case.

Chapter 6 is devoted to the analysis of the data, with a view to resolving the research question(s). Several distinct traditions are discussed. The use of theories holds a far more central position in this text than in most publications on this topic.

Finally, in Chapter 7 several remaining topics, such as styles of reporting, the use of mixed methods and meta-analysis, are discussed.

Methodological distinctions and debates covering a wider field than case studies alone are summarily explained in some appendices. The book contains a 30-title annotated bibliography on case studies, where the reader can use the asterisk symbol (*) as a guideline to key publications.

The present text is based on an earlier version in Dutch, *Case study's: wat, wanneer en hoe.* (Amsterdam: Boom Publishers, 1996, 2000, 2003). Based on class-room experiences with several types of student, it has been thoroughly re-written since its first publication, and hopefully improved. I owe a lot to Iris Westall, who was very helpful in translating, and to many PhD students and course participants.

Peter G. Swanborn
Oosterbeek, The Netherlands, Summer 2009

ONE

What is a Case Study?

In this chapter we distinguish between extensive and intensive research in social science (section 1.1). The object of case studies – a social phenomenon – is discussed in section 1.2. After surveying some historical origins of the case study in section 1.3, section 1.4 examines the research question as a methodological point of departure. It determines which general type of design is to be used: an extensive design (e.g. a survey) or an intensive one (e.g. a case study). A definition of the case study is presented in section 1.5, and expanded upon in section 1.6. The popular point of view that a case study is characterised by an holistic approach is explained and discussed in section 1.7. In section 1.8 we review the contents of this chapter and we draw conclusions.

1.1 Introduction

In social research, we describe and explain certain phenomena that relate to people, groups, organisations, communities, large towns or even countries. Such phenomena are, for instance: leisure time activities; the treatment of an ADHD child; the determinants of individual health; the way in which people use their social network; how people cope with a disaster; riots; strikes; the process of adoption of an organisational innovation in a hospital; the principles according to which political coalitions are formed; or, an arms race between nation-states. In order to study social phenomena, we use a diversity of approaches or strategies. They can roughly be divided into two general types: extensive approaches and intensive approaches.[1]

In an *extensive approach* we collect information about the relevant properties of a large number of instances of a phenomenon. We draw our conclusions by putting together all the information and calculating and interpreting correlations between the properties of these examples. For instance, in a study about the conditions for and causes of riots (the phenomenon under study) we may start by making an inventory of, say, 200 riots using documentary sources. We establish the 'scores' of

---

[1] This pair of concepts is popularised by the British philosopher of science and social scientist Rom Harré (1979: 132–135).

each riot with respect to a set of properties (such as the number of people involved, the extent of damage to property, the weather conditions), and study the correlations between these properties (these are usually called variables) in order to construct a model of causes and consequences.

In extensive research, we use a large set of events, people, organisations or nation-states to ground our conclusions about the phenomenon. In sociology, in the political and educational sciences, as well as in several other disciplines, large-scale surveying of people is the dominant extensive strategy to collect empirical data. Hundreds or even thousands of respondents may be involved to study a phenomenon. This might, for instance, be the causation of (non-)smoking habits in individuals. Each survey respondent provides information in the form of answers to a series of standardised questions. These answers are *not* used to study the development of the phenomenon within *this* individual person. They are *aggregated over all respondents* to create information about frequency distributions and relationships between the variables under study which might be helpful in understanding and explaining the phenomenon.

Alternatively, in applying an *intensive approach*, a researcher focuses on only *one* specific instance of the phenomenon to be studied, or on only a handful of instances in order to study a phenomenon in depth. We would therefore be inclined to study *some* riots, or *some* young people, or *some* traffic accidents, or only a *handful* of schools by probing into the details of the process (i.e. the phenomenon) we are interested in. Each instance is studied in its own specific context, and in greater detail than in extensive research. Data is collected using many sources of information, such as spokespeople, documents and behavioural observations. There are not only many separate variables to measure, but a phenomenon is also followed over time by repeatedly measuring some of these variables. This explains the label 'intensive'. Monitoring helps us to describe and explain the history, the changes during the period under study and the complex structure of the phenomenon. Each instance, or example, is usually called *a case*. Therefore, an intensive approach is generally called a 'case study', or a multiple-case study if more than one instance of the phenomenon is studied. The word 'case' originates from the Latin '*casus*' (*cadere* = to fall); it simply means 'event', 'situation' or 'condition'.

Let us take an example, such as the origins of (differences in) civic participation. An intensive approach often takes the form of a field study within a specific local setting. As a 'case', we might select an election campaign in a small town: a clear, local, manifestation of political participation (or the lack of it). We may even restrict ourselves to the membership of one political party in that town. The researcher monitors the process, by reading all available documentation, interviewing people who were, or are, involved in the case in order to get first-hand information, and – if possible – by using observation in the field as a technique to widen understanding of what happens in this case. To lay a hand on the phenomenon, we focus, *within each selected case*, on the relationships between a number of variables and the ways in which the scores on pairs, or sets, of variables simultaneously change *over time*. For instance, during a municipal election campaign we monitor the political participation of party members and other volunteers, and their changing expectations, attitudes, decisions as well as their influence on each other.

Alternatively, we could select participation in a trade union during a certain period as our case. Evidently, on the basis of our results, we will not be able to say much about the 'political participation of the adult population in this country' or about 'participation in trade unions in general'. However, we can probably formulate very interesting conclusions about how differences in participation developed *within this selected case*. And this might suggest some tentative ideas about the phenomenon in general, and at least provide us with suggestions about designing further research. So, in a case study, the researcher collects information by studying the characteristics of those people who are/were involved in the same case and their relationships. Instead of the word 'people', one could use the words 'organisations', 'events', 'nation-states' or any other entity. But even in studying entities like these, one should not overlook that it is people who act and react to each another within the given case.

In these examples, comparisons between the researched cases – if more than one election campaign, party, or more than one city, is involved in the study design – are of *secondary importance*. In selecting more than one case, the usual procedure is to design a tentative model based on the results of the first studied case, and to adjust the resulting model when and where necessary while studying the other cases, until the designed model fits all cases. Alternatively, we may discover that different models are necessary to fit different cases, depending on certain conditions. But the focus is on the description and explanation of developments *within one case*.

Evidently, an intensive approach may provide us with tentative ideas about the social phenomenon, based on knowledge about the studied event or about this specific person, organisation or country, and 'how it all came about'. That is to say, a case study is an appropriate way to answer broad research questions, by providing us with a thorough understanding of how the process develops in this case. Whether its results can be generalised in other contexts remains an open question, to be answered by complementary case studies and/or an extensive approach.

In Box 1.1 we give two examples of an intensive role of case study research and an extensive approach. Both examples are selected to demonstrate a dual strategy. Phenomena can often be studied in both ways. However, as we will see in Chapter 2, for solving some research questions a survey is to be preferred (it might even be the only way to obtain useful results). For other questions, or under some special circumstances, a case study is far more appropriate. It goes without saying that there are several research designs 'in between' an extensive and an intensive approach. Moreover, not all research designs can be easily labelled in this respect, but the intensive and extensive concepts are at least workable.

BOX 1.1

Example 1. Let us assume that a sociologist or a policy scientist intends to study the integration of ethnic minorities within the local municipal services in some Western European country. An *extensive* approach would be to conduct a mail survey among the heads of personnel departments of some 200 municipalities. In a precoded questionnaire, a set of precisely formulated questions are posed about the participation of members of ethnic minorities in civil service jobs in the respondent's municipality. An *intensive* approach would be to conduct participatory observation and interviews in say three municipalities during a six month period. The researcher hangs around in three departments, observes patterns of interethnic social interaction in corridors and restaurants, interviews people at several places and on different occasions. (S)he studies documents about decision-making as it takes place in the municipal council and in the mayor and aldermen's deliberations, and (s)he interviews as many employees as possible about the topic in question. Attention is paid, for instance, to the reactions of departmental heads to decisions from higher levels when these are made against their advice. Finally a research report is drawn up. Sometimes, a draft of the research report is discussed with stakeholders in several rounds.

Example 2. We could tackle the problem of the relation between formal education of school leavers and the labour market by administering some hard variables to a national cohort of school leavers: what exactly was their formal education; how long did it take them to find a first job, etc. Alternatively, we might focus on one specific local group of school leavers, and organise intensive group interviewing as well as individual interviews. From this, it may become clear how these boys and girls perceive their own situation; how they evaluate their experiences with potential employers; how they perceive the experiences of their friends; how they influence each other, and so on.

In the social and behavioural sciences the popularity of case studies has a fluctuating character.[2] Several contemporaneous social science disciplines, such as sociology, show a rather one-sided emphasis on the extensive, large-scale strategy. One of the causes of this lack of balance is that an extensive approach easily allows

---

[2]Feagin et al. (1991) construct a challenging distinction between modern 'article sociology' (as represented in the *American Sociological Review* and the *American Journal of Sociology*) on the one hand, and 'book sociology' on the other hand. In their opinion, the articles, based as they are on 'the scientific method' (the variable language), are almost irrelevant and are largely ignored, whereas book publications – especially those based on case studies – are the focus of public attention. There is an element of truth in this undoubtedly one-sided view. The fate of sociology and of some other disciplines is still the lack of consensus with respect to a methodological core, a consensus that might enable scientists to distinguish between what is acceptable and what is not.

for quantification. Multivariate analysis of data, and statistics, together with the advance of computers in data analysis, has facilitated an extremely rapid development in the field. At the same time, however, modern social science is confronted with many problems that cannot be solved by an exclusively extensive approach. That is why, especially in applied research, a sub-stream of intensive studies grows in importance. In several fields, such as the educational sciences, an intensive approach is already frequently employed; in others, for example organisational studies and the nursing studies, it is even dominant. In the last decades of the twentieth century the *combination* of a survey (as a strategy 'in width') with an intensive counterpart (the 'in-depth' strategy) gradually developed as the standard approach in applied research projects. It is generally called a mixed-method approach (see Chapter 7).

To summarise:

	Extensive research	**Intensive research**
Example:	survey	case study
Comparisons made:	*between* units of observation (i.e. between males and females regarding their political participation)	*within* the unit of observation (i.e. between different stakeholders in an organisation)
Global character:	'in width'	'in depth'

1.2 Phenomena and cases

Social science phenomena studied by case researchers are as diverse as:

- individual health histories or labour market careers,
- production processes or innovations in organizations,
- riots, strikes, protest marches,
- selection procedures,
- initiation rituals,
- industrial mergers,
- collective decision-making,
- procedures of quality care,
- attempts to de-bureaucratise a public service sector merger,
- inter-organisational efforts against drug use,
- implementation processes of a governmental policy,
- alliance formation or war termination between nation-states;
- socialisation processes,
- election campaigns,
- causes of traffic accidents,
- effects of restrictions on the 'policy space' of policy-makers.

In a case study on the causes of traffic accidents (involving pedestrians (e.g. pedestrian/ motor vehicle collisions) we may, for instance, select from documentary sources of, say, ten accidents that occurred within the boundaries of a selected city. Cause within this specific type of traffic accident constitutes the phenomenon, and the ten *accidents* constitute the (ten) cases. Within the study of each accident, the regulations and specific features of the local situation as well as the characteristics of the participants involved and the actions of the local police are taken into consideration. In another example – a case study about fatal decisions on battlefields (the phenomenon) – the study may consist of an intensive analysis of documents concerning some fatal decision in five great battles (the five cases) in the Second World War.

Note that in a survey about political attitudes and behaviour, involving several thousands of people, the respondents are usually not labelled as cases. Not only because of the numbers involved, which exclude an intensive approach, but principally because the individual respondent is not studied primarily as a specific example of the formation of political attitudes; (s)he acts only as an 'informer' about a set of scores on variables that are taken together with those of all the other respondents in data analysis. Explanations are based on correlations between variables that are regarded as either causally independent, or as causally dependent.

A phenomenon may involve only one actor, such as in a study about the trajectory of terminal illness in one individual person. In other examples, such as in studying the development of friendships in a classroom, a riot or an industrial merger, *each case or manifestation of a phenomenon may often involve many individual as well as collective actors.* Hence, a case does *not* necessarily involve *only one* 'actor', such as a person, an organization or a local settlement. Depending on the phenomenon of interest, the actors involved in a case may be located on the micro-level (persons and interpersonal relations), and/or the meso- (organisational, institutional) level and/or the macro-level (large communities, nation-states).

Micro-level, focusing on one actor:
For example, clinical research, such as description, diagnosis and monitoring the treatment of individual patients; or historical research such as biographies of famous politicians.

Micro-level, more than one actor involved:
For example, people in a restaurant; some people together in an elevator (the phenomenon might be how people bring a conversation to an end or the continuous adjustment of physical positions in the elevator).

Meso-level, only one actor:
For example, an organisation, such as a firm or a department; a police station; a hospital; a voluntary association.

Meso-level, more than one actor involved:
For example, co-operations or networks, such as between four local primary schools and a school for special education; conflicts between public service and private enterprise in the renovation of an inner city; co-operation of industrial firms and educational institutions with respect to the labour market and learning places.

Macro-level, only one actor:
For example, a local social system such as a street or, a village; a nation-state, a civilisation.

Macro-level, more than one actor involved:
For example, an arms race; the process of organising a common European foreign policy.

A combination of micro- and meso-level actors:
For example, socialising newcomers into an organisation.

By far the most popular branch of case studies relates to organisations. Substantial fields where case studies are used include marketing, human resources management, management information systems and strategy.

However, on the micro-level as well as on the macro-level, there is an important research tradition that has its own specific character, even though it uses the label 'case study'. This begs for some elaboration.

On the micro-level, the label 'case study' is often applied to the tradition of single-subject research[3] (in earlier days called 'N=1 research'), well-known in cognitive and developmental psychology, in counselling and psychotherapy, and in

---

[3]Single-subject research has a long tradition. Over the period 1939–63, Dukes (1965) already counted 246 N=1 publications in American psychological periodicals. We mention some references for information. Barlow and Hersen (1984) is a useful textbook for design and analysis of single-subject research. It contains an historical overview, and discusses in a reasonably systematic way, starting from the A–B design (A = 'baseline', B = treatment), several of the more complex time series designs. Comparable is Kratochwill (1978). The first part of the book offers a complete introduction to single-subject research. It is compatible with Cook and Campbell's (1979) book on quasi-experimental designs. As a consequence, both books can be studied very well together. Some of the other chapters have a statistical-technical character and are aimed at the clarification of specific problems. Kratochwill and Levin (1992) contains an overview of historical developments since 1978, and is state of the art. This publication offers many interesting bibliographical suggestions. It limits itself to methods of analysis, including meta-analysis, for case study researchers. Another source is Bromley (1986), in which – exclusively in its qualitative interpretation – single-subject research is discussed, with the help of some clinical cases. The author applies Toulmin's argumentation-analysis (1958) on his case reports. In this logic, arguments are weighed. The trust of the speaker or writer in the argument, and the explication of assumptions are of central importance. A view on actual developments is offered in the e-journal *Pragmatic Case Studies in Psychotherapy* (2007, 3 (4)), with contributions by Clement, Kazdin and Barlow.

health studies. In this approach, an individual is monitored during a certain period. In health studies, the researcher focuses on a few variables only, for instance the introduction and dosage of medication, and the patient's status on a handful of health indicators. If the number of moments of measurement is large (above 50), this kind of research constitutes a tradition of its own. Quantitative analysis is possible, and may be highly sophisticated. This mostly refers to monitoring the development of the client after the introduction of a treatment, and assessing the effects. In psychotherapy, many characteristics of the client are usually monitored and carefully documented.

Although this type of research (only one or just a few 'case(s)', and multi-moment research) is in some respects related to the intensive approach, it also shares common ground with the scientific tradition of experiments. It belongs to the broad category of evaluation research, which nowadays is undoubtedly the most popular branch of applied research. In evaluation research, both extensive and intensive approaches are used. Nonetheless, in the fields of psychology, psychotherapy and medicine, the label 'case study' is generally used for this kind of research. In this book, this micro-level tradition is not where our main interest lies. Rather, for readers wishing to pursue this tradition, see Fishman (1999).

On a macro-level, the dominant tradition is represented by those case studies in political science and the economy, in which certain phenomena (i.e. peasant revolutions, wars) are connected to a restrictive set of causative 'hard' variables, such as population size, climate, economic development or armament level. An exemplary study might be about the impact of electoral systems on the number of parties in a country. Data is obtained from documentary sources. The political sciences and economics traditions stand apart from the case study tradition in sociology, the administrative and management sciences, health and social care sciences, and most other disciplines. Although this tradition is largely beyond the focus of this book, we pay attention to the methodology of the 'case-comparative methods' in the political sciences in section 4.4. The central topic – how to ground causal conclusions on data from a restricted set of cases – certainly is of general importance. We will present examples, and discuss aspects of this strand of research. Appendix 2 presents a (very short) description of the history of the debate.

Both the clinical approach and the political sciences approach are focused on the study of causal relations – does the therapy work? What were the causes of this revolution? But we have a wider interest. It is not only causal relations we are interested in, but we focus on case studies aimed at detailed description, at uncovering a phenomenon that is situated in the context of this special case. Our emphasis is on an exploratory approach.

One should keep in mind that the researcher is interested in the general phenomenon, and not in the more or less accidental case, or 'instance', in which the phenomenon manifests itself. This is not self-evident because already some definitions of the case study may put you on the wrong foot, for example: 'a case study is *an intensive study of a single case* (or a small set of cases) with an aim to generalise across a larger set of cases of the same general type' (Gerring 2007: 65).[4] A more appropriate expression would be that a case study is *the study of a phenomenon* or a process as it develops within one case. The point needs to be emphasised, particularly where only one actor (person, organisation or local setting) is involved. In intensively studying the medical history of a person, or the development of some public service, sometimes the researcher's attention gradually shifts towards this specific, selected person, organisation or nation-state, while the phenomenon in general more or less remains backstage. If we asked what constitutes 'the case' in a case study on hysteria, researcher A would perhaps answer: 'hysteria in person P', while researcher B would reply: 'person P' (person P happens to be hysteric). The danger implied in the second point of view is that one focuses on irrelevant features of the actor, 'the bearer of the phenomenon', and that one overlooks the original intention to study the case for its representativeness of the phenomenon in general.

We do not argue that, in so far as applied science is concerned, the psychologist, psychotherapist or doctor does not have the health of the individual patient or client as a focus of interest. Of course the patient or client is 'central'. But in so far as the goal of the project is to use the research results of cases for comparative purposes, the phenomenon (e.g. the treatment of ADHD) is central.

Confusion between the phenomenon and the studied social unit(s), however, is to be expected in view of the fact that, mostly, the boundaries of the phenomenon to be studied are not yet clearly defined. In other words, often it is not yet clear which features are relevant to a general model and which properties are irrelevant. This explains a report writer's reluctance to leave out local and often colourful details, and the sometimes over-abundance of irrelevant aspects. It may put some report's readers – and sometimes the researcher him/herself – on the wrong foot: to erroneously regard the selected case, instead of the phenomenon to be studied, as paramount.

BOX 1.2

Yin (1994: 16) presents Bernstein and Woodward's *All the President's Men* (1974) on the Watergate scandal as a fine example of a journalistic case study, in which the case is defined as 'the cover-up'. As often happens, however, it is unclear whether the Watergate scandal can be used as an empirical case from which to generalise about the domain of (Presidential) scandals, or to some other broader phenomenon. Anyway, one would prefer to have 'cover-ups' defined as the central phenomenon, and 'Watergate' as 'the case', that is to say if the Watergate book is considered to be a contribution to scientific knowledge.

---

[4]Additionally, we do not see 'the intention to generalise' as a definitional property of the case study. In Chapter 2, the difference between the study of 'stand-alone cases' and '*pars pro toto* cases' is elaborated.

There is another implication. At the start of a case study we should know which phenomenon to study. If we start, however, at the wrong side, by selecting an individual person, organisation or setting, and only afterwards start thinking about *which phenomenon* to study, complications are certainly to be expected. A researcher who starts studying 'something' in a selected place, but doesn't know 'of which phenomenon this place is a case', is comparable to the secondary school pupil who starts writing a paper without having an idea about the topic, but afterwards deciding that it has to be about his/her own school.

BOX 1.3

The researcher's choice of the phenomenon, a specific topic, is the primary choice that should be expressed in the research question. Somebody who is going to study a computer factory where a new 'generation' is being developed is still rather vague. What is the phenomenon to be studied? Procedures in R&D departments? Problems connected with outsourcing? Conflicts between engineers and marketing people? Communication processes in general? Many possibilities present themselves to the naïve researcher. Selection of a certain enterprise and within this context the selection of a certain generation are secondary aspects. In applied research, generally the choice of the case(s) is not up to the researcher, but this doesn't imply that the relation between the phenomenon to be studied and the case(s) is much different: the phenomenon deserves to be central.

1.3 Historical background

Writing and speaking about case studies, one experiences some frustration: the label 'case studies' seems to be used for many purposes. One is confronted with several different strands of case study research. This is evident already by glancing at some of the classic popular texts in the area: Glaser and Strauss (1967); Stake (1995); Yin (1994, 1989) and Miles and Huberman (1984, 1994). Each one of them has little in common with the others. On the other hand, in this field several labels are in use, sometimes addressing the same subject, sometimes used for very different things: case report, case history, case biography, case study and case method.[5] The confusion relates to the fact that case studies originate from many traditions. We mention the most important ones here.[6]

---

[5]The term 'case study' may refer to the process of research as well as to the end product of such a process. To put an end to this confusion, Stenhouse suggested using the term 'case record' for the end product, but this suggestion has not been followed (L. Stenhouse, in R.G. Burgess (1984)).

[6]An outstanding historical overview of the role of the label 'case study' in American sociology is presented by Jennifer Platt (1992).

- The growth and development of many sciences, such as the health sciences, clinical psychotherapy and law, went hand in hand with the study of cases. Description and attempts to explain the peculiarities of a case precede, or are part of, steps towards generalisation. In the teaching of these disciplines, cases still play an important role as a didactical vehicle.[7] A similar orientation on cases can be observed in fields that developed later on, such as political science and organisational studies.
- A specific source of inspiration in social science is constituted by the traditional study of a village or local setting in cultural anthropology (Malinowski, Margaret Mead and many others).
- A third source is the sociological Chicago School. *Street Corner Society* (Whyte 1941); *The Jack Roller* (Shaw, 2nd edn 1966); *The Taxi Dance Hall* (Cressey 1932); *Boys in White* (Becker et al. 1961) and many other monographs illustrate this tradition. In this tradition, it is not always evident that it is a general phenomenon, not the local setting itself, that constitutes the focus of research.
- In political science, historical roots include a strong tradition building on case studies. Later on, when the methodology of the behavioural sciences became dominant, this tradition was partly replaced. Debates between proponents of the case study method (only one case) and those of the comparative method (a few cases) and finally the correlative method (many cases) still colour the field.
- Well-known from the field of psychology are the studies of Sigmund Freud and other psychoanalysts. Later on, the study of individual persons (cases) on other domains, such as personality psychology and clinical psychology, developed.
- More recently, the study of cases in many policy fields (e.g. social work, youth support, labour market intermediary, the integration of ethnic minorities) presents new impulses. Case study research in these fields is not seen as an admission of weakness, as it is in some domains, but as one of the central strategies for research.

In recent decades, confusion increased because the character of case studies changed rapidly within the social and the behavioural sciences. While in the past basic research, by means of a qualitative, exploratory approach, dominated the field, nowadays attention has shifted to applied research. The present-day popularity of terms such as 'policy experiment' and 'evaluation research' (both strands often using case studies as their preferred research strategy) is an illustration of this development.[8] Another relatively recent development is the blending of qualitative and quantitative approaches (see section 7.2).

---

[7]Concerning the use of case studies, or rather more or less 'extensive case reports' in education, see Lee (1983). The 'Harvard Business School' tradition is well known (see, for instance, Stein 1952). This is an example of an education-guided compilation of cases for management scientists. The cases, which are described in great detail, concern the change of production from military purposes to civilian aims; and collective decision-making in the United States during and after the end of the Second World War. Other examples of the use of case descriptions in education are given by Towl (1969) and Windsor and Greanias (1983). The most useful book on this topic is perhaps Easton (1992). Learning to summarise information, to understand, to diagnose, to invent alternative scenarios, reduction and selecting from alternatives are illustrated with the help of an example of an industrial take-over. A web source is: ublib.buffalo.edu/libraries/projects/cases/case.html

[8]The distinction between basic research and applied research is highlighted in section 2.4.2.

1.4 Methodological point of departure

This book is based on a simple central principle: the idea that different traditions in, and strategies for, social science research are complementary rather than incompatible. Therefore, we emphasise a common methodological core for case studies and other types of research. This strongly contrasts with the majority of methodology texts, in which a major split between 'the scientific method' and the 'case study method' dominates. For 'science', labels such as 'quantitative' and 'hypothetico-deductive method' are used; in the context of 'case studies', labels such as 'qualitative' and 'holistic' are more common. In debates on the results of case studies (e.g. with respect to the relevance of an evaluation research project), not infrequently invalid arguments are used to upgrade or, conversely, to downgrade, research results. The know-how to posit case studies in a rational way in the general scientific enterprise seems to be lacking. As far as is evident from these texts, one assumes that intensive research methodology is quite different from extensive research methodology. Especially with respect to applied research, it seems necessary to correct this exaggeration.

Literature on the methodology of case studies is, comparatively speaking, not vast, and is actually very heterogeneous. The relative lack of reflection on the methodology of case research means there are few additions to the existing literature. Researchers cite the already well-known texts; newer publications refer to the older ones. Often it is insufficiently clarified what additional value case studies contribute to the results of a survey, and vice versa. Many researchers experience difficulties in formulating conclusive results based on their case studies, in sharp contrast to their ability to do so in the field of survey results (compare Yin, 1993: 70). They seem to rely on the premise that descriptions and interview reports speak for themselves (this especially is the case when quotations from interviews are exclusively used for illustrative purposes) and pay little attention to the specific research question.

1.5 Definition

To elaborate our introduction into the difference between intensive and extensive research, let's try to attain a sharper outline. Case studies are already difficult enough to define as a research strategy, because typologies of research strategies are generally based on different sources of data. A case study, however, is compatible with many data sources, and therefore hard to posit in a system of strategies.

The case study may be defined in different ways, one definition being broader than the other. We prefer to offer a definition that includes those properties that are present in *most case studies*. We attach the word 'most' to several of these properties in order to indicate that not all aspects are always present. This implies that a debate about the question of whether a certain research project is a case study or not is not always fruitful.[9]

A case study refers to the study of a *social phenomenon*:

- carried out within the boundaries of one social system (the case), or within the boundaries of a few social systems (the cases), such as people, organisations, groups, individuals, local communities or nation-states, in which the phenomenon to be studied enrols
- in the case's natural context
- by monitoring the phenomenon during a certain period or, alternatively, by collecting information afterwards with respect to the development of the phenomenon during a certain period
- in which the researcher focuses on process-tracing: the description and explanation of social processes that unfold between persons participating in the process, people with their values, expectations, opinions, perceptions, resources, controversies, decisions, mutual relations and behaviour, or the description and explanation of processes within and between social institutions
- where the researcher, guided by an initially broad research question, explores the data and only after some time formulates more precise research questions, keeping an open eye to unexpected aspects of the process by abstaining from pre-arranged procedures and operationalisations
- using several data sources, the main ones being (in this order) available documents, interviews with informants and (participatory) observation
- in which (optionally), in the final stage of an applied research case study project, the investigator invites the studied persons and stakeholders to a debate on their subjective perspectives, to confront them with preliminary research conclusions, in order not only to attain a more solid base for the final research report, but sometimes also to clear up misunderstandings, ameliorate internal social relations and 'point everyone in the same direction'.

It is a wide definition. Perhaps too wide? What does it exclude?

---

[9] Almost every author on the topic 'case study' presents his own definition. In most of them some of the elements of our encompassing-definition are mentioned or emphasised. An overview of definitions would serve some academic purpose, but is not useful in the present context. Here, we limit ourselves to a comparison with Yin's definition. In his view, the case study is determined by the 'how' and 'why' research questions; by events in which the researcher has no control, and is restricted to contemporary situations, not to situations in the past. In the 1994 edition of *Case Study Research*, Yin adds two more elements: the real-life context, and the fact that the boundaries between phenomenon and context are not clear. We do not agree with Yin with respect to the necessity of contemporary phenomena. With regard to phenomena in the past, a retrospective approach is fitting, and can be put into practice in a case study (although observation as a research technique is excluded). Furthermore, the fact that researchers have no control over actual behavioural events is only relevant in so far as causal research questions are at hand; it is less relevant with respect to descriptive purposes, for which case studies can be used as well (Yin, 1994: Chapter 1). The argument about the necessary vagueness of the boundaries between phenomenon and context is represented in our definition in two places: studying a phenomenon in its natural surroundings is based on this argument as well as using an 'open approach'.

Excluded are, of course, extensive approaches, the most typical of them being social surveys. In a standard social survey many people are approached, but in their capacity as mutually isolated individuals, generally at only one specific moment, using one data source exclusively (verbal responses). Also excluded is a standard survey even if it takes place in one bounded social system, for instance a village. Some methodologists would call this a case study too, especially if that village is selected from a set of villages about which the researcher wishes to draw conclusions. But here the label 'case' means that *for practical purposes only* the sample is restricted to one local setting. Other characteristics of such a project are typical for standard extensive research. From a purely formal point of view, one could likewise label a survey on people's norms and values in France a case study, especially if the domain of the wider project is, for instance, Western European countries, and the project is repeated in other countries, such as Belgium or Norway. But this use of the label 'case study' has nothing in common with what is defined as a case study in this book.

In identifying 'case studies' with 'intensive research' and focusing on the perceptions, interactions and decisions of people, we attach a substantive meaning to the label 'case study'. This contrasts with a purely formal approach, in which a case study would relate simply to the study of one case versus other approaches that involve a number of cases. It might be possible to combine both points of view and state that some research project (such as the survey in France) is a survey as well as a case study. For reasons of clarity, we avoid this ambiguity in using the label 'case study'.

Excluded, too, are laboratory experiments and simulation studies because some of their essential characteristics include manipulation and isolation from the natural context. When taken in a strict sense, our definition also excludes the two powerful sub-traditions focusing on individuals, respectively on nation-states, as practised in psychotherapy on the one hand, and by political scientists/economists on the other hand. If we follow a more ecumenical course, however, by leaving some aspects of the definition out, these approaches would fall well within the boundaries of our definition.

1.6 Additional remarks about the definition

The label 'case study' nowadays is not only used in connection with the study of one case, but includes the study of a small number of cases as well. 'Small' means that normally not more than four or five cases are included in a study. Exceptions, however, exist, in which the number of cases may be as many as 40 or 50, particularly when individuals are cases. In the older literature, a sharp distinction used to be maintained between 'non-comparative' or 'case studies' (N=1) and the 'comparative method', in which more than one case is included (Lijphart 1971;

Eckstein 1975; George 1979).[10] The latter approach was called the 'case-oriented comparative method' by Ragin (1987), and later on 'diversity-oriented methods' (Ragin 2000). The generally used label nowadays is 'comparative politics'. The reader should be aware of the fact, however, that *all* research boils down to comparison. Even if only one case is studied, implicitly comparisons are made with a standard or an ideal case, or with the case itself in an earlier phase of development. Hence, from a methodological point of view, the fading away of this distinction is not regrettable. In this book, wherever useful, we apply the labels '*single-case studies*' (N=1) and '*multiple-case studies*' (N>1).[11]

The phenomenon is studied in its natural surroundings because, at the start of the research, it is not yet quite clear *what the spatial and temporal boundaries of the phenomenon are*. In other words, it is not yet clear which properties of the context are relevant and should be included in modelling the phenomenon, and which properties should be left out. Therefore, for the time being it is better not to isolate the phenomenon from its context.

Studying 'a phenomenon in its natural context' means that the researcher does not set apart individuals from their normal life situation, such as in a standardised interview, or that (s)he models a social process under the simplifying conditions of a laboratory experiment, but that (s)he studies social phenomena with as little disruption of the original setting as possible. Moreover, because the research takes place in the natural context of the phenomenon, we may be able to explore – in repeated case studies – the significance of *different* social and physical contexts and their impact on the social process.

BOX 1.4

A complex phenomenon in an open social system such as those described in Box 1.1 is far removed from examples we meet in our natural or physical environment. For the malfunctioning of an electric circuit at home, three explanations may suffice: a defective bulb, a defective switch or some loose contact in the wiring. Each

(Continued)

---

[10]In political science, the struggle with one of its sources, the historical sciences, has triggered a protracted debate, in which authors such as Verba, Lijphart, Eckstein and George argued, about the role of case study research (N=1) as opposed to the strategy called comparative method (N>1). A summary of the debate is included in Appendix 2.

[11]Yin (1994) uses the labels 'single-case designs' and 'multiple-case designs'. Miles and Huberman (1984) discuss 'within-site analysis' versus 'cross-site analysis'. In the second edition of their *Qualitative Data Analysis*, these labels are replaced by 'within-case displays' and 'cross-case displays' (Miles & Huberman 1994).

(Continued)

of these explanations may be tested by one simple experiment. Characteristics of the house or its surroundings are irrelevant. However, with broad social science problems, many factors come into play. For example, in fractured relations between the established insiders and the outsiders in a little town, one always wonders whether it is a specific problem of this town. Or is it the same as in other, surrounding, towns? Or can it even be broadened out and applied to problems of immigration in western European countries? Or do we deal with a clash between very specific cultural subgroups, subgroups that get into trouble wherever they come into contact with each other? Does the local press play a role, or is it the national media that triggers the emergence of riots? What are the reference groups (or cultures) of different stakeholders? Thus, it is often impossible to define the relevant contextual properties of the phenomenon at the start of a study.

The monitoring approach differs strongly from the one-moment measurement in a survey. This is so even if we compare the case study's monitoring with a 'multi-moment' survey, such as a panel survey, that is a 'repeated' survey. In a case study it is generally not possible to distinguish sharply between different measurement 'waves'. Normally, observations are collected continuously but irregularly during the relevant period (e.g. a 10-day period, a month or six months). Research designs in which relevant variables are measured at several moments, and in which changes in the environment can be monitored at the same time, provide many advantages over the 'one-moment survey', certainly where time-lags regarding the impact of one variable on the other are concerned. Our insight into the association of successive events and conditions is much furthered by longitudinal research compared to transversal (= cross-sectional, one-moment) research.

In order to describe and explain (parts of) social processes, doing a case study presents a unique opportunity to focus on social interactions and the developing meanings that participants in the system attach to each other, and how they interpret each other's acts. Another object of our attention is the existence of multiple realities: the different, and sometimes contrasting, views participants in a system have, and their diverging interpretations of events and conditions. Moreover, in applied research of innovations, one of the standard foci is on factual and perceived physical and social bottlenecks, and how people cope with them. These aspects of the research approach are elaborated in section 2.2.1.

As in all research, in doing a case study we focus on the problem we want to solve. Whatever research project one has in mind, the research question is the point of departure. In the majority of case studies the researcher starts with a rather broad and perhaps sometimes still vague question. If little is known about the object one can only pose broad 'what' and 'how' questions. This does not exclude the fact that the researcher, after defining the problem, proceeds by selecting some possibly applicable theories. Generally, during the research process the broad question develops into a series of more precise questions. In most case studies the researcher tries to maintain a maximal openness towards unknown aspects, and to 'let the object speak' (serendipity![12]). This implies – for most case studies – an exploratory approach (see section 2.2.3).[13] However, occasionally, a case study starts with precise questions, or even with an hypothesis to be tested (see section 2.2.2).[14] The latter requires an all but exploratory approach.

In case studies several data sources are used. Obviously, documents as well as interviews and observational data are not always available. In the eyes of many scientists, the case study is more or less identical with field research in a natural context, as is well known from cultural anthropology. A case study, however, need not necessarily include participatory observation. The possibility to observe behaviour renders the case study exclusively apt for studying contemporary phenomena. But we also use the label 'case study' for some forms of historical studies in a not too distant past. One may afterwards collect information about developments during a specified period. In *historical* case studies, exclusive use is made of documents (or, if the recent past is concerned, of oral history). Particularly with respect to organisational studies, in which we want to understand an extant situation by reconstructing developmental processes through the use of documents and/or interviews with participants, but also on the macro- and micro-levels, retrospective case studies are carried out. Asking retrospective questions may give us some insight in what happened in the recent past, or about the perceptions earlier people had about each other and about the process itself. However, apart from the fact that we do not always know the proper questions to ask because of lacking information, or that we even don't know the suitable informants, answers on retrospective questions are notoriously liable to bias. If possible, collecting data 'on the spur of the moment itself' is to be preferred. Being critical about the data and the way they are gathered is one of the key requirements of the researcher's attitude. 'The most important rule for all data collection is to report how the data were created and how we came to possess them' (King et al. 1994: 51).

---

[12]This nowadays well-coined term refers to the fairly common experience of observing unanticipated, anomalous and strategic data which may start the development of a new theory or extend an existing theory (see Merton 1945; Merton & Barber 2004).

[13]The ideal goal of an exploratory researcher is, of course, that some day (s)he may stumble upon a great discovery, such as Beveridge (1950), who describes how, in 1889, a laboratory assistant accidentally observed the urine of a dog whose pancreas had been removed. The amount of sugar in the urine led to the discovery of the relation between the pancreas and diabetes.

[14]A hypothesis is a precise question with an answer to that question, accompanied by a question mark. The aim of the researcher is to test whether the question mark can be omitted.

Often in case studies, the applied researcher deals with several (groups of) stakeholders, each with their own perceptions, interpretations, arguments, explanations and prejudices. It may be very useful to confront each of these groups with the ideas and opinions of some of the others in order to better understand the history of sometimes long-standing controversies or prejudices. Also, the researcher may take the opportunity to present his/her preliminary results to the participants in order to gather last-minute corrections and additions. The general expression for this procedure is 'member checking'.

In some forms of applied case research a further step is being taken. If it is detected that different groups of stakeholders have different views, the researcher may see it as his/her task to bring all participants to agreement. Now, the researcher's role is linked to a change agency role. This generally implies lengthy workshops, in which the researcher invites comments of all stakeholders, where groups present their opinions, etc. This merger of research and action agency is generally called 'action research'. It is representative for much of modern qualitative approaches in applied sociology. In this book action research is not our focus of interest.

1.7 An holistic approach?

Often, in defining 'case studies', some expression indicating a 'holistic approach' is added.

> The case study … is a way of organising social data so as to preserve the unitary character of the social object being studied. (Goode & Hatt 1952)

> Case studies are those research projects which attempt to explain (w)holistically the dynamics of a certain historical period of a particular social unit. (Stoecker 1991)

The label 'holistic' means we have to take into account that behaviour of people and social phenomena, in general, are determined by a complex set of causes. As a consequence, simple causal models, such as those used in most survey analysis, are not adequate.

In a more technical language, statistical interaction (between causal and contextual variables) is the rule; simple models of additive independent variables are not adequate. Put in this way, one cannot but agree that 'holistic researchers' have a point. However, if this leads to radically refusing to think in terms of variables, one is likely to throw away the baby with the bathwater. Compare the following quote:

> In most variable-oriented work, investigators begin by defining the problem in a way that allows examination of many cases (conceived as empirical units or observations); then they specify the relevant variables, matched to theoretical concepts; and finally they collect information on these variables, usually one variable at a time – not one case at a

time. From that point on, the language of variables and the relations among them dominates the research process. The resulting understanding of these relations is shaped by examining patterns of co-variation in the data set, observed and averaged across many cases, not by studying how different features or causes fit together in individual cases. *The alternative case-oriented approach places cases, not variables, centre stage.* (Ragin, in Ragin & Becker 1992: 5)

The following sour comment on the analysis of survey data is also very illustrative:

...the person disappears from the analysis, which instead merely compares traits. The person who is recorded on a polling schedule is not only dissolved by becoming a set of traits individually tabulated; he almost fails to exist from the beginning by virtue of the narrow range of the data concerning him. (Goode & Hatt 1952: 331)

The comment of the clinical psychologists Gordon and Shontz (1990: 16) is very apt:

A suitable guideline (in a case study, PGS) is to formulate the research problem by stating: 'I wish to study a person who...' and following that with a description of the condition, experience or circumstances of interest (the obvious contrast is with the classical formulation: 'I wish to test the hypothesis that...') after which a specification of the reasons why the study is important, is to follow. For example, I wish to study a person who is adapting to the prospect of dying from a terminal illness, because facing death is a universal problem, and what I learn about that person will reveal one of many ways to experience and deal with it. Knowing in detail how one person does so will open up possibilities for studying how other persons deal with it and eventually for discovering which aspects are universal, which differ as a function of general characteristics of people (traits, values, motives, aptitudes and abilities) and which are idiosyncratic. Used appropriately, such knowledge will promote understanding among counsellors and give guidance to others who face similar problems in the future.

In holistic explanations in the classical sense, one doesn't take recourse to general laws and initial conditions from which an occurrence or condition is deduced, but explanation is based on 'the pattern' of the existing situation, which is called 'a type'. In this view, the difference between *explanans* (the statements that explain) and *explanandum* (the thing to be explained) disappears. An explanation is never 'ready', but is continually elaborated. Because each element of a pattern can change, it may influence other elements. Such ideas are easily recognised in many arguments for qualitative research [15] but they are not accepted in the mainstream of social science research.

The battle between the 'variate language' and a 'typological approach' is almost as old as science itself. In this context, reference is made to a 'Galilean

---

[15]See, for instance, Glaser and Strauss (1967) and Denzin and Lincoln (1994/2000). A first examination of the holistic point of view in science is offered by Diesing (1972).

approach' versus an 'Aristotelian approach'. Our view on this matter is that it is a misunderstanding to think that researchers are interested in 'the complete person' or in an exhaustive description of all the ins and outs of a social system. Researchers who emphasise the 'holistic character' of a case neglect the fact that, starting from a research question, the researcher omits many specific factors and conditions that (s)he considers irrelevant, to be separated in analysis from the relevant properties of the *phenomenon to be studied* and the general factors that influence it. That is, the researcher is interested in general or at least generalisable phenomena and does not follow an idiographic interest (i.e. is only interested in this particular case). A researcher always selects, looks at the world from a certain point of view, and reduces the complexity of reality to a simplified model that seems to be adequate for the solution of the research problem. Failures are possible of course; some observed and measured data may afterwards prove to be irrelevant, while some relevant properties are erroneously left out in the initial modelling. But we do not make any scientific progress if we keep thinking in terms of 'we must observe the whole', instead of thinking in terms of properties or variables.

What is the origin of the point of view that case studies should be 'holistic'? It originates from the usual situation that a case study is undertaken because it is not (yet) possible to isolate the phenomenon under study from its environment: *we simply do not yet know which variables are relevant for the model and which variables are not.* In such a situation it seems wise not to be too selective in the choice of variables. That is not to say that we, as an unguided missile, are going to observe everything (if that would be possible). Making use of available theoretical knowledge is always to be advised. But arguments for an holistic approach in our view should be taken as a warning against

- a premature selection of aspects by the researcher
- a premature closure where one is not open for unexpected aspects
- too simple models of reality, in which, for instance, interactions are not taken into account between several independent variables and neither are non-linear associations[16]
- a premature closure of schemes for data collection and data analysis (on the contrary, one should always be ready to follow unexpected leads in the data as this implies a general search for a flexible research practice)
- negligence of the fact that human beings attach meanings to occurrences, facts, circumstances, other people, and that these meanings differ between persons and are liable to change in the course of the social process.

Holism, in this sense, is not a vague concept, but an intelligent choice as long as a satisfying model of the phenomenon is not attained.

---

[16]A non-linear relation between two variables means that their relationship cannot be portrayed by a straight line, such as the relation between length and weight of people (linear between certain boundaries).

In the same vein, we add that a case study is not necessarily 'qualitative'. In most textbooks an 'open' approach is strongly associated with a qualitative style of analysis and reporting (analysis and reporting in *words, not numbers!*). That is why many scientists in cultural anthropology and sociology identify case studies with a qualitative approach. However, case study research is not to be identified with qualitative research. First, qualitative research contains many more approaches (such as using focus groups, or performing a qualitative analysis of documents, or doing an extended series of non-structured interviews). Second, in several case studies the wealth of within-case data about sub-units[17] requires a strongly quantified measurement and analysis. And in political science case studies, the interest in generalisation, and in systematic quantitative research in order to reach comparability of cases, has been present almost from the beginning. Besides, the qualitative/quantitative dichotomy is used in many different ways, and the use of numbers to represent categories of variables is of minor importance from an epistemological point of view. That is a general reason why we prefer to abstain from these labels.

1.8 Conclusions

There are two ways to learn how to build a house. One might study the construction of many houses – perhaps a large subdivision or even hundreds of thousands of houses. Or one might study the construction of one particular house. The first approach is a cross-case method. The second is a within-case or case study method. (Gerring 2007: 1)

This quote may act as a very apt and short formulation of what a case study is about. A case concerns a specific instance or manifestation of the phenomenon to be studied. A case study may be based on one case (a *single-case study*), or on several cases (a *multiple-case study*). Furthermore, a case may involve only one actor, such as a person, an organisation or a village, or it may involve several, sometimes many, interacting actors (such as in studying a conflict between organisations, a conversation between people, a riot involving hooligans and the police, or a traffic accident).

At least three traditions can be distinguished depending on the level of the inquiry. At the micro-level, in the health sciences, psychology and psychotherapy, a strong tradition exists of N=1 studies, aiming at the healing of this patient or helping this client. While in earlier times many of these studies lacked a firm methodological framework, nowadays most of them are much more disciplined in the striving for comparable data and in the general goal of understanding an illness

---

[17]For instance members of a studied organization, or people living in a village destructed by a typhoon.

and finding an adequate treatment. At the meso-level, disciplines such as sociology, anthropology, history, the administrative and organisational sciences, education and many others use the label 'case studies' in research with an emphasis on detailed description and an understanding and explanation of a social process or phenomenon. At the macro-level, the political sciences and parts of economy apply the label 'case studies' mostly to those research projects that try to uncover relationships between causes and effects using a small number of units, mostly nation-states.

In this book, our focus is on the meso-level.

A case study is defined as the study of a social phenomenon

- in one, or only a few, of its manifestations
- in its natural surroundings
- during a certain period
- that focuses on detailed descriptions, interpretations and explanations that several categories of participants in the system attach to the social process
- in which the researcher starts with a broad research question on an ongoing social process and uses available theories, but abstains from pre-fixed procedures of data collection and data analysis, and always keeps an eye open to the newly gathered data in order to flexibly adjust subsequent research steps
- that exploits several sources of data (informants, documents, observatory notes)
- in which sometimes the participants in the studied case are engaged in a process of confrontation with the explanations, views and behaviours of other participants and with the resulting preliminary results of the researcher.

By the research strategy that is called 'case study' many different phenomena may be studied. The case study has its own place in the gallery of social science strategies. It is, together with other strategies, based on a common methodological framework. However, a clear positioning of the case study between the others is still lacking. This is one of the consequences of the complex origin of the case study: it has its roots in several disciplinary traditions.

EXERCISES

1.1 In addition to those given in Box 1.1, find another example of a social phenomenon that can be fruitfully studied in an intensive as well as an extensive way. Define a research question. Elaborate in not more than 15 lines the main steps taken in each research approach.

1.2 In section 1.2, 16 examples are presented as phenomena that can be the subject of a case study. (a) Define the level (micro-, meso- or macro-) for each example. (b) For each example, define a research question. (c) For each research question, select one or more cases to study. (d) With each case, which actors are involved?

1.3 Find one or two monographs on a case study in a policy field in a library. Make sure the monographs are less than 10 years old. (a) Why do you define these monographs as case studies? (b) Detect the phenomenon to be studied and the research question(s) asked. (c) Write down the selected cases and the units involved. You will be asked to use these monographs for answering more questions in following chapters.

1.4 Scrutinise the cases in the selected monographs for the elements of the definition of a case study presented in this chapter. In which respects do the cases agree with the definition, in which respects do they differ?

1.5 Do the authors of the selected monographs use the idea of an holistic approach? How do they define this? What is the importance of their arguments?

1.6 Some forms of desk research exist that are sometimes considered to be examples of case studies as well. An example might be a comparative study of styles of reporting the same crime in several national newspapers during a certain period. On the basis of our definition, check in which respects this kind of research qualifies as a case study, and in which respects it does not.

KEY TERMS

extensive research
intensive research
phenomenon
case
micro-, meso- and macro-level
confusion of phenomenon and case
historical origins

natural context
continuous monitoring
multiple data sources
exploratory approach
action agency
single- and multiple-case studies
holistic approach

TWO

When to Conduct a Case Study?

In this chapter we are in search of the conditions that invite us to select a case study as our research strategy. After an introduction (section 2.1), we illustrate the type of research questions that are typical for most case studies (section 2.2). In section 2.3, we discuss several specific sets of research conditions that may prompt us to perform a case study. Some further dilemmas have to be taken into account before embarking on a research project (section 2.4). We need information about the 'context' of the project. For instance, is it an autonomous research project, or is it typically additional or auxiliary research, preceding or following a survey? It may even be part of a broad research programme in which documentary analyses, surveys, perhaps experiments are additional components (see section 2.4.1). Another preliminary question is about whether we deal with basic research or applied research (section 2.4.2). A third question concerns the targeted domain of generalisation: do we intend to generalise results to a larger, non-studied set of cases, or are we satisfied with the results for the specific cases under study (section 2.4.3)? In section 2.5 the contents of this chapter are summarised and conclusions are drawn.

2.1 Introduction

Whether it concerns an experiment, a survey, a case study or whatever combination of strategies, we always have to:

- first, carefully acknowledge and formulate the problem(s) we intend to solve with this research endeavour, and
- afterwards, carefully evaluate to what extent we have been successful.

In other words, answering the research question is central. This basic principle is obvious, but it tends to be neglected now and then. Naïve researchers may assume that 'their interest in phenomenon X' sufficiently legitimises their work. Research, however, is a costly enterprise. Defective research implies a waste of (mostly, taxpayers') money. In our view, the researcher has the obligation to conceptualise as sharply as possible which problems have to be solved and which questions have to be answered in order to design an adequate research project. Without a research question to answer, the researcher is liable to endlessly continue collecting and analysing data without ever reaching a satisfying goal. Moreover, it would be impossible to decide which research steps are relevant, which ones irrelevant. Finally, if one cannot relate the outcomes of a research project to the initial research questions, it is impossible to evaluate the research project itself.

The type of *research question* determines to a large extent whether we select an extensive or an intensive strategy. Therefore, in section 2.2, we tackle the types of research question that prompt us to carry out a case study.

The character of the research question, however, provides not the only rational argument for conducting a case study. Other rational arguments relate, for instance, to the *specific conditions* where a case study is the research strategy to select, such as in working on design questions or in doing action research. But these specific conditions include as well research endeavours where other strategies, such as randomised experiments, might be used or even be preferable, but cannot be realised.

2.2 Research questions

2.2.1 Broad questions on social processes

Which research questions turn a case study into the preferred strategy?

If the impetus for our research project lies in some *broad, familiarizing, questions about a social process*, doing a case study seems to be a fitting approach. Some examples are given in Box 2.1.

BOX 2.1

- Which forms of discriminatory behaviour are present in this organisation?
- What is the state of affairs in this village with regard to relations between the established insiders and the outsiders?
- In what manner does this small group of youngsters belonging to an ethnic minority develop into a gang?
- What are the careers of these drug users?
- In which ways do the French railways obtain public support for the planning of a route for the high speed train?
- How does an in-company price adjustment system work?
- Why is absenteeism at this conveyor belt higher than at another conveyor belt?
- Why has the merger process of these hospitals developed in a conflicting way, and in other hospitals more harmoniously?

Generally, posing a broad research question results from a relative absence of knowledge about the process to be studied, otherwise one could have phrased a more specific, precise question or even an hypothesis to begin with. Starting with a broad question usually results, during the process of research, in many detailed questions.

Focusing on social processes, what might be the main groups of variables we are interested in? First, people's thoughts, values, expectations, motives, opinions, experiences, attitudes and behaviours. We emphasise that we do not simply aggregate over individual's various opinions or attitudes, but we explicitly pay attention to *differences* between values, norms, opinions, attitudes and behaviours of various (groups of) people involved in the phenomenon. If we wish to gain insight into the worlds of several groups of stakeholders, in contrasting visions, into the way people perceive bottlenecks and the way they find a solution, we obviously select a case study instead of a survey or an experiment as our research strategy. We want to discover the world as seen by participants in the system, and try to explain why they see it this way. A case study enables us, furthermore, to reliably monitor *changes* in these characteristics by continuous monitoring, or at least by repeated measurements.

It also implies asking people about how they perceive each other and influence each other. In interviewing people about characteristics of other participants in the system (What did board member John do at that moment? What were Bill's ideas?) we are able to check how far John's reality concurs with the reality of others. If we are able to elucidate with each individual his/her ideas about the opinions of the others, we may compare these perceptions mutually, and compare them as well with the model of reality constructed by the researcher so far. The object of study is dynamic. Intensive research includes studying features of the social environment as transitory interpretations constructed by different groups of stakeholders. In the literature about this topic, it is emphasised that a story of this type results from negotiations between the researcher (who poses the questions, presents stimuli) and the researched. However, the interpretations of the researched are sometimes difficult to detect, for example in children, mentally deficient people or foreign language speakers. In addition, the utterances of the researched people are in no way 'the ultimate truth' or sacrosanct: they reflect only the views of some people and there are many different views. Nevertheless, ample attention for participants' own stories is one of the central strong points of almost every case study in the social sciences. In social psychology, the participant's story is called an *account* or a *narrative account*.

Furthermore, we focus on (changes in) social interactions between people. As a result of communication and social interaction, ideas about each other start to develop, ideas that stimulate individual behaviour and new interactions. Particularly, as is often the case in policy research, if the focus is on success or failure of policy measures, it is important to trace the ways in which behaviour is influenced by the interaction of people, and when and how behaviour changes. But also, more concretely, it is important to discover who helps or hinders whom, who tries to influence who and which bottlenecks occur.

By describing certain successive behaviours or situations in detail, accompanied by a description of the motives people attach to a change in their behaviour and the changing perceptions they have about each other, we may obtain insights into micro-level social processes which would remain hidden if we were restrained to simple survey-like cross-tabulations. In doing a case study, we obtain solutions for explanatory problems on the micro-level that can be embedded in social science theories.

Summarising, if we want more information about what (groups of) people perceive and decide, in relation to their interaction during a certain period, a case study seems to be the optimal strategy. While at the start of a research project we perhaps had a rather simple causal model in mind, we are now actually searching for the 'intervening variables in a causal chain'. Factors and circumstances mentioned by people can help to fill in the causal process (see Box 2.2).

BOX 2.2   Detailing a causal chain

It is known from documentary evidence and surveys that immigrant children do better at integrated schools than at 'segregated' schools. An easy interpretation is that the probability of being befriended by native youngsters is higher in integrated schools, and therefore the probability of picking up the language and other useful subcultural habits at school may and integration into society generally. A case study showed that the improved results were partly caused by the ambition 'to do better than the natives youngsters', an ambition that does not develop at in segregated schools, where pupils feel less challenged.

An approach such as this is already more or less standard in education/labour market research and in health and social care studies: what has been the career of a specific person?; which schools?; why a switch?; what changes of jobs and periods of joblessness?; what explanations does the individual offer for each change?

The following quotes of qualitative researchers may illustrate the importance of this approach:

> Studies of individual cases allow the researcher to learn the intricate details of how a treatment is working, rather than averaging the effect across a number of cases. (Kennedy 1979)

> We uncover all kinds of relationships in our 'hard' data, but it is only through the use of this 'soft' data that we are able to 'explain' them. (Mintzberg 1979)

The word 'only' in this second quote is a bit exaggerated, but Mintzberg drives home the point. When one is led by these desiderata, and when there are no practical or financial hindrances, a case study is an appropriate strategy to choose.

2.2.2 Precise research questions and hypotheses

Discussing the importance of research questions and immediately embarking upon one special type – broad, orienting research questions – the reader may wonder what other types can be distinguished. In this section we grasp the opportunity to elaborate this point. Research questions may differ in at least two respects.

The first criterion refers to the classic distinction between

- descriptive
- explanatory, and
- predictive (or rather, in applied research, design) research questions.

Descriptive research questions are 'what' or 'how' questions. Explanatory research questions are 'why' questions. Prediction questions have the format of 'what will happen if' questions. Design questions (see section 2.3) refer to designing an intervention: 'What is the best way to change…?'

The second criterion relates to the state of our knowledge. In this light, research questions can be distinguished by degree of completeness or precision, into

- object demarcations
- broad questions
- precise questions, and
- hypotheses.

In the following, we elaborate this second distinction.[1]

1. '*Object demarcations*', such as '(a study of) six general elections in Britain' have little content, and consequently are of little importance, because a real question or problem is not yet indicated. A study such as this may refer to a N=1 case study (with Britain as the 'unit'). It might also, in the frame of a study into the changing political climate, refer to a N=6 study (that possibly may also be regarded as a case study; the research question may refer to changing non-response habits in Britain), or refer to a N=120,000,000 study (the units are the voters and the research question may refer to individual determinants of voting behaviour) (this is Eckstein's example, see Eckstein 1975).

2. When we know little about our object, we are restricted to *broad, orienting questions*. Such questions characterise many case studies, and tackling them requires an exploratory approach (see section 2.2.3). We emphasise that despite its broad character, in order to fulfil its function as a 'leading guide' in research steps to be taken, the *wording* of any research question, also the 'broad' ones, should be as transparent and precise as possible!

---

[1]This distinction is derived from Bunge (1967).

3. Sometimes, however, it is possible to start a case study with a series of *precise questions*. In case studies, they are used if one can build on earlier research. A popular topic is, for instance, the description of an innovation in an organization, and the different views of stakeholders on the matter, hindrances and bottlenecks. Examples are the introduction of a computer network in an office, a new patient's intake system in a hospital, or a reorganisation after an industrial merger. We can build already on research traditions in these fields because much is known about the relevant variables, and the problems that may arise. Accordingly, a new research project need not start with a broad, orienting question, but it is possible to start with a series of closed, precise questions. Another example refers to studying the causes of traffic accidents, as mentioned in Chapter 1. Much earlier research has been done, and a rather precise model of the phenomenon can already be constructed. In this example, we will certainly collect data on the age of the people involved, their yearly mileage, the type of car they use, weather and road conditions, time of the day, and so on. Those variables are included in a first model of the phenomenon because we expect them to be relevant.

4. If we dispose of earlier research results, laid down in a theory, we may even accompany such precise questions with a preliminary answer. That is to say, we start with an *hypothesis*: a combination of a precise statement followed by a question mark. Our research project aims at eliminating the question mark, and by doing so, at confirming (or falsifying!) the statement. Hypothesis-testing research is a standard approach if we dispose of a theory that enables us to predict that in a certain situation X will occur, and not Y or Z. Research like this is especially interesting if we wish to decide between two or more theories leading to conflicting predictions. Applications of theory testing are rather rare with case studies. One famous example is Festinger et al's *When Prophecy Fails* (1956) (see Box 2.3).

BOX 2.3   When Prophecy Fails (Festinger et al., 1956)[2]

Festinger and his colleagues infiltrated a group of people who were members of a UFO doomsday cult in order to test his 'cognitive dissonance theory'. Cognitive dissonance is an uncomfortable feeling caused by holding two contradictory beliefs simultaneously. This will lead people to change their beliefs to fit their actual behaviour, rather than the other way round. The book documents the increased *proselytization* (increasing efforts to find new followers) these people

(Continued)

---

[2]Adapted from en.wikipedia.org/wiki/Cognitive_dissonance under a Creative Commons Attribution – ShareAlike 3.0 Unported License (creativecommons.org/licenses/by-sa/3.0/).

(Continued)

exhibited after the leader's prophecy failed to come true. The prediction of the Earth's destruction, supposedly sent by aliens to the leader of the group, became a disconfirmed expectation that caused dissonance between the cognitions 'the world is going to end' and 'the world did not end'. The members lessened the dissonance by accepting a new belief that the world was spared because of the faith of the group. The results confirmed the cognitive dissonance theory.

2.2.3 Exploration of data versus a stricter approach

One of the reasons for the overwhelming use of broad research questions in case studies is that at the start of a research project we do not yet have a sharply bounded model of the phenomenon, that is to say we do not know which properties of the context of the case under study are relevant. Assuming our phenomena to be dependent on a variety of unknown contextual characteristics, it seems wise to start by monitoring one case or a few cases *in their natural context* and study them as thoroughly as possible.

Likewise, there is no complete inventory of variables available, nor measuring instruments ready to use. Neither are procedures for data collection, nor codings and ready-to-use procedures for data analysis. Our first research steps are tentative, and we are ready to change direction as a consequence of our findings. This is what is called an *exploratory* research approach. Typical for an exploratory approach is its flexibility and openness towards the phenomenon under study. No hypotheses are formulated in advance. Research decisions follow the data; diversions are allowed. One tries to get out of the data what's in it. Flexibility instead of fixation ahead is characteristic for an exploratory approach. Therefore, the odds on *discovering* relevant aspects and finding really interesting results is much larger than in doing research that follows routines that are already fixed and would be closed to unexpected developments or new discourses findings.

This does not mean that we start our research without any ideas at all. The often very sketchy theory we start with is instrumental in providing us with some guidance, to help us in the preliminary selection of concepts and variables. During the research process, the rudimentary theory is further developed, specified, perhaps even modified or replaced by a more appropriate one.

Obviously, there is another side to the coin. One disadvantage of an exploratory approach is that it requires much time. Researchers show a tendency to drift around; a research project never seems to be terminated. A second disadvantage is that as a consequence of the continuous adjustments in the process of research, there is ample space for the researcher's personal and situational biases to enter research results. If the results of an exploring researcher are being criticised by a colleague, (s)he can 'always find a way out', for instance by adding another variable to the model. In this way, the research results are invulnerable to critique and scientific progress is aborted from the beginning. Third, there is always the danger of falling into the trap of capitalising on chance: a finding that is specific for the researched case – and only for that case – is interpreted as a fact of general significance. With exploration, the odds with respect to bias are much larger than with testing, and accordingly the range, or scope, of research results is more modest. Therefore, the explorer's results should almost always be provided with a question mark.

Some researchers are proponents of the idea that in following this bottom-up approach a theory can be *developed*. Glaser and Strauss (1967) introduced the expression 'grounded theory'; Bromley (1986: 2) uses the label 'case-laws'. But, apart from the fact that we do not start without some preliminary ideas, the development of a theory on the basis of research with one, or a few, case(s) cannot be more than a starting point. Testing the model or theory is necessary, that is to say, if we aim at a theory that covers more instances of the phenomenon than the one studied. A testing approach requires more research and more (independent) cases, and, especially, an a priori fixed approach that minimises the odds for the researcher's biases.

In a testing approach, the researcher states his/her findings in clear and unambiguous propositions that do not leave escape routes: either an hypothesis is confirmed or it is falsified. At least, this is the basic idea in testing what is called a deterministic relationship, where no exceptions are tolerated. In research practice we take errors in measurement and perhaps even argumentation into account, and usually we continue testing an hypothesis or a theory in several other research endeavours. In recent methodology, the concept of 'deterministic' is even 'softened up' in several ways, as Box 2.4 and the discussion of Ragin's solutions in section 4.3 will show.

In a testing approach, there is another side to the coin as well. We might miss findings that were not expected, we might overlook the richness and peculiarities of the phenomenon under study.

BOX 2.4   Exploring data versus testing data

The classic pair of polar concepts, 'exploration' and 'testing', probably requires some updating. To start with, these labels are extremes that define a continuum. This continuum refers to the explicitness of procedures (are they 'written down' in advance of the project and followed in the course of the project?) and the researcher's accountability.

Exploration means that reality is approached with few pre-arranged ideas about how to handle the research object. The research is carried out following hunches, changing direction, sometimes in a very quick succession, and the researcher is unaccountable for all 'thinking and changing'.

(Continued)

(Continued)

On the contrary, the other extreme implies fixing all procedures beforehand, and the researcher following a pre-arranged routine. In case of a deviation (s)he is expected to carefully document her/his steps. The rigour of the method is necessary in order to realise the idea of testing. It should be crystal clear whether the initial statements about reality are rejected or accepted – for the time being.

But all types of scientific endeavour have in common the 'empirical cycle' of research:

Problem
Tentative solution
Data collection and analysis
Confronting the tentative solution with the data, often leading to a new problem and a new cycle of research.

In testing research, the 'tentative solution' is a precise statement (question + answer) that is called an hypothesis. A simple experiment may serve as an example. The cycle is carried out only once, and it is carefully documented.

In an exploratory approach, cycles are carried out repeatedly (and they sometimes remain undocumented and even unremembered!), leading to many iterations and many intermediate 'tentative solutions'.

The distinction between exploratory and testing approaches nowadays is less important than it used to be. In quantitative research, the classical distinction has become less useful because of the practice of multivariate analysis methods such as Generalised Linear Models, in which a continuous adjustment of models replaces the old dichotomy 'conjecture' versus 'refutation'. Second, the occurrence of one falsification of a prediction is seldom handled as being definitive. It is to be expected that the gradual disappearance of the earlier sharp distinction will make it easier for survey researchers to accept the 'weaker' case study methodology. Eventually, the pair of concepts relates to the degree of self-criticism of the researcher; of his/her critical attitude versus data and interpretations. The stricter your approach is, the less ambiguity and the fewer interpretations your data permits. Thereby, in following a stricter approach you make yourself vulnerable; you are making it easier for an opponent to criticise you; there are less ways out. This is a good methodological principle to keep in mind. So the essence of the continuum defined by a flexible approach versus a fixed approach is in heightening the researcher's awareness of the possible impact of one's biases in a flexible approach as well as the danger of premature closure in a more rigid approach.

2.3 Specific conditions

In section 2.2 we explained that the impetus for doing a case study often is a broad research question. We added that certainly sometimes a precise research question or even an hypothesis is used at the start of a case study. Irrespective of the type of research question, there are some specific conditions that prompt us to carry out a case study.

Design problems. One of these situations refers to the presence of design problems, which are often solved with the help of a small-scale or case study approach. In basic (and applied) research, we try to solve problems of description ('what is' and 'how' questions) as well as problems of explanation ('why'- questions). Besides, in basic research, problems of prediction arise ('is our theory sufficiently articulated in order to predict future situations?'). In applied research, *problems of designing* replace *problems of prediction*. A design may consist of a policy advice about a certain mix of policy measures. It may also be, in a more technical sense, the design of a curriculum, of software, of an industrial strategy (a budgeting system; a planning strategy; a stock control system) or of a part of the organisation. In research such as this, it is assumed that, to start with, descriptive problems with respect to the actual situation have been solved in earlier research. Furthermore, it is assumed that, with the help of theories, the extant situation is explained. Now the essence of design research is to deduce the specific conditions under which another, more desirable, state of the system can be attained, using these same theories. A specification such as this results in a policy advice, a mix of measures, a *design*. Often, we cannot be certain, however, about the adequacy of a proposed policy measure or a package of measures – usually *'ceteris paribus'* clauses are abundantly used in formulating the policy advice. Therefore, we are not satisfied with the blueprint alone. Its implementation has to be monitored (by process- or formative-evaluation). In process-evaluation the researcher is enabled, during the process, to adjust policy measures if they do not function satisfactorily, preferably in an experimental or small-scale environment where not much harm can be done and that is not too costly. Therefore, case studies are often used as an aid in solving design problems. A series of preliminary designs of policy 'packages' ('try-outs') is carried out within a handful of specific small social systems (e.g. school classes) to study the consequences, in order not to cause any harm to the larger domain for which it is eventually designed. A specific asset of a case study is that it enables us to understand emerging problems and their practical solutions in the social system under study. Gaining insight into these aspects is very profitable in optimising our design or policy advice. Typical for design research is the occurrence of many *iterations*. One 'unit' or a few 'units' (e.g. a school class or a department in a factory) are involved in a series of trials, in which successive variants of the policy measure are implemented. Cycles in which a minor or a major change in the design of the measure is implemented are repeated. With the help of a theory, we describe what is done in each cycle, we explain why the design is not completely satisfactory, we deduce which modifications are needed to lead to the desired result, and we test our deductions in the next cycle. Finally, at the end, its overall success should be tested. This is product- or summative-evaluation.

Action research. Some researchers explicitly link their research activities to change agency. They are not satisfied by measuring opinions, attitudes and behaviours of groups of stakeholders, but by confronting these with each other and bringing them together in sessions under a professional 'moderator'. In this way they try to 'all head in the same direction'. In situations such as these, a combination of research and action agency/social assistance is at hand. Obviously, this type of research is only possible in the specific social system one intends to change, so a case study is the fitting strategy to use.

The rarity of the phenomenon. Another specific condition refers to the rarity of the phenomenon. Certain phenomena are very rare, such as, fortunately, some epidemics or disasters. Well-known examples relate to the behaviour of a group of sectarians who kept predicting the decline of the world after this prediction had been falsified (see Box 2.3), the flood disaster in New Orleans in 2005, or a terrorist attack on the scale of 9/11. The researcher deserves congratulations if (s)he succeeds in studying an example (e.g. people's behaviour under a terrorists attack) from inside. In policy research, the domain is often rather small. Consequently, it is not suitable for extensive research when one needs quite a number of units. If we decided to study AIDS policy in the EC countries, or the procedures followed by parliamentary survey committees since 1980, the maximum N is 20 or 25. Furthermore, in evaluation research, the policy to be evaluated is often rather new. As a consequence of this only a few cases are available that contain enough information that justify their inclusion in the sample. One has to search for a long time to find some cases that are functioning long enough to provide interesting information. Anyway, case studies are the indicated research strategy.

Feasibility. A fourth rational motive for selecting a case study as a research strategy refers to restrictions implied by the research – or the researcher's! – context: another approach might be preferable, but a case study is the only feasible one. An emphasis on these restrictions, which have little to do with the research question itself, can be found, for instance, in the writings of a well-known author on case studies, R.K. Yin. This need not surprise us since this author has his origins in experimental psychology. He favours the experiment as the Kings's way to solve a causality problem, and posits other approaches in a context 'where a real experiment is not feasible'. First, a phenomenon, such as a riot or a strike, cannot be invoked or simulated at will in a psychology lab. The researcher will have to patiently wait until 'it happens' in reality (and it will be over before a survey can be organised!). Second, it may happen that some policy experiment on a small-scale is undertaken, but the policy agent decides on the selection of participants in the experiment, and/or self-selection occurs. Here, the researcher has no say in the selection of experimental or control groups, which generally results in bias. If, owing to circumstances such as these, we have little or no control over the objects of study, an experiment is replaced by a (multiple) case study as a next best solution.

2.4 Further considerations

Before actually embarking on a case study, some preliminary questions have to be asked and answered, questions that relate to the wider context of our research endeavour:

- Is the planned case study intended to be an autonomous research project, or is it a minor study, additional to a large survey, or is it part of a complex strategy (section 2.4.1)?
- Does our project concern basic research or applied research (section 2.4.2)?
- Is it our intention to generalise results from the studied cases to a larger set of cases, or are we only interested in the cases actually studied (section 2.4.3)?
- Are we free to restrict or enlarge the domain at will (as often is the case in basic research), or are we dealing with a domain already demarcated by the client? This final question is tackled in Chapter 3.

2.4.1 Autonomous research or additional strategy?

A case study can be a quite autonomous project. But it may also be part of a complex of several research approaches within a larger project. In the research report, the role of the case study has to be made quite clear. In this second context, case studies often play a role as pilot project: the results of a prior case study may help us to design a more extensive (survey) approach. Furthermore, a case study may produce specific knowledge that can be used to design questionnaires and other instruments for the main research effort (instrument construction). A case study can also function in the reverse order: after studying a phenomenon in its 'width' by means of a survey, it is additionally researched in its 'depth' by the study of some cases. In this way, the latter functions as a complementary design in order to help in explaining, especially if a survey produces ambivalent or non-interpretable results, or if the (multiple) case study is used for research on deviant cases. Logically, research in the order 'cases → survey → cases', is possible as well. In Chapter 7 we will extend the discussion about the use of 'mixed methods'.

2.4.2 Basic research or applied research?

Basic research is characterised by research questions aimed at developing, illustrating or testing general theories. Applied research aims at providing knowledge that can be used in solving practical problems. Obviously, results of basic research might eventually find usage in solving practical problems, whereas applied research might in the long run help in establishing theories. But these are unintended functions. This is not to say that the report of an applied research project always contains policy advice. Sometimes it is restricted to descriptive knowledge, or perhaps also explanations are offered; the wording of policy suggestions is left to the reader. If, however, policy suggestions are formulated, this means that the researcher has tackled one or more design problems, a type of scientific problem that is absent in basic research.

An obvious criterion to judge the quality of the results of an *applied* research project is that results should be *usable* for the client, and hence the results of an applied case study project should be usable too.

It is worth adding a few lines about quality criteria for results in scientific research. The *standards for research quality in social science are valid for case study research as well as for all other research strategies*. They are treated in almost all textbooks on methodology, which is the reason why we do not extensively discuss this topic here. We mention them here briefly, just as a help to memory.

1 *Construct validity*: are your tests, instruments, questions and observation schemes measuring the concepts they intend to measure? Valid measurement in this sense means that variations in measurement results are caused by variations in theoretical concepts, and that we can explain why the variation in measurement results is caused by variation in the concept.
2 *Reliability*: are the results of your measurements stable over time, independent of the researcher(s), and independent of contextual properties? That is, in so far as your results are intended to be stable over time and independent of contextual properties. As implied in earlier sections, in case studies the 'contextuality' of some measurements is accepted.
3 *Internal or causal validity*: is the relation between variables, interpreted by you as causal, really causal? Or are the correlations resulting from other factors?
4 *External validity or generalisability*: are the results of your research project generalisable to the targeted populations or domains?

In the world of qualitative research, many other systems of quality criteria were introduced in the final decades of the twentieth century. Guba and Lincoln (Guba 1981; Lincoln & Guba 1985; Guba & Lincoln 1994) are well known for their publications in this area. Criteria such as trustworthiness, credibility, confirmability, transferability, and many others have found their way into research projects and reports.

We do not consider it useful to define, compare and discuss these terms and systems here. It would require a lot of space, while leading us to not much more than variations on the concept of usability (see above). Besides, we consider the development of alternative systems of quality criteria, each one to be used for a separate strand of research (such as qualitative and quantitative) as one of the less fruitful enterprises in the social sciences.

The one and only central quality criterion that distinguishes applied research from basic research is the striving for usability for the client of applied research results. Starting from the idea of usability, several practical hints can be developed (Swanborn 1996a).

A sharp distinction between applied (respectively, design) research and basic research sometimes serves as a justification for the fact that in applied research certain methodological benchmarks cannot always be attained (time is too short, informants refuse to co-operate, several stakeholders take a counterproductive attitude or have strongly contrasting expectations regarding the result of the research, etc.). Regrettably, these are very realistic circumstances, but all this does not liberate the applied researcher from his/her duty to do his/her utmost to keep to the traditional methodological criteria as much as possible – criteria that are no different for basic and applied science. In basic research as well, practical restrictions lead to the fact that a study can almost never be undertaken under perfect conditions. Scientists who make a sharp distinction in this respect seem to neglect that methodological criteria, such as reliability and validity, concern rules *one has to strive for*. Included in these rules is the obligation to report one's research steps explicitly, and to locate weak points in order to enable the reader to value the results.

BOX 2.5   A special methodology for 'design research'?

In several applied sciences, such as educational science, organisational science, the policy sciences and the socio-technical sciences, the special character of a separate 'methodology for design research' with specific quality criteria is argued. We are of a slightly different opinion. Instead of emphasising the differences, we are inclined to stress that from the start the methods of the 'design sciences', or applied sciences, policy sciences, practice-oriented sciences, change-directed sciences, or whatever they are called are quite comparable to the methods of basic research. Second, prediction problems in the basic sciences and design problems in the applied sciences both originate in the solution of explanation problems, because theories are at the base of all these problems. In applied research one uses theories that are developed and tested in basic research. Obviously, we admit that an explanation for an existing situation does not 'automatically' provide us with the instruments to change the existing situation into a better one. The necessary conditions, specified in the theory, have to be realised; variables have to be manipulated; several criteria, such as timing and social acceptability, play a role. We do not deny that in applied research there is often a long way to go between the first ideas, resulting from theory-based predictions, and a blueprint of workable interventions. Evidently, severe practical and technical problems have to be resolved. But this hardly necessitates a separate 'design methodology' in social science.

2.4.3 The domain: cases as *pars pro toto* or stand-alone cases

In case studies we study one example, or a very restricted number of examples, of a social phenomenon. A central preliminary question is: do we intend to generalise our research conclusions based on this example or this small set of examples, to a larger set? If this is our intention, we use the expression *pars pro toto* (a part representing the whole) research. Alternatively, if it is not our intention to generalise our conclusions beyond the researched case(s), we use the expression *stand-alone cases.*[3]

There is an important difference between basic research, in which we always want to generalise, at least in principle, and applied research, in which the intention to generalise from the studied cases to a wider domain may or may not be present. We illuminate this point below. In *basic research*, the collected knowledge primarily serves to develop, to illustrate or to test scientific theories. If practical interests are served as well, so much the better, but this aspect is not emphasised. In basic research we are not especially interested in the phenomenon as it manifests itself in this selected researched case, but the domain of the research question is larger: we want to generalise, on the basis of the case, to a larger set of cases. That is because theories and models transcend the specific case. They are abstractions of concrete manifestations of the phenomenon. A selected case always deviates more or less from a theory or model. From the start, the researcher is interested in the question of which concepts and variables are of general interest: the selected case is a more or less accidental 'bearer' of the phenomenon. Researchers strive for a domain that is as large as possible.

Publications of researchers such as Glaser and Strauss (1967), many anthropologists and the Chicago School sociologists fit into a basic, theory-oriented tradition. With some case studies from the famous Chicago School, it perhaps seems that the author presents a description of a local community or organisation without the intention to generalise to a larger set of cases, but this is mostly a misinterpretation. The studied community is seen as representative of many others. Compare titles such as *Small Town in Mass Society* (Vidich & Bensman 1958), *The Conduct of the Corporation* (Moore 1967), *The Dynamics of Bureaucracy* (Blau 1955) and *Middletown* (Lynd & Lynd 1929/1956). Here *pars pro toto* research was conducted.

Sometimes we stumble upon seemingly 'basic' case studies in which generalisation is not the objective. *All the presidents men*, by Bernstein and Woodward (1974) on the Watergate scandal, might be an example. It is not applied science, but is it basic science? It is perhaps better not to perceive this kind of research as science, but to perceive it as pre-scientific, journalistic work. That does not exclude the fact that publications of this kind can be used as raw material for generalising studies. Indirectly or unintentionally, such studies may contribute to the making of

---

[3]In the context of 'stand-alone cases', Stake (1995: 3) uses the label 'intrinsic case studies', and in the context of cases as *pars pro toto* the label 'instrumental case studies'. Gerring (2007: 187) uses the unfortunately chosen labels 'single-outcome studies' and 'case studies'.

theories. Descriptive monographs can later be used by researchers in their efforts to reach a higher level of abstraction, and to cover larger domains (see Box 2.6 for examples of this).

BOX 2.6 Examples of basic *pars pro toto* research

- A group of American sociologists (Becker et al. 1961) conduct a research project on a medical campus to identify the ways in which students identify with their new professional field and their teachers.
- Dutch criminologists (Bovenkerk 1977) study the behaviour of disco bouncers within the frame of a general research programme about racial discrimination.
- Lipset, Trow and Coleman (1956) study a trade union that showed a peculiar deviation of Michels's theory of oligarchisation, to detect the conditions under which this general theory is invalid, or to detect a more general theory that enables scientists to explain the existing findings as well as the exceptions.
- Glaser and Strauss (1965) study social interactions and processes of meaning in hospitals around terminally ill patients. The social context was the hospital ward. Within the ward the individual patients and their social contexts can be distinguished. The researchers did not aim at describing a specific ward; their goal was to develop, to 'ground', a theory on social processes in general. The theoretical concepts that, according to the authors, were developed in this study, such as 'awareness context' and 'social loss', illustrate this.
- Allison's *Essence of Decision: Explaining the Cuban Missile Crisis* (1971, 1999). In this study several theories to explain the origins and solution of international political crises are discussed and tested.

In *applied research*, however, the ambition to generalise our results beyond the case(s) studied may or may not exist. Generally, policy-makers are only interested in the improvement of the situation of one, or a few, specific social units. The aim is not to develop, illustrate or test general theories. The collected knowledge has to be usable for:

- practitioners (management, therapists, action agencies, technical personnel, CEOs) in order to change part of reality, be it an individual (a clinical problem), an organisation (e.g. with an eye to a go/non-go decision regarding a production line), a local community, nation-state, or whatever.
- the design of (packages of) policy proposals, material objects such as computer hardware and software, budget systems or whichever measures are deemed useful to change an undesirable situation. We certainly do *apply* general theories, but these are used to select concepts and theories and to provide an interpretative scheme.

If our targeted domain[4] is not larger than the cases selected for the study, we use the term 'stand-alone cases'. The domain may be the schools for special education in a certain city; the four production departments in a factory; the institutionalised care for asylum seekers in a certain region; a community; a hospital; a police station or whatever organisation the policy refers to. In applied research the researcher will be less inclined to eliminate specific, local characteristics of the case as irrelevant. If the policy is directed towards that case, all factors, also case-specific ones, may be of importance. This leads to the conclusion that in applied case studies, more than in basic case studies, attention is drawn to the local situation and concentrates on the embeddedness of the phenomenon in local contexts (see Box 2.7).

BOX 2.7   Examples of applied, 'stand-alone' research

- With respect to the intention to locate departments with a high level of interaction with each other in each other's vicinity, the interaction intensity of all departments of a community police force in a city are studied, the mutual perceptions and appreciations are monitored, and wishes with respect to the future location are inventoried.
- An evaluation research project into the intended and realised functions of a social centre for prostitutes in a Red Light district.

However, in applied science, case studies are not, by definition, restricted to stand-alone cases. Quite another situation exists when the set of cases in the research question is much larger than the set of cases taken into empirical study. Just as in basic research, these cases function as *pars pro toto*. So-called policy experiments also fit this category (see Box 2.8).

BOX 2.8   Examples of applied, *pars pro toto* research

- In a London police station, a researcher studies discriminatory behaviour by male officers towards their female colleagues. The aim is to identify problems and find practical solutions, which can then be used in other police stations as well.
- The Ministry of Education is interested in how a new curriculum is being introduced into primary schools. Research is undertaken in several schools

---

[4]The term 'domain' perhaps requires some comment. It simply means the set of all cases the researcher wishes to generalise to. In a statistical context it is more often labelled as the population or the universe.

that are in different phases of developing the curriculum. The results of the research are expected to be useful for all schools in the country.

- The Department of Traffic organises a research project within eight communities to discover the impacts of limiting the use of private cars in those areas. The aim is to detect successful strategies that may then be adopted in other communities.
- An umbrella confederation of action groups in the field of regional planning has carried out a study into factors influencing the success and failure of some well-known action initiatives. The objective is to better fund future action initiatives.

Some researchers, for instance Yin (1994)[5] and Gerring (2007), even conceptualise case studies exclusively as *pars pro toto* studies. In this way, however, an important category of case studies is neglected. The fact that a distinction between cases as *pars pro toto* and stand-alone cases so far receives little attention causes much confusion. It is very common, for instance, to speak about the lack of external validity or generalisability of a case study. Apparently it is often overlooked that in 'stand-alone cases' the problem of external validity does not present itself.

2.5 Conclusions

The selection of the case study as a research strategy is primarily guided by the character of the *research question*. If it concerns descriptive and/or explanatory broad questions about a social process in a situation in which we have *little knowledge of the phenomenon*, and specifically if we are interested in the ways several individuals and groups of stakeholders interact with each other and interpret each other's behaviour, and the ways in which they cope with problems, we need to explore one or more cases to clarify the intricate web of social relations, perceptions, opinions, attitudes and behaviour. Besides, case studies as a main research strategy are selected under one or more of the following set of conditions:

- the impossibility to isolate or simulate (properties that are relevant to) the phenomenon
- the rarity of the phenomenon
- design problems
- the intention to combine research and action.

---

[5]In Yin (2003: 16) this point of view is corrected.

Some general background questions have to be posed and answered:

- Are we dealing with an autonomous case study, or is the planned case study part of a complex of strategies to tackle the same object. If the latter is the case, how does the case study fit in with respect to the other strategies?
- Are we dealing with basic research or with applied research?
- Do the cases to be selected figure as *pars pro toto* or as stand-alone cases? Often we want to generalise to a larger set of cases, but sometimes we are only interested in the specific cases under study. In this context, the demarcation of the phenomenon to be studied as well as of the units or cases, the bearers of the phenomenon, is of primary significance.

In the reality of research practice, several non-rational factors may also be involved in selecting a research strategy. Some proponents consider the case study as the one and only strategy in social science. They tend to ignore the fact that many research questions, for instance those with respect to frequency distributions,[6] simply cannot be answered by a case study. Some others consider the selection of a research strategy as almost completely dependent on their own subjective priorities and preferences. One could say that the case study selected them, rather than the other way around. Indeed, some students do have an inborn preference for large-scale surveys, others for intensive field studies within one social system, such as a village, a hospital, an organisation, or a sex club. Actually, in such cases the researcher's personal preferences precede formulating the research question. One cannot object to this state of affairs as long as a relevant research question is posed and the research strategy is an adequate choice. But, in the harsh reality of social research, many exceptions to this rule exist! There are also those who regard the case study as only a second-best choice, when for practical reasons other preferred strategies are excluded.

The fact that rational arguments do not always dictate the choice of a strategy disturbs the picture of the research landscape. Sometimes it seems methodologically sound to organise a survey or an experiment, while for reasons of time and money a case study approach (or vice versa) is chosen. A researcher is not always fortunate enough to choose the optimal strategy. Student research proposals often fall in this category. Often a school class, a hospital ward, a police station or another local institution is turned into the object of scientific attention, depending on its vicinity, already existing contacts or the expectation of easier access. Again, one cannot object to this, as long as relevant research questions are posed and the

---

[6]Frequency distribution problems (i.e. 'how much' questions) cannot, or can hardly, be solved by case studies. Doing a case study to answer such questions makes little sense because there is not much to count, and if there is anything to count, this has little use because the selected cases are not representative for the intended domain of cases. How many ethnic youngsters drop out of school because of conflicts with their parents is not a question to answer with a case study. For some 'how much' questions, however, a case study is the only way to get an (approximate) answer. If we want to know how many youngsters took part in a riot, or how much damage was inflicted upon property, a case study is the relevant choice of method.

case study can be expected to produce an answer to such questions. But it is not uncommon that research questions are posed that lead to uninteresting results and that the case in question could have been tackled much more effectively by a nation-wide survey, for example.

There is one more factor that may affect the choice of a research strategy. This factor is the perceived difficulty of a strategy. Generally, case studies are perceived as 'easier' to bring to a good ending than, for instance, experiments or a survey. This idea is wrong. Exactly because there is no fixed procedure to follow, and exactly because the 'social sensitivity' of the researcher as well as creativity and methodological sophistication play a major role, a case study is more difficult to perform than following a strategy of several phases, each phase more or less dictated by 'how to do' handbooks. Flexibility and a potential for quick learning in the field are the necessary characteristics of the case study researcher.

EXERCISES

2.1 Try to draw a provisional picture of a case study prompted by the broad question: 'How does a small group of boys of an ethnic minority develop into a gang?' Formulate at least five more precise research questions that might arise in the course of the study. Do the same for: 'Why has the merger process of these schools resulted in conflict whereas in other schools it progressed harmoniously?'

2.2 (a) Replace the broad research questions of Exercise 2.1 with one of the more precise research questions. How would this change your research design? (b) Reformulate your precise questions as hypotheses. Using these as you starting point for research, how would this affect your design?

2.3 Using the monographs of Exercise 1.3, scrutinise the texts on the intended domain (of generalisation). Carefully read the arguments used – if any – about the actual domain of the conclusions. Are they convincing?

2.4 In section 2.3, the specific conditions for doing a case study include 'design problems' and 'action research'. Both deviate from our 'cover all' definition of case studies in Chapter 1. Analyse the respects in which they differ and the respects in which they agree with the definition.

2.5 (a) Referring to the first example in Box 2.6, formulate the research question(s) in a precise way. Do you think the exploratory approach is still necessary? Or would you be able to document (most of) the research decisions and steps in advance? (b) Although the policy domain is rather restricted, this case study might produce some results that later on prove to be valuable for other policy fields as well. Which results, would there be?

2.6 Intended *pars pro toto* research might fail to reach conclusions that go beyond the domain of the (few) cases studied. One of the examples (in Box 2.8) attempts to limit the use of private cars. What factors might account for a lack of generalisability in this case study?

KEY TERMS

broad research questions

detailed analysis of social processes

precise research questions

hypotheses

exploration

impossibility to simulate/isolate

rarity of the phenomenon

case studies in design research

case studies in action research

autonomous case studies

case study as additional strategy

cases as *pars pro toto*

stand-alone cases

THREE

How to Select Cases?

Uncertainty and uneasiness about the number of cases, and about selection procedures for cases, result in some frequently asked questions (section 3.1). In section 3.2 we discuss the demarcation of the domain to study. We proceed with methods to select cases from within the domain. In section 3.3 we illustrate several situations in which no selection at all takes place. Random selection is discussed in section 3.4. Section 3.5 covers selection on practical grounds, and section 3.6 selection on substantive grounds. The generalisation problem is tackled in section 3.7. Finally, in section 3.8, questions and answers are neatly arranged and some conclusions are drawn.

3.1 Introduction

As in all research, an early and careful demarcation of the domain under study is essential. We have to determine beforehand the domain (i.e. the set of cases) for which our conclusions should be valid. Hence, don't start by picking a case and postponing the demarcation of the generalisation domain to a later time, but start by defining the targeted domain, and then select the case(s) accordingly.

Next, the question of *how to select* cases from the domain arises. Here, three problems need to be solved:

- How to go about finding cases in research practice?
- How many cases to select?
- If selection is necessary, which criteria should be used?

The *first* question can be answered relatively simple. That is to say, nothing much can be said about it. Finding cases can take a lot of time. Problems and opportunities with detecting cases are not principally different from those with sampling in extensive research. We mention four possibilities here:

- Drawing a sample from a list or frame covering all units belonging to the domain. If the domain refers to recognisable social units, such as pupils, or shopping malls, companies, municipalities, etc., more often than not a frame exists. In applied research, a frame is often put forward by the client. However, if one wants to select cases with the help of certain criteria, it is of little use when these criteria cannot be identified in the frame.

- 'Reputation' samples, where experts, key persons, authorities 'in the field' are asked to provide information or possible informants, and with their help the researcher composes a frame of all eligible cases. Such people may also be useful in establishing contacts in the field. However, we need to guard against the fact that some informants may be influenced by these 'intermediaries' which may affect their participation in the research. To avoid this scenario, it is always advisable to consult more than one person or representative of an institution.
- Sometimes network or snowball sampling is used where finding one possible case can lead eventually to a long list of cases. Examples are found in research among small or specialist groups: drug users, prostitutes, women in higher management jobs, etc.
- 'Open applications' via mass media can also be used, where cases can be found from advertising in newspapers, professional group papers, on the television or on the web.

Regarding the *second* question, we can also be relatively brief. Starting from the obvious reliability principle 'the more cases, the better', we prefer two cases to one, and three cases to two. This is reliability in the classical sense: a multiple-case design is considered to be a series of replications of measurement of the same phenomenon under different, but hopefully irrelevant, conditions. The idea is that the more cases one studies, the better the chances to separate the general (relevant) from the specific (irrelevant) features of a case. This ideal can only be attained with a large number of units, where the specifics of each are supposed to cancel each other out in the long run. The argument is based on straightforward statistical estimation theory. In doing a multiple-case study, one cannot do more than take a few steps in this direction in order to obtain at least some information about the reliability of the results. Leading to the same conclusion, but based on a different argument, is Yin's remark:

> You may want to settle for two or three literal replications[1] when the rival theories are grossly different and the issue at hand does not demand an excessive degree of certainty. However, if your rival theories have subtle differences or if you want a high degree of certainty, you may press for five, six or more replications. (Yin 1994: 50)

The reader may understand this argument more or less intuitively. We elaborate on the use of theories in case study research in Chapter 4.

Often, the number of cases to select is limited by financial restraints. In selecting cases, the extra value of each new case – in other words, the efficiency of adding more cases – has to be estimated in advance. The boundary is determined by the cost/benefit ratio. To summarise, within the limits of our budget we try to replicate the study of one case by studying as many cases as possible, but depending on

---

[1]For Yin (2003: 47), a literal replication implies that in going from one case to another the expectations are the same; the 'conditions' are kept identical as much as possible. In theoretical replication, on the contrary, the conditions are intentionally changed from one case to the other, and the researcher is interested in the domain of the initial theory – in other words, whether the theory will stand under varying conditions or whether it needs to be adjusted.

the variance of the cases and the degree of our knowledge, we sometimes need more cases than at other times.

The *third* question – which criteria to use in selecting cases – is far more complicated, and answering it will take up a major part of the rest of this chapter. But first we have to discuss the demarcation of the domain to be studied.

3.2 Demarcation of the domain

A careful delineation of the domain of the research question generally precedes the process of drawing a sample from that domain. It actually is the domain we want to say something about, not the selected case(s). *The domain is the set of all cases we wish to refer to in our research conclusions about the phenomenon to study* (see Box 3.1).

BOX 3.1

If our study concerns, for instance, a phenomenon on the meso-level (of organisations), do we include 'all' organisations? Profit and non-profit organisations? Companies? Production companies? Production companies within a certain sector? Only companies with over 100 employees? Specific departments within such companies? Also, and very importantly, demarcations have to be made according *to place and time*. In actual research practice it is, unfortunately, not uncommon for a researcher, first, to search for 'some' cases to study, and only afterwards strive for a demarcation of the domain of interest. Sometimes even a definition of the domain remains absent.

In testing research, one of the absolute demands put to the researcher is, of course, the a priori demarcation of the population, that is to say before the actual case selection and data collecting proceeds. Otherwise one could shrink or expand the domain at will to get results that are in accordance with the hypothesis. In descriptive research as well, the boundaries of the domain are to be defined in advance.

But in research of an exploratory character the delineation of the population might be one of the things to be explored. Sometimes, one only has vague ideas about the boundaries of the targeted domain. One may start, for instance, with defining a very wide phenomenon, to discover afterwards that it is only partially covered by the selected cases. The phenomenon the researcher is interested in might be 'the room for public policy and its determining factors'. We may end up with the description and explanation of youth welfare policy in a certain nation during a certain period. Obviously, there is a long way to go back from the empirical results of a handful of cases to the very broadly worded phenomenon. The *domain* is gradually delineated through successive steps, such as selecting a field, a country and a period. The originally targeted domain is only partially covered.

Furthermore, the role of domain demarcation is different in basic research compared to applied research. In *basic* research, the researcher is principally at liberty to restrict or enlarge the domain. Whether this liberty is real is another matter. Whatever the design may be, the restriction or widening of the phenomenon itself, or the domain of the phenomenon, falls within the authority and freedom of the researcher (see Box 3.2). In *applied* research, however, the domain of targeted units is generally determined by the client who orders and finances the research project, and it is sharply demarcated. The researcher is not free to change the boundaries of the target set at will. Yet, even when, initially, the domain is sharply demarcated, its boundaries may become the object of negotiation between the researcher and the client in dealing with the problem of sampling. We illustrate this with an example from empirical practice (see Box 3.3).

BOX 3.2

In a basic research project on the topic of 'bullying' in three school classes, in which pupils are seen as the 'physical units' involved (better would be pairs of pupils), it is possible for the researcher to restrict the phenomenon of 'bullying' to one of its specific forms, or to widen it to all other forms of non-adjusted or harmful social behaviour, in order to arrive at a higher level theory. In the same vein, (s)he may restrict the study of bullying behaviour to interacting boys, or to girls, or to a specific type of school or age category. It may be desirable, for instance, to start with homogeneous groups in one specific context, in order not to jump higher than one's capacities allow.

BOX 3.3

In a study about how schools deal with perceptions and interests of different groups of stakeholders (parents, teachers, pupils), for instance about the balance between education in school and education at home, the question may arise which schools, and how many, should be selected in a case study. The original domain to study is defined as all primary and secondary schools in a country. Let us assume that, financially, as well as from an organisational point of view, room exists for a maximum of five or six cases. Arguments may run as follows: one has to select primary schools as well as secondary schools of different types. Also, the denomination of a school might be important because, for instance, protestant/Calvinist schools might be opposed to an emphasis on the educational

---

influence of the school as compared to the family's influence. Also, one has to take the socio-economic composition of the school population into account. A preliminary conclusion might be that if we wished to represent each combination of different characteristics by one school in our sample of schools, we might already need more than 10 or even more than 20 schools in our study. A design such as this is only possible if the case study budget for each school is strictly limited, and this implies that the research design is gradually to be more survey-like than a case study. Alternatively, we could select only a few cells from the cross-tabulation, and represent one or two schools in each of these cells. The client, who intends to cover 'the complete educational system', is probably opposed to this latter choice.

One can conclude that at the start of the project prolonged negotiations are needed to demarcate the target population. It is simply not possible to cover, within the context of a real (multiple-) case study, all variants of schools, even if we represented each cell by only one school (and that would be useless because we would not be able to interpret differences between schools in a reliable way). The population has to be restricted from the beginning (e.g. to only public secondary schools).

Next, some cases may be selected from this layer, or one decides to conduct a survey first in order to supply some 'in width' knowledge. If we follow the first approach, and if almost all schools produce the same results, then we are lucky in a certain sense: the stratification variables do not seem to be relevant, and we have more or less convincing results 'for all public secondary schools in this country'. If, however, and more probably, different results are produced, it will be very difficult to interpret these differences. By the level of education? By denominational character? By socio-economic differences? Even if not one, but several schools 'per cell' are included in the design, the only results we may hope for depend on exploratory interpretations; we have to add the inevitable 'more research is necessary' to the conclusions.

Furthermore, in policy research, demarcation of the domain might have some special implications. As a policy measure generally will not be put into practice for several years to come, the domain of units as it will be in the future seems to be more relevant than the domain of the same units as they are now. Regrettably, we cannot, of course, draw a sample from a domain-yet-to-come, but we can implement this idea by taking a couple of 'vanguard' units, units that are more advanced or modern than others. It is difficult to say whether we are dealing here with a population (i.e. domain) or a sampling problem. It is clear, however, that with respect to a future policy to be implemented in a heterogeneous domain of cases, selecting some vanguard organisations or social systems in general (e.g. schools, urban neighbourhoods) is more appropriate than selecting some 'retarded' or backward social systems.

In the following paragraphs, we discuss several alternative procedures for selecting cases.

3.3 No selection at all

If a domain is small, we do not select cases, but we may try to include all cases that constitute the targeted domain. In applied (policy) research this domain may be small: the public hospitals in *this* city; the departments in *this* organisation. It may even consist of only one case. But if there are more, we will probably do everything in our power to include all cases in our study, finances allowing. Goetz and LeCompte (1984) call this situation 'comprehensive sampling'. Evidently, our task is to formulate policy advice for the whole domain, and the researcher cannot permit him/herself to leave four cases out, when, for instance, the complete domain consists of six cases. Should it be impossible to study all six cases intensively, we may choose between several alternatives: doing a pilot study on, say, two cases in order to study the rest in a (to be hoped for) follow-up project, or studying all six, some of them more intensively than others. A dilemma like this will often lead to intensive and time-consuming, but mutually enlightening, negotiations between researcher and client.

Quite another situation exists when the domain is large (at least too large to include all elements in our study), but we experience so much trouble in finding a case, that if we find one, we are only too glad to include it in our sample. Inaccessibility of the domain may lead to a restriction of a project to one or two cases. A lack of co-operation is not the only cause for a large domain resulting in few available cases. On the meso-level, this situation often occurs in premature evaluation research, for instance with educational innovations. The government is so keen on having a new policy evaluated that researchers have great difficulty in finding cases with enough experience. A new policy needs time for implementation. In other words, fresh cases are often not informative enough! Should one nevertheless wish to do research in an introductory period, perhaps only one hospital or other institution is available. Here, the domain is large, but only very few cases are available, or we have to wait a long time before the research can be undertaken.

Turning to basic research, Yin (2003: 42) mentions some specific situations where, evidently, a case study might be restricted to only one case:

- *The critical case* where studying one case may be decisive with respect to the choice between rival theories (see section 3.6).
- *The unique case*, for example patients with a very rare injury or disorder, or murderers of presidents. Any single case found is worth documenting and analysing because of its rarity.

- *The representative or typical case* where a rather homogeneous domain of cases indicates that selecting one or the other case is irrelevant. The collected information is interpreted as valid for all of the cases. It goes without saying that this presupposes knowledge about the composition of the domain.
- *The revelatory case.* This situation occurs when, by pure luck or accident, the researcher has access to a group, situation or person *that has not been studied before*. Sometimes by accident, for instance when a researcher is called upon to act as a member of a jury, or when (s)he gets involved in a hostage affair. Other examples involve a strike or a heroin-taking prostitute. It is told that the famous German physician Ernst Mach he had a stroke during a train trip. He used this situation to systematically study which movements he still was able to make, and which not. He observed himself as a black box with his will as input and movements as output. The phenomenon is often rather common, but it is apparently very difficult to gain access to a case.
- *The longitudinal case* studies where for one unit or case a series of measurements on a time scale is available.

With respect to these situations, in selecting a case to be studied no criterion is intentionally applied; each case is, in principle, fitting and is gratefully accepted. The intensive study of one single case may function as an eye-opener, as a highway to new scientific knowledge about a large group of phenomena. The researcher will seize every opportunity with both hands.

3.4 Random selection

In extensive research (in other words, in a survey), the usual practice is random sampling. However, statistical induction, the 'sample-to-population logic', is not applicable if it comes to generalising from case(s) to domain in intensive research. The number of studied cases is far too small. Even if we selected, for example, ten cases, the sample would be too small to reliably estimate population parameters, let alone if our case study is restricted to one case or a handful of cases. Parameter estimations will be located in intervals that are so wide that they are almost non-informative. Besides, a random sample of, say, three cases can be far off the mark with respect to some important variable. In fact, a random sample may be worse than any other sample, considering the small number of cases. Second, random selection presupposes that, for all units or cases in the domain, a frame from which to sample exists. Often, no such frame is available, for example homosexuals, owners of a weekend or holiday house, organisations that employed an interim manager in a certain year. Consequently, random selection is not an important criterion in case study research. It may, however, be used additionally, after having composed, on other grounds, a list of eligible cases.

3.5 Pragmatic grounds

Frequently, rather trivial criteria, such as proximity to the researcher's university, personal interest and involvement, incidental contacts or the researcher's network, determine which cases will be included in the research project. In American literature the expression 'convenience sample' is used. A pragmatic solution for the sampling problem is the selection of all cases that satisfy a certain simple objective criterion, for instance all cases located within a radius of a 15-minute car journey from the research institute, or the selection of the maximum number of cases within the research budget. If the domain concerns individuals (where sometimes relatively large groups are involved), quota sampling is applied. This implies the construction of certain categories or strata that are subsequently filled. Phrased more generally, decisive selection factors are distance, time and money. Sometimes cases are selected that are in the public eye or, more often, cases that get less public attention. Evidently, criteria such as these are additional, in the sense that they may help to select cases out of a larger group of eligible cases that satisfy more substantive criteria. Pragmatic criteria are often combined with substantive criteria.

We usually apply pragmatic criteria in basic research. This is less obvious in policy research, in which the domain of cases is often, as said before, prescribed by the client. Probably, additional pragmatic criteria will be applied only in dealing with a large and homogeneous domain.

3.6 Substantive criteria

Finally, we arrive at those selection criteria that relate to substantive properties of the cases themselves. Foremost, it is important to keep in mind two general principles, whichever special criteria are used. First, we should look for *informative cases*, that is cases that are expected to represent the phenomenon under study quite clearly. In evaluation research, with respect to an innovation, we only include cases in which the innovation has been implemented for a certain period – long enough for the expected effects to materialise. Some prior knowledge is assumed, of course. Second, we prefer – independent of the use of other criteria – *representative cases*, that is cases occupying a modal position on putative relevant variables. Or, if a specific causal relationship is the point of departure for selecting a case, we select a case that does not deviate from the regression line or, rather, select cases that occupy different positions along the regression line (but that deviate little from that line!). The expressions 'typical cases' and 'representative cases' are also used.

Sometimes these criteria are sufficient to select some cases or perhaps only one case. In this way, the Lynds

> selected a single city to be as representable as possible for American life. Specifically, they were looking for a city with: 1) a temperate climate; 2) a sufficiently rapid rate of growth; 3) an industrial culture; 4) the absence of dominance of the city's industry by a single plant; 5) a substantial local artistic life; and 6) the absence of any outstanding peculiarities or acute local problems which would mark the city off from the midchannel sort of American community.

> After examining a number of options, the Lynds decided that Muncie, Indiana, was more representative than other midsized cities in America, thus qualifying it as a typical case. (Gerring, 2007: 92)

Preceding the actual sampling process one may use a 'sampling plan', as applied in extensive research, for instance aimed at stratification based on some relevant variables. Sometimes the expression 'dimensional sampling' is used. It is often applied in actual research practice, especially in the frame of evaluation research. Here it is assumed that we have some knowledge about an applicable theory and about the case(s), which, however, isn't always present. A sampling plan will surely be used if we start from precise questions or hypotheses. If we have a broad initial research question, it is possible, though not necessary, that, starting from a more or less fortunately chosen case, during the process of data collection we decide which other cases to include in the sample, depending on the results thus far obtained. There is no prior sampling plan: the selection of each next case depends on our interpretation of the results of the cases already studied. This procedure, known as 'theoretical sampling', is advocated by Glaser and Strauss (1967).[2] The expressions 'opportunistic sample' or 'ad hoc sample' are used as well. In an approach such as this, data collection, interpretation and analysis occur more or less simultaneously. During the process it is decided what additional data are desired and where such data are to be found. In this way, for instance, we may develop the expectation that with cases belonging to a slightly different category the results thus far obtained will not apply. We are studying, for instance, the quality of services delivered to the public by a heterogeneous group of institutions. Thus far we only included banks and travel agencies in our sample. The expectation emerges that adding local tourist information desks and some community-level agencies to our sample might change research results. With 'theoretical sampling' it is not clear beforehand when sampling comes to an end and, consequently, how many cases will be involved in the study. As stated before, in research practice, usually financial

---

[2] In research literature (Goetz & LeCompte 1984; Miles & Huberman 1994; Kuzel 1999; Patton 2002), we come across several labels for selection on theoretical grounds. Terms used are: 'theory-based cases', 'critical cases', 'confirming' and 'disconfirming' cases. The term 'theory-based cases' means that we select cases from which we expect an illustration of a theory. The word 'theory' here is mostly used for a 'construct', such as 'image building' or 'awareness context'.

and practical considerations determine when and where to stop sampling. In texts on the methodology of theoretical sampling, the principle of 'saturation' of the sample is advocated. This principle indicates an approaching end to sampling if we discover that new cases no longer add information or that the cost/benefit ratio is going to be negative in continuing sampling. However, this principle is only applicable with domains counting a relatively large number of relatively cheap cases (e.g. individual persons to be subjected to an in-depth interview). The principle of saturation can be applied to answer the question whether, after having interviewed 25 people, it is useful to add another ten interviews. This question does not apply if we consider, after having included and studied three organisations in intensive research, whether to include a fourth or fifth organisation. Evidently, almost any fourth organisation will add new dimensions to our results. Whether we use a prior sampling plan or apply the 'saturation' approach depends on the character of the research question, and therefore on the state of our prior knowledge.

A said before, frequency of occurrence together with pragmatic criteria may be a sufficient base in selecting cases. Often, however, additional substantive, that is to say theory-related considerations, are applied. This is especially the case in dealing with one or more clearly defined central causal relations, such as in evaluation research. Several alternatives for case selection are available. They are discussed in the sections below.

3.6.1 Homogeneous on the independent variable(s)

In speaking about selection on one or more 'independent variables' (variables that are expected to influence the process), this label stands for 'causes' in a broad sense: contextual characteristics, background variables, and conditions.

If the model or the theory is still new, and has not yet been submitted to intensive testing, it is generally advisable to *minimise* between cases-variance.[3] The idea is to look for some 'modal instances' of the phenomenon. The argument runs: let's first have a look whether a common model is possible for a reasonably homogeneous set of frequently occurring cases. An exclusive orientation on the frequency of occurrence can even be the deciding criterion in selecting cases, especially when we know very little about the effects under different conditions.

---

[3]The distinction between minimising and maximising variance was introduced by Glaser and Strauss (1967: Chapter 3). Curiously, these authors do not indicate which variables are to be used as criteria for minimising or maximising. Glaser and Strauss avoid the labels 'dependent' and 'independent variables', they do not use the word 'variables' at all. Instead, they unfortunately use the expressions 'categories' and their 'characteristics' without defining these things explicitly. The resulting vagueness and terminological confusion has cost the scientific community a lot of time, but we won't repeat this debate here. In covering the topic of selection principles for case studies, this distinction is very important. So far in the literature, the distinction between independent and dependent variables has not been made in this context. Taking the long history of 'qualitative research' into consideration, this is understandable. But surely, in applied research, where effects of policy interventions are studied, it cannot be omitted or neglected.

Minimising variance in fact means that an initial study done on one case is replicated with other cases from which we expect comparable results. Yin (1994) calls this literal replication. It is a sensible first option if we are not yet knowledgeable in the field. However, some methodologists view this approach as inferior. It is even made suspect by using the label 'case contamination' (see Appendix 4). If cases are very comparable or even dependent or related, knowledge based on these cases is less respectable, less informative (Swanborn 1996a). It is of course true that this approach is not a very bold one; it is rather modest indeed. But it is not an inferior strategy. On the contrary, it has to be recommended under the circumstances discussed above. Nevertheless, we should be aware of its limitations.

To start with, it is a modest approach in the sense that if four cases are drawn from the *same* context, nothing can be said about the role of that context, because it doesn't vary. A case study including four departments of the same directorate can never, with certainty, explain results in terms of characteristics of that directorate. In other directorates, results could be just the same. It is possible as well that our tentative causal conclusions within this homogeneous subset are conditional upon the context. Seemingly causal relations are spurious: the context is the common cause (but cannot as such be identified empirically because it does not vary). This context may have a temporal, a spatial or a social-network character. A next step would be, of course, to study departments taken from other directorates.

One should keep in mind that selecting extra cases from a homogeneous subset is a cautionary strategy, but the law of diminishing returns plays its role: adding another case gradually adds fewer new elements to our knowledge. The 'x-th' replication under exactly comparable conditions has a very small chance of being refuted if the model is not refuted after studying all foregoing cases. Each added case is less informative. A statistician would express this in terms of degrees of freedom: as cases are dependent, the number of degrees of freedom (see Chapter 5) is no greater than one would superficially think. The real significance of 'contamination' is that the more our cases are 'contaminated', the less informative they are. On the one hand, we need to be aware of this and on the other hand, it inspires a next step in selecting cases: the introduction of variance on one or more of the independent variables; selecting another cohort; or selecting another way of studying the limits of our temporary model or theory. Replications under varying conditions have a smaller chance of producing the same result, and therefore are more informative and methodologically more interesting. Replication under *simultaneously varying conditions* is, however, less useful because deviating results are hard to interpret. The conclusion is a strategy of 'small steps'. In replication we vary only one condition at the same time.

3.6.2 Heterogeneous on the independent variable(s)

The reverse strategy is the selection of cases that largely differ on the independent variables. Which circumstances would prompt this approach? When, by means of an exploratory study of some comparable cases, we arrive at a common model for all cases studied, perhaps the time is ripe to test the extent of the model or its sensitivity to varying parameters of the context? We select cases that contrast on some relevant independent variables, cases that clearly differ from the ones chosen earlier. Sometimes the expression 'polar types' is even used. Starting with the most frequent categories of the independent variable(s) may be wise. One may start with a simple cross-tabulation (e.g., a 2 × 3 table) of some of these variables, and select an informative representative case for each cell of the table. It is *not* necessary to represent all categories of a relevant independent variable if some of its categories occur very infrequently. Relevant independent variables in a study on organisations may be, for instance, economic sectors (primary, secondary, tertiary or other) and size of workforce. Replications in other communities, in another period, with other circumstances can fall under this heading as well. The argument is not of a statistical nature, but it fits an exploratory approach: we want to have some idea about the fit of the model under alternating conditions. In studying aspects of an organisational process in hospitals, assuming we include four cases in the study, it would be possible, for instance, to include two large and two small hospitals. The argument for a strategy such as this does not refer to the usual stratification argument, that is that it would enable us to generalise separately to large as well as to small hospitals. The numbers do not allow that. The argument is more modest: in our exploration we wish to bring some variance on putative important properties in order to get an impression – not much more than that – about the range of our conclusions.

If results prove to be stable under varying conditions of that dimension, the dimension obviously seems to be irrelevant. This constitutes no objection to the procedure. On the other hand, it is of course conceivable that some relevant dimension remains hidden.

In a later phase of the study, if a model is relatively well fixed and if we are able to predict when it will be verified and under which conditions it will be refuted, we may test whether, according to the theory, contradictory, or deviating, results appear. Still another procedure consists of selecting cases (at least three) that represent different positions on an ordinal independent variable. If these cases, after data-collection and analysis, show monotonously increasing scores[4] on the dependent variables, our conclusion with respect to the effects of the independent variable is considerably strengthened.

Problematic to these approaches is that an intelligent choice is only possible on the basis of knowledge we generally don't have. The model or the theory has not yet been formulated. The solution to this typically methodological problem is using a 'bootstrap' approach, in which, starting from weak subjective knowledge, a first effort is

---

[4]Monotonously increasing means that if case A scores higher on an independent variable than case B, its score on the dependent variable should always be higher than, or the same as, the score of case B.

made, and thereafter other steps, one by one (or a step backwards is done), etc. In short, this implies exploration, also with respect to the selection of the next case.

Although all of these approaches seem to be rather obvious, much can be improved with respect to current research practice. Sometimes, variables are quite automatically regarded as the relevant ones. Replacing this automatism by a little more reflection, and the use of available actual expertise about the subject, from the field as well as from science, we may obtain a more appropriate choice of independent variables. We may start with those variables everyone agrees on to be important and then move on to the variables whose effects the experts disagree about. Consulting experts is the best way to detect variables that effect contrasting and therefore interesting results, and that clarify the background of such effects – the determining causal processes. Naïve exploration of material may be partly replaced by testing assumptions.

3.6.3 Selection on the dependent variable(s)

In speaking about selection on dependent variable(s), the latter concept represents 'consequences': central characteristics of the *process* and positive or negative *effects*. Let's have a look at several possible situations. Most of the practical solutions restrict the range on the dependent variable(s) in selecting cases.

The *first* method, very popular in evaluation research, consists in selecting 'success stories' or 'best practices'. However, without variance of the dependent variable this design is useless from the point of view of causal analysis. It is not known whether perhaps the same conditions that characterise success stories would be present in the less successful cases as well. A control group (based on random selection) or comparison group (comparable, but not randomly selected) is absent. In no way can insight be gained into the factors that determine why school leavers get a job, if we restrict ourselves to the pupils who actually do find a job. We cannot explain variance on a variable that doesn't vary. We cannot aim for more than some tentative ideas.

Close to the first method is a *second* method: restriction of range on the dependent variable. Figure 3.1 shows the dangers with respect to a causal conclusion implied by this approach. In this figure (adapted from King, Keohane & Verba 1994: 131), the correlation between the number of courses taken and the earned income in the first job is portrayed. Roughly, with one additional course one gains an additional $10,000. The regression line shifts considerably, however, if we restrict our study to people who earn at least $100,000. Now, one additional course results in only $5,000 more, hence the causal effect is strongly underestimated.

Examples of false conclusions are not always as obvious as this. Selection may take place by restricting oneself to one side of a variable that is correlated with the dependent variable: the same biased results may be expected. Such a bias may result from self-selection. If we study the relation between academic performance and labour market success, and we would depend on self-selection of people, it is to be expected that especially people with a good job and good earnings volunteer

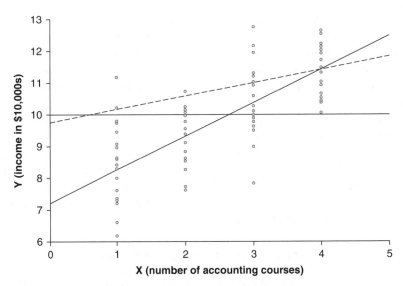

Figure 3.1   Bias by selection on the dependent variable

as respondents. The result is comparable to the situation portrayed in Figure 3.1. Self-selection may not be the only factor at the basis of such bias. Successful people can be detected more easily, whereas unsuccessful people gradually disappear from sight and are liable not to be included in a sample. Almost any inventory of ex-students or ex-whatever, composed by the enthusiastic collaboration of some 'networkers', is biased in this sense. The *accessible domain* is already biased. This often happens in *retrospective* research on nations or organisations as well as on people: units have disappeared or died or cannot be reached anymore, in whatever way. Far better would be *prospective* research, in which one starts with a sample from the original domain, and where the process to be studied is going to be continuously monitored. The example of (extensive) designs in health research on the relation between smoking and lung cancer is illuminating. Retrospective studies with persons above a certain age only deal with *survivors* and are consequently biased. Prospective research, starting from school age, is much better, but takes many years. Restriction of range at one side of the dependent variable endangers our conclusions and should flatly be avoided wherever possible. Retrospective and prospective research is more fully treated in section 3.6.7.

A *third* selection procedure lies at hand: restriction of range to groups or cases that are extreme on both sides of the set of values of the dependent variable. This is not too far-fetched. Often selection on the dependent variables comes down to the selection of some success cases ('best practice') as well as some 'failure' cases. In other words, maximising the variance. Sometimes even in calls for proposals in policy research it is demanded that the design contains some cases that show good practice and other cases showing bad practice. Yet enough reasons exist as to why we should be very reticent with such designs here as well. Selection in this way might not lead to an underestimation of the causal effect, but it is impossible to reach conclusions with respect to *differential* effects of several causes, which is the aim of much causal research. The crux of the matter is the 'confounding' of independent variables. Blalock (1964) already showed the serious disadvantage of selecting on the dependent variable. In setting apart successful cases and failure cases, one actually constructs two sets that are contrasting *on several independent variables simultaneously*. The result is that causes cannot be disentangled; they are hopelessly 'confounded'. At best we describe, on the one hand, situations in which a number of factors are positive, and on the other hand, a situation in which the same factors are all negative. But there is no way to gain insight into the relative strengths of each of these independent variables, and into their correlations and interactions. Besides, the regression effect might play a role. We mostly select cases according to the results of measurement at one moment, and we cannot be sure that they are that stable and that selection at another moment would have produced the same results. A comfort might perhaps be that with measurement error and instability present, it is to be expected that the selected extreme groups actually are less extreme than we expected them to be.

If we could base our selection on the mean of scores from several points on a time scale, or on summative scores over several dependent variables, we could perhaps more or less avoid the regression effect. But in performing an evaluation of recently implemented social experiments, we generally are glad when at least one effect-measurement can take place.

The objections against selection on dependent variables are in fact grave. In general this procedure has to be advised against. At most, we could think of it as a first gross search for possible causes. But even then it would be more efficient – for instance, if we studied only four cases – to immediately introduce some contrast on those independent variables that are deemed most important. Even if we can avoid the regression effect, these procedures are not efficient because we cannot get hold of the relative weights of several causes.

A fine-tuning of the procedure may, however, lead to a certain acceptability. If several dependent variables are measured and we decide to select those cases that score high on *all* dependent variables, the regression effect will partly be excluded. There remains the confounding effect. It can partly be avoided, after selection on the dependent variable(s), in complementing the procedure by selecting contrasting cases on one or two important independent variables. In this way, at least the effects of these independent variables are more or less controlled. Recently, more methodological advancements have been made in the field of matched-pairs selection (Imai, King & Nall 2008). As these are highly sophisticated in their statistical properties, we do not discuss them here. More improvements in specific situations are conceivable, improvements that condition and perhaps mitigate the recommendations laid out.

The reader might wonder whether a discussion of statistical matters is appropriate in a book on case studies. Actually, it is. We have no intention at all to turn (especially qualitative) researchers into statisticians. But while arguments of a statistical nature mostly remain hidden in a report of a seemingly simple sample selection procedure, they may be very real and grossly bias results. That's why at least awareness and caution in this respect are needed.

3.6.4 Selection on the causal relationship

Suppose that from a survey or from documentary sources a correlation between some clearly defined variables emerges, and a causal interpretation presents itself. We are eager to know more about the range of the domain, that is we want to know more about the conditions that play a role, and we want to know more about the causal mechanisms. Here, with a bivariate situation, one might portray the correlation and contrast some cases that lie on the regression line with some other cases that are 'deviant'. The aim is to detect conditions that might be in favour of (or even necessary) for the relation between the two central variables, and conditions that might constitute a handicap. In a multivariate situation, one might calculate the general regression formula as well as the residuals for each case. Finally, one might select cases with a very small residual as well as cases with a larger residual.

Selection on the basis of a causal relationship takes a special format in the so-called selection of deviant cases. If it is found that a lot of cases fit a common model, that is to say that a theory is found but that it turns out that there is one stubborn exception to the rule, it is time to perform a 'deviant case study'. A famous example is Lipset, Trow and Coleman's exploratory study of the International Typographical Union (1956) (see Box 3.4).

BOX 3.4   The ITU case[5]

Michel's Iron Law of Oligarchy states that all forms of organisations will eventually develop into oligarchies. As organisations increase in size, the bureaucracy will grow as well, and leaders of bureaucracies will use their position to increase and entrench their power. Lipset et al.'s book is a case study of one particular organisation, the International Typographical Union, an organisation that seemingly disproved Michel's Iron Law. The exception was explained by the fact that the ITU was founded by a group of local unions, valuing their autonomy. The

---

[5]Adapted from en.wikipedia.org/wiki/Union_Democracy under a Creative Commons Attribution-ShareAlike 3.0 Unported License (creativecommons.org/licenses/by-sa/3.0/).

existence of factions within the democratic structure and elections within the union prevented the leaders from becoming corrupt, as each faction was willing to expose the wrongdoings of another. They also pointed out that similarity in background (most of the leaders coming from middle class) further encouraged democratic decision-making processes. The authors tested Michel's theory in the first place, and being confronted with a falsifying instance of the theory, they explored their case in search of an explanation, in this case adding some new elements (conditions) to Michel's theory. Having learned from the Festinger et al. (1956) example (see Box 2.3), one could also remark that Lipset et al. found a way to cope with their cognitive dissonance ... which is not always bad at all!

Deviancy refers to a causal relationship, not to the position of a unit relative to its position on a variable. Deviancy is always relative to a theory or general model. Perhaps after a deviant case project, the theory can be adjusted and the selected case is – after all – not deviant any more. Many deviant case analyses result in the addition of other variables to a theory ('conditioning the theory'), or in the adjustment of the form of the relation (say from linear to curvilinear). Sometimes it is shown – after a re-operationalisation or recoding of one or more crucial variables – that the case was not a deviant one after all (but be careful with this type of welcome result!).

This approach is adequate at the end of a programme cycle. Careful conditioning of a theory could, in principle, be the result of an analysis like this, as well as designing a deeper theory (covering more cases) that includes the non-fitting cases too.

3.6.5 Selection on developmental phases

Still another possible selection strategy is selecting cases that represent different stages or phases of a developmental process. One often encounters this approach with one of the most popular applications of case studies: research into the factors that facilitate or hinder the implementation of an innovation. As with most innovations, a complete implementation of the trajectory takes several years. Only a restricted period is available for research, so there is an obvious need to select cases accordingly. After the selection of sub-populations on the basis of temporal points, or cohorts, a subsequent random selection of cases, or one of the above-mentioned principles of selection on the independent variables, may follow. Selection on the dependent variables is not applicable because most cases have not yet reached the final stage. Selection on developmental phases can be very efficient, but it is based on the partly untestable assumption that cases from different cohorts are comparable. Therefore, in practice, researchers often struggle with ambiguity of interpretations.

3.6.6 Selection of critical cases

The practice of 'selecting a critical case' has to be posited in the context of *testing* a causal proposition within a well-articulated theory. As we will see later on, this is a rather exceptional use of case studies. A beautiful example is the study of a girl who from her birth till the age of 13 spent her life in almost complete social isolation. She became as a test case for the competing language development theories of Noam Chomsky and Erik Lenneberg. At the same time, this is an example of a 'revelatory case'.

In its original format (often labelled 'crucial case'), it refers to a deterministic proposition that can be corroborated or falsified by studying one case. This is a rather academic concept. To say the least, almost always we struggle with measurement errors in the study of social life, a fact that makes research results in deterministic terms highly improbable.

In a mitigated format, reference is sometimes made to the so-called *most likely* and *least likely* case selection. Here, we do not assume a deterministic relationship, but allow for the more 'normal' situation in which a series of factors is responsible for the effect Y. In the 'most likely' approach, in testing an X/Y relationship, a case is selected that represents as many factors (X_1, X_2, ... X_k) as possible that may cause Y, except the factor of interest to the researcher, namely X. If the result is non-Y (the most likely result to expect would be Y), there is fairly strong evidence that the only remaining factor, X, is causative. In the 'least likely' approach, in testing a X/Y relationship, a case is selected where all other possible factors that might cause Y are absent, but X is present. The argument is that if in this least likely situation the effect Y presents itself, the only factor that may cause it is X (and Y will certainly be manifest in a situation where other factors that contribute to Y are present). In Popperian terms this refers to a 'risky prediction', and risky predictions are the things upon which progress in science is based (Popper 1963).

Other approaches in a testing frame relate to techniques such as those applied in experiments, for example using pairs or small sets of cases that are comparable on many variables but that contrast on the variable of central interest, commonly known as matching techniques. In the political sciences, where theories as well as comparable scores of nation-states on many (relatively hard) variables are available in data banks, testing methods such as these are practised.

Still, in many of these research projects, a result in terms of 'this confirms' or 'this disconfirms' a theory is to be regarded as preliminary. Too many non-measured factors may affect results. However, researching cases along these lines may be very worthwhile in detecting or questioning possible causal links or alternative explanations. But here we are, exploring again... In Chapter 4 we will tackle this topic again.

3.6.7 Prospective and retrospective research

The subject of prospective and retrospective research designs is often treated within the context of causal analysis, when a real experiment is not feasible, for instance because the causal process needs a very long period, or when independent variables cannot be manipulated by the experimenter. Actually, we made some references to it already in sections 3.6.1–3.6.4, especially where we commented on combining success and failure cases in a project. It is useful to provide a link between case studies and these (quasi-) experimental designs. Using retrospective or prospective designs is also relevant for the methodology of case studies, as Box 3.5 at the end of this section will show.

Samples may be drawn at random, not at random or only partly at random, but control of the 'experimental conditions' is much more difficult than it is under laboratory conditions. In both designs, samples are drawn of groups that differ on one of the essential variables.

In a *prospective* design, the presumed causal impact has not yet taken place: we 'look into the future'; a prospective project has to be carried out. In prospective research about the impact of one supposedly causal variable, the researcher selects *cases contrasting on the independent variable*. One is relatively free to choose design and data collection according to his/her own ideas, but if the time span between cause and effect is large, a prospective research project is not feasible. In fact, if you wish to determine the long-term effects of smoking at an early age, you cannot wait till all people in your sample of youngsters have reached the age of 80 (or have died). A more fortunate example is studying the relations between social background, education and choice of career, and one may follow a group of youngsters from contrasting social backgrounds in their development at school and into their professional careers (for as long as your research interests and funding allow!).

In a *retrospective* design, the impact on the dependent variable(s) has already taken place: we look 'backwards'. Now there are two possibilities: to select on the independent variable (called a 'retrospective cohort' approach) or to select on the dependent variable (called a 'case/control' approach). In order to apply a cohort approach, data from the past should be available, for instance from documentary sources.

A 'cohort' approach is an efficient design if the population distribution on the independent variable is very skewed. If you wished to carry out research on the relationship between working in coalmines and lung cancer, in using the case/control approach you would identify only a small number of ex-miners in your samples. This would be a very inefficient design. In the 'cohort' approach one is able to select the sample from two equal groups, one of young people who went on to be coalminers, and one from the same population who took other professions.

Contrarily, a 'cohort' approach is very inefficient when the distribution on the dependent variable is very skewed. If one desired to study the impact of religion on suicide, one would need very large numbers to draw conclusions with a certain level of reliability because very few people commit suicide. It seems more sensible to start with a sample of people who committed suicide, and compare this sample to a comparable group of people who did not attempt suicide. A 'case/control' approach would be more appropriate.

The 'cohort' approach has other disadvantages:

- The sample mortality, as a consequence of death, removals, those no longer willing to participate, etc., may be large, and accumulates the longer the research continues. The problem is that this mortality may be related to the independent variable.
- The researcher is likely to be biased if (s)he is acquainted with the subjects' score on the independent variable, especially if (s)he has to attribute in-between cases to one or the other group. If the researcher does not know the score on the independent variable, the research project is called a 'blind' experiment. If researchers and subjects do not know their score on the independent variable(s), it is called a double-blind experiment. Literature on this topic is abundant in the health sciences and a standard text on methodology is Cook and Campbell (1979).

A 'case/control' research project into the characteristics of people who died from the Mexican swine flue epidemic in 2009 compared to people who were infected but did not die could probably be carried out by studying a number of characteristics of 50 people who died (the 'cases'), and 200 comparable infected persons who did not die (the 'controls'). Cases and controls are selected so that they can be compared to variables that are assumed to be correlated with the cause of the illness ('risk factors' such as air flight passenger, age, general health factors, time and duration of exposure, etc.). A number of about 250 persons would do, while with a 'cohort' approach (say, a sample of all air flight passengers coming from Mexico in 2009) one would be obliged to start with tens of thousands of people, to detect a handful of persons who were actually infected.

As is the case with all non-random selection processes, the generalisability to the intended general population remains an open question. Special attention should be paid to the comparability of cases and controls. Several years ago it was made public that the risks of a heart attack for heavy consumers of black coffee were twice as large as for others. 'Cases' were drawn from a coronary diseases department in a hospital and 'controls' from other departments of the same hospital. The 'cases' counted twice as much coffee drinkers as the controls. A sceptical comment was that about 60% of heart attack victims died before reaching the hospital, and that the conclusion might be that those who reached the hospital in time owed their life to the fact that they were heavy coffee-drinkers. Apparently, the inversed conclusion is not excluded! More generally, the people entering our research group as cases or controls may constitute a non-random selection from the intended populations. We may compare cases and controls, but little can be concluded about the populations they originated from because of mortality, migration, disappearance from the administration, or odd selection procedures that change the samples.

In using a case/control approach, the variance on the dependent variable is maximised. As indicated in section 3.6.3, if several causes are involved (such as predominantly occurs), it is almost impossible to estimate the separate effects. This is because in one sample the 'beneficial' values of all variables are combined, and in the other group the unfavourable conditions are combined. In other words, the independent variables are maximally correlated. If we only measured the effect of one central variable, the effect on the dependent variable is expected to be overestimated.

BOX 3.5

A good example of retrospective as well as prospective case study research is Van den Berg, Denolf and van der Veer (1997). Their object of research was finding the success and failure factors in a recently developed, tailor-made system of job intermediacy in parts of the Netherlands and Belgium. They started with the retrospective part: exploratory interviews with 14 job intermediators. The interviewees were asked to consider a successful case and a failed case (no job found), and then to reconstruct the history of this person. Ample attention was paid to the characteristics of the jobseeker as well as of the intermediator and the other people involved with this person, and to the networks of the people involved and critical incidents (e.g. a remark made during an interview, or a new friend or colleague who opened up another perspective) that also played a role. The interviewees were explicitly asked to mention the factor(s) that were decisive in making their case a success or a failure. Only after detailing these cases were the intermediators asked which general factors, in their opinion, were crucial in job intermediacy. One of the findings was that the level and quality of information about the capacities of the jobseeker and about the specifics of the job was important. Another discovery was that staff members who did the intake and the staff who were the real intermediaries often had a difficult relationship because of status differences and uncertainty about the expected behaviour and 'output'.

For the research team, this was not enough. They were sceptical about the reliability of the memory of people, especially where socially desirable behaviour was involved. They also wanted to know more about the implementation of the intended intermediacy policy. That's why they started a prospective multiple-case study. Some of the topics were: (1) Which decisions are taken at which point on the time-line? (2) How do staff members collect information about the jobseeker and how is this information used? (3) How do staff members see their role in the relationships between employers and jobseeker?

Based on the findings of this retrospective pilot studies, a list of potentially relevant factors was compiled. Then a carefully selected group of 40 people – according to country of origin, sex and some other criteria – was followed, starting from the intake. All were of allochtonous origin, as candidates from other countries had the weakest position on the labour market. Per case at least four interviews were held (one or more with the jobseeker, other interviews with intermediators and other

(Continued)

people involved). There are two methodological comments one can make about this approach. First, the shortcomings of selecting on the dependent variable in the retrospective part of this project (see section 3.6.3) are corrected by adding the prospective part, in which the outcomes for each case were unknown. Second, this was not a research project that was aimed at estimating the impact of one independent variable on a dependent variable; it is not an example of what, in policy research, is called 'summary evaluation'. Instead, it aimed at discovering elements of the long process of implementation of a new policy, such as unpredictable reactions of people and organisational problems. Therefore, there was not a real selection 'on the independent variable' at the start. The researchers composed their sample simply by order of intake of jobseekers, thereby taking care that their cases were evenly distributed over several countries of origin and age groups (factors that *might be* of influence in the causal process).

3.7 The problem of generalisation

Over and over again in debates about the merits and disadvantages of the case study, the problem of generalisation is raised, with single case studies as well as with multiple-case studies. In short, the question reads: on the basis of the results of our researched case(s), what can be said about non-researched cases?

To start with, we have already seen that hardly ever enough cases can be studied to use inductive statistics for generalisation to the intended domain in the way it is usually done in extensive research. According to Yin, in case studies the role of inductive statistics is replaced by what he calls 'analytic generalisation'. In his view, cases are not considered as units of research, but each case, in the tradition of laboratory psychology, is to be treated as a new experiment. A case study is an experiment to test a theory. Yin's motto runs as follows: 'case studies, like experiments, are generalisable to theoretical propositions and not to populations or universes' (Yin 1994: 10). Compare this to Niederkofler (1991): 'The case study investigator's goal is not to demonstrate the validity of an argument for statistical populations or universes. Rather, he aims to create and expand rich theoretical frameworks that should be useful in analysing similar cases.' Consequently, in case study research, it is assumed that we do not deal with a sample-to-population logic, but with generalising from case results to a theory or model. The label analytical (or theoretical, or logical) generalisation has been established in the literature (see for instance, Firestone 1993). Yin's argument, however, deserves further analysis.

In the *first* place, Yin presents the comparability of case study and experiment rather easily. Typical for an experiment is the care researchers show in trying to model reality in the situation under study, in order to let only relevant variables play a role, and the care with which it is isolated from sources of error . The results of a laboratory experiment are therefore, in principle, directly translatable in terms of the theory that inspired the experiment. This means that the theory is confirmed if the results are as expected, or that the theory is conditioned or extended if unexpected results emerge. Typical for a case study, however, is a natural situation in which variables of all types are entangled. Interpreting the results of one case, or a few cases, in terms of a theory, depending on the state of our knowledge, is therefore a hazardous matter. The odds are that relevant variables are not included in the model or that we discover something 'interesting' simply by accident. The central problem is that we think we can replicate a case study in which only one aspect of the context is changed (e.g. a study about the police force in a small city being replicated in a large city), but that in doing so we change many other variables simultaneously. Producing different results, one can hardly state 'it depends on the level of urbanisation of the context', or, in the case of comparable results, 'look, the level of urbanisation doesn't play a role'. Results obtained in this way – replication with one or a few cases – have an hypothetical character, and of course need further testing. And they need to be explained. An answer to this kind of question can be approached by:

- replication with new cases
- comparison with dispersed results of earlier studies
- argumentation and presentation of the argument to a forum of experts. If a heterogeneous group of experts cannot think of any plausible argument why our results cannot be generalised, our position is strengthened.

BOX 3.6

If we want to study, in 2010, the effects of innovation X in a number of medium-sized chemical industrial enterprises in state Y, we take, for instance, a sample of five or six cases. Our argument probably runs that one is allowed to generalise to all medium-sized enterprises in state Y. It is not a watertight argument in view of the sample. Our position is strengthened if, in every enterprise, we find the same results. It is weakened if there is variance among cases. Generally, there is ample space for subjective evaluations by the researcher.

Often, researchers take another step. We may assume that 'state' or 'region' is an irrelevant variable, and draw the conclusion that we are allowed to generalise to comparable enterprises in other states. Hopefully, research in other states can be undertaken, but in practice we formulate our conclusions without any empirical base. In the same vein, we may conjecture that our conclusions are also valid for small enterprises in the chemical branch, or for the non-chemical sector, or for 2018. The *assumptions* about comparability remain untested.

In using informal procedures such as these, we often read the expression 'theoretical generalisation'. This can be allowed in so far as a striving towards abstraction and perhaps conditioning is at the basis of the argument, and as long as we remember that the end result has an hypothetical character. Obviously, this uncertainty is applicable to statistical generalisation as well, so in the end there is perhaps not much difference. But in 'qualitative generalisation' there is more room for intersubjectively different trust in the assumptions used. Yin (1994; chapter 5) cannot be accused of neglecting such difficulties. He indicates several ways by which the researcher can strengthen his/her conclusions. They all boil down to 'enlargement of data points' (see Chapter 5).

Second, the difference between generalising to a broader domain and generalising towards a theory is not as large as it seems at first sight. The expression 'theoretical generalisation' may often be read as 'domain generalisation'. It often comes down to generalising to other populations, other places or times, other circumstances, other operationalisations, etc. Only in the latter procedure do we deal with generalising from operational variables to theoretical concepts, or from an operational model to a theory. *Our central focus is to show that in all these forms of generalisation steps are taken that are not only (or not at all) supported by empirical evidence, but above all by interpretative argumentation by the researcher.* The researcher, implicitly or explicitly, handles a model of relevant variables. The leading idea is that the more the non-researched cases are similar to the researched cases, the more valid the generalisation is. The assumption is that given the background and contextual variables the studied cases have in common, the researcher is allowed to generalise to cases comparable on those dimensions. The free use of untested hypotheses needs not to be rejected. It is standard procedure. This is immediately clear in thinking about the time aspect. If we did not use the untested assumption that, for instance, the year the research is carried out is irrelevant, all evaluation of policy interventions would be irrelevant, since policy research is of course meant to be useful for the future.

The standard view with respect to generalisation on the basis of a case study is that, owing to the small number of cases, statistical generalisation cannot be applied in case study research, and that, in this sense, case study results are far less generalisable than survey research results. Curiously, in the literature we some-times encounter the statement that case study results are more generalisable than results of other research strategies.[6] This contradiction can be explained as follows. In comparing a case study with a laboratory experiment, we may conceive a case study that is undertaken in a natural context, as more 'true to reality' than a

---

[6]A superficial, but frequently heard, commonplace about case studies is that their strong side is the internal validity, but their weak side is the external validity or generalisability. This means that in a case study we might be able to discover causal mechanisms rather well, but that we often have no idea about the possible domain of cases. Often one speaks about a 'trade-off' between both types of validity. Bonoma (1985) sketches a two-dimensional space, in which many research strategies (including experiments, tests, surveys and case studies) are located. The horizontal axis represents 'currency', meaning something near to generalisability, and the vertical axis a combination

psychological experiment in an artificial situation with the proverbial psychology students as actors. Especially when – and here we return to the conditions that prompt us to carry out a case study – problems are complicated and the phenomenon to be studied cannot yet be isolated from several contexts, we do well to undertake research in 'the natural environment itself'. Even if we could establish causal relationships in an experiment quite well, a result of this kind would only cover a minor aspect of the total problem, and we are not able to generalise. This is a way of viewing, for instance in the context of market research (Bonoma 1985), that may be legitimately defended.

Whether result R of a case study can be generalised to domain D depends on the result of the following considerations:

- the homogeneity of results over the cases studied so far (reliability in the classic sense)
- the internal or causal validity of result R. This validity depends on the quality of the study, on the success or failure of ruling out alternative causal interpretations, on the number of data points, the plausibility of the interpretation, etc.
- the construct validity of the applied indicators of the relevant variables
- the complexity of the set of relevant variables, and whether the phenomenon can be isolated from contextual influences (if the model contains only a few variables that can be isolated from contextual characteristics, generalisation is much easier than when we deal with a complex model that cannot be isolated from its context)
- the similarity of relevant (that is to say, R-influencing) variables between the studied case and D. As D mainly contains non-researched elements, knowledge can only be of an hypothetical character
- the precision of the statement we want to generalise. The more precise or informative the statement is (i.e. the more content it has), the harder it is to generalise. For instance, a typology is easier to generalise than a statement regarding the relation between two variables, especially if we specify (some aspects of) the frequency distribution.

We must also point out one unfortunate practice that is often encountered in case study reports, that is the habit of discussing a specific studied case, without *explicit* generalisation, in terms of a very broad domain. One reads conclusions such as:

---

of reliability and internal validity. Curiously, the author locates case studies in the lower right corner: low internal validity, high 'currency'! This is the consequence of a totally unsatisfactory definition of the criteria used. If we compare a case study with a laboratory experiment, evidently case studies lack randomisation and control groups. Consequently, causality (internal validity) is harder to obtain than with a real experiment (however, the extra data points and detailing in a case study offers us other possibilities of control). And with respect to generalisation, Bonoma apparently has something like 'reality-near' in mind when he values the currency of a case study more than the currency of an experiment. Generalisability, however, means that it has been proved, or at least made plausible, that a case study's results are valid for such-and-such non-researched cases, and in this respect the case study generally scores very low. An objection with respect to the 'trade-off' idea refers to the suggestion that quality of data is interchangeable with generalisability. Obviously, widening the possibilities to generalise is useless if nothing of value can be offered. Besides, the exact mix of methodological demands with which to confront a research design is dependent on the character of the research question.

'in a medium-sized enterprise in sector X it was found that…, while in a small architect's firm it was found that…'

or:

'in a highly developed Western country it was found that…, while in an African development area it was found that…' .

We tend to forget that in the first study only two specific enterprises were studied (the object was the phenomenon of profit sharing), and in the second study two very specific countries, countries that differ from each other on 1,001 aspects. Besides, they are perhaps not very convincing or fortunately chosen representatives for all 'Western communities' or 'African developmental areas'. Especially if interpretations of the detected differences are interpreted in terms of these contexts, the suggestion is made that the selected cases represent all medium-sized enterprises in sector X, etc. Obviously, a researcher is allowed to present tentative interpretations of discovered differences, but many more interpretations are possible. Besides, some reflection on the limits and homogeneity of the involved domains is necessary. To summarise, the validity of our conclusions with respect to non-researched cases is a matter of more or less plausible arguments. In follow-up research our extrapolations may well be refuted. And in general, it remains a difficult task to generalise results from studied cases to other and larger domains of cases.

3.8 Conclusions

Before reflecting on the selection of cases, we have to delineate as precisely as possible the domain under study. In an exploratory approach, however, we have to be aware of the fact that the actual boundaries of the domain may shift. Furthermore, in basic research one is generally free to restrict or enlarge this domain at will; in applied research the boundaries of the domain are often prescribed by the client and/or the subsidising agency.

A selection problem with respect to the cases is not universal. We pointed out several situations in which the researcher tries to include all cases of the domain in his/her sample as well as the situation where the researcher is just pleased to accept any case because of the rarity of the phenomenon. We also examined the use of the case as a decisive factor between two competing theories.

If, however, one has to choose one or more cases from a domain containing many cases, one should keep in mind that the standard procedure in extensive research – random selection – finds little recognition in intensive research, simply because of the fact that rarely is the number of cases large enough to warrant a reliable estimation of domain parameters. Only when, with the help of other criteria, a large inventory of eligible cases presents itself, can one additionally apply the principle of randomly selecting cases to be included in the study. Whichever other criteria are used, the selected cases should be informative as well as representative for frequently occurring types of case. Very rare types of case might be interesting, but for policy research goals, the selection of the more frequently occurring types is more efficient.

Other criteria are of a pragmatic or a substantive nature. Practical arguments for selection deal with distance, time, money and accessibility. Substantive arguments deal with the variance of independent or dependent variables or with developmental phases. The following list presents a summary:

All available cases	• when the domain is very small • when the cases are very inaccessible • with 'critical' cases • with 'unique' cases • with 'revelatory' cases
Random selection	• only as an additional criterion
Pragmatic grounds (distance, time, money, accessibility)	• preferably only as an additional criterion
Substantive criteria	
1. Homogeneous on the independent variable.	• advisable at the start of a research programme
2. Heterogeneous on the independent variable.	• advisable to explore the limits of a theory
3. Homogeneous on the dependent variable.	• not advisable
4. Heterogeneous on the dependent variable.	• not advisable
5. Selection on developmental phases comparable?	• good, but are cohorts
6. Selection on the causal relationship	• can be used in special situations
7. Selection of critical cases	• can be used especially when testing a theory

Whichever procedure is used, conclusions with respect to differences between cases, and the causes thereof, cannot possess more than an hypothetical status (for the moment assuming that no sub-units are involved). Generalising to sub-domains (large and small enterprises, Eastern states and Western states) is only tentatively possible. On the other hand, if we consider case studies as complementary to extensive research, this problem is less important; other research instruments may provide answers about frequency distributions and statistical relations. The problem of case contamination has to be tackled in the context of successive phases in a case study programme. Generally, when little knowledge is available, one starts with comparable cases, drawn from a sub-domain, and afterwards, one explores the boundaries of the mode by gradually varying dimensions.

EXERCISES

3.1 Select three case studies from your library or web sources. Scrutinise the case selection procedures. To which class (see this chapter) do they belong? Are there, in your view, other (better) ways to select cases? In your opinion, which research decision was taken first – one regarding the intended domain, or one about the selected cases? What about the number of cases in each study?

3.2 Read Chapter 3 of Glaser and Strauss's *The Discovery of Grounded Theory* (1967). Write a commentary on this chapter using no more than 400 words.

3.3 In an evaluation of a reorganisation of healthcare services in Mexico, areas were selected (i.e. local clinics and their catchment areas, the clinics being within a certain distance from all points in the area). From the original 12,284 areas, 100 were selected in co-operation with the Mexican authorities. These were matched as equal as possible on a large number of characteristics into 50 pairs. One member of the pair was selected randomly for the treatment, the other was used as 'control' area. What types of selection were combined in this approach?

3.4 Read again the concluding remark in Box 3.4. One could expand this remark by stating that scientists regularly, or even normally, ground their activities on a dissonance between two or more ideas, beliefs or findings, and then try to explain the contradiction by expanding earlier explanations and theories. What is the difference between a new theory and a statement such as 'The Earth was saved because of the faith of our group'?

KEY TERMS

critical case study
unique case
revelatory case study
random selection
selection on pragmatic grounds
substantive criteria
homogeneous on the independent variable
heterogeneous on the independent variable

selection on the dependent variable
selection on developmental phases
selection of critical cases
retrospective research
prospective research
statistical generalisation
analytical (theoretical) generalisation

FOUR

What Data to Collect?

In this chapter, we discuss, rather briefly, three data sources used in case studies (section 4.1). In section 4.2, with the help of an example, we argue that some obvious theoretical notions should guide data collection. In section 4.3, we discuss, with Lieberson as our guide, the specific difficulties regarding causal conclusions in situations where we collect observations on a few cases and a few variables. We also refer to Ragin's approaches of the causality problem. In section 4.4, a summary is presented and conclusions are drawn.

4.1 Introduction

The usual sources of data are field documents, interviews with key persons or informants, interviews with 'members', and observation. Our discussion in this chapter refers predominantly to the case studies of organisations.

An effective way to get to grips with a case study subject is to study any relevant *documentation*. A first orientation by means of the study of *documents*, if present, is obviously an efficient approach: agendas and minutes of meetings, self-evaluations, earlier research reports, letters, memoranda, newspaper clippings, programme proposals. Archives are also a good source: for example, the number of clients per period, geographical characteristics, inventories of members, service records, electoral results, and many other statistics. Documents and data such as these are very stable and, unlike interviews, they are outside the researcher's influence. They may, however, be biased towards the institutions and persons who constructed them! This should always be borne in mind when using such data.

Interviews are the next data source to be discussed. A necessary first round of interviews not only gathers information in an efficient way, but also allows the researcher to gain admittance to the site and key personal such as area experts, branch experts and historians. 'Common' members of the group should be interviewed next. This will result in a number of interview transcripts.

Observation mostly serves a complementary purpose. It focuses primarily on human behaviour, but observation of physical artefacts, material resources and of people's surroundings may also help to develop insight in the processes at hand. It need not necessarily be participatory observation, that is observation in which a researcher fulfils a functional role in the social system under study during a certain period. Alternatively, observation may be carried out during a field visit or during the research phase of interviewing. Observation is an important element of case study research and cannot be omitted on some occasions. As a main method, however, it is a time-consuming and expensive approach. It results in a lot of observer notes of various types that have to be analysed! If the processes and phenomena to be studied took place in the recent or distant past, observation is obviously excluded.

With respect to *interviews*, we make a distinction between informants and respondents. Key personnel are designated as *informants*. In selecting key persons, we do not proceed randomly, but generally focus – for instance by means of a snowball procedure and an accidental initial contact – on well-informed individuals. Mostly, we interview people who have a leading role in the organisation or who have an otherwise important position. In organisational research the persons who are strongly involved in the phenomenon under study are contacted directly, possibly by telephone. Another point of entry is via the highest level in the organisation, and a third is via 'external experts' who know the field as well as the targeted social system. An approach by telephone or email, followed up with personalised postal correspondence is preferential to an anonymous approach or a speculative letter.

Informants, in the first place, supply general information about the phenomenon and the social processes in which they are involved. Their personal experiences are, for the time being, less central. However, they may also report about their own experiences, social relations, perceptions, attitudes and behaviour. With this information, the investigator can construct a detailed picture of how the process goes on and is to be explained. However, we do not yet know whether our informants are representative of the group or solely of the layer they are assumed to represent. We could construct hypotheses, of course, but we would be looking too far ahead and jumping to conclusions about differences between groups of actors based on the utterances of a small number of people. Conclusions such as these are only possible if we, preferably by means of a random sample and a standardised interview, conduct a survey of a reasonably large number of people.

In a survey we use the word *respondents*. A standardised survey-approach offers the opportunity to reliably describe perceptions, attitudes and behaviour of different groups, and to test explanations about the process based on the properties of individuals. If the individuals, for instance the employees of an enterprise, represent a lower level of aggregation (the enterprise being the original level, the case), we deal with 'nested units' and a 'nested case study' (see section 5.3)

With respect to the selection of informants, in small organisations we will include perhaps all members of the organisation in the study. In medium or large organisations, after stratification according to relevant characteristics, within each layer a sample can be drawn. In school research, for instance, the differences between 'members of the management team', teachers, administrative and technical staff, pupils, parents and parents' council are relevant. We may represent strata such as these by different numbers of informants. If, for instance, it seems important to represent opinions within a certain small group reliably, the number of respondents in that group may be enlarged.

Data collection naturally implies selection: selection not only with respect to people, but also with respect to roles, activities, processes, events, temporal points and locations. It is important to document the many selection decisions and choices we make beforehand, in a *protocol*. This not only refers to the questioning of informants in interviews (and respondents), but it concerns the whole field of possible data sources. It indicates whom, and how many persons, one is going to approach; which documents to study; and whether one conducts interviews by telephone or face to face. A protocol, prepared in advance, helps us not to lose sight of the central research questions. It demonstrates the researcher's use of a comparable approach by going from one case to the other, and that (s)he uses identical questions. When several researchers are involved, the use of a protocol also ensures that differences between interviewers or observers biases are minimised.

However, in our view, a protocol is only one side of the picture. In practice, each researcher deviates from a protocol to a greater or lesser extent. It is therefore important to carefully record the researcher's actual behaviour while conducting the case study, for instance in a research *diary*. A diary also offers the opportunity to maximally profit from unexpected outcomes of the case under study so that the protocol for the next cases can be adjusted. In this book we leave further suggestions and ideas with respect to the implementation of data collection in the field to the reader. There is an abundance of manuals and handbooks to help the reader in this subject.[1]

The protocol and the diary help to realise two goals that are central to data collection (Yin 1994: 94–9). The first is the creation of a case study database; the second is maintaining a chain of evidence between data and conclusions. According to Yin (and we fully agree), 'every case study project should strive to develop a formal, presentable database, so that, in principle, other investigators can review the evidence directly and not be limited to the written reports' (Yin 1994: 95). In survey research it is far more generally accepted than in case study research to consider the database and research report as different things. This situation needs to be changed. Case study investigators should make explicit and retrievable their 'notes, documents, tabular materials and narratives' (Yin 1994: 95). This advice should not be taken as a hint to fully edit all the material one collects and produces during the research process. This would take far too much time, and seldom do other researchers ask for the original data. But the principle of making your data available and retrievable should be kept in mind in all circumstances. It also serves

---

[1] The reader may want to consult the following (old, but not obsolete!) titles: McCall and Simmons (1969); Schatzmann and Strauss (1973); Bogdan and Taylor (1975), but see also the updated version of Taylor and Bogdan (1998).

another function for the original researcher: often an important interpretative step can be taken in a flash of inspiration or on the very weak basis of a single observation or one utterance of a key person or respondent. Being forced to reflect on situations such as these, a good researcher asks him/herself to search for more empirical evidence in support of the given interpretation, as well as for evidence to the contrary! Sometimes, it may be impossible to find more evidence. This should be made transparent as well as it may be a quite defensible position under the circumstances. Making explicit the chain between data and conclusions is another goal all researchers should strive for. The report's readers, who want to find the empirical evidence for a certain conclusion, should be able to verify the link.

4.2 Data and theories

With respect to a research project's relationship with 'theory', four options may be distinguished:

- No theory is used in the research project. A phenomenon is described using everyday terms, without scientific abstraction. Using an old label for this practice, we call it 'idiographic' research. In such cases, the researcher selects what to observe, perhaps making use of earlier research.
- The project aims at the construction of theory. In this case, we need an exploratory approach; to be open to whatever reality has in store for us. However, at the beginning of the project we will head to select some (probably) relevant variables and leave out some (probably) irrelevant ones.
- An extant theory is used in the research project. In applied as well as in basic research, an extant theory is used to describe and/or explain a phenomenon, deduct predictions about a future course of events or to develop interventions. Furthermore, in basic research it may be that a case study is used for the sole purpose of illustrating a theory. Here, the theory offers relatively clear indications about what variables to use and what not to use.
- The project aims at testing a theory. The result of a testing approach is that an hypothesis, formulated in measurable form at the start, is confirmed or refuted, or (an unfortunate result) that the result remains undecided.

In a case study, the initial theory often consists of only some vague ideas about reality. A case study in basic research is mostly directed towards the (ongoing) development of a theory. Rarely does one start with a well-articulated complex of related propositions about reality in order to test or illustrate this theory. In applied case study research, the use of theory is strongly advocated. In applied research no *intended* theory construction or testing takes place. Of course an exploratory approach may be followed. The aim, however, is not to construct a theory (a theory may result as a by-product) but to familiarise with the case, to describe relevant characteristics, and to search for general theories that might be applied to explain things. Also, in applied research we may test a theory, for instance if we desire to check thoroughly whether a certain theory might be applicable before using this theory as a frame for description, explanation and designing policy means. But also, in this case, the result for the theory is a by-product. *In applied research existing theories are used; it is not the researcher's explicit intention to develop or to test theories.*[2]

The following scheme summarises these alternatives:

Relation to theory	Basic research	Applied research
None	Not applicable	To be avoided
Theory construction	Yes	Not intended
Use of theory	Yes; a case can also be used as an illustration	To be advocated
Theory testing	Yes	Not intended

4.3 An application of theory

To answer the question which types of data are to be collected, we focus on the same topic as Miles and Huberman did (1984, 1994): innovation processes in schools. This topic, conceived by us in a wider sense as *success of innovations in organisations*, constitutes one of the important fields of application of modern case studies. We question what data are collected in a study such as this, which generally takes one or two years of research. In an applied research project such as this, we use theoretical ideas based on rational choice theory and the Fishbein/Ajzen-model.[3] This certainly doesn't mean that we accept these theories as unquestioned complexes to explain our observations. For instance, it is evident that many choices in human behaviour are not very rational (see also section 4.3.5). But a theoretical starting point is instrumental. *It enables us to make a grounded choice out of all pos-*

---

[2]Instead of setting out with the usual distinction between exploratory, descriptive and explanatory case studies, we prefer to use the character of the research question as the starting point. After all, a research design doesn't come from out of thin air, but is a consequence of the research question. Moreover, most designs are mixed because research questions of a diverging character are to be answered (e.g. exploratory *and* descriptive questions, or exploratory *and* explanatory questions). Furthermore, we do not agree with Yin's distinction between exploratory, descriptive and explanatory theories (Yin 1993: Chapter 1). Overall, the same theory can be used for very different purposes. Furthermore, Yin uses a rather strange definition of theory: 'the design of research steps according to some relationship to the literature, policy issues or other substantive source' (Yin 1993: 4). This has little in common with the generally accepted definition of a theory, focusing on a net of propositions about an empirical domain.

[3]See, for instance, Ajzen and Fishbein (1980) and Swanborn (1996b).

sible variables, and to have a frame for the interpretation of results. We use knowledge gathered by earlier investigators as well, of course.

In this substantive field much research has been going on, and we know the main relevant variables. Actually, the work done by Miles and Huberman themselves has contributed considerably to our knowledge because these authors have already constructed an inventory of variables and concepts that are considered to be relevant in innovation processes.

We focus on the behavioural choices of individual persons. Participants in a social system are continuously confronted with choices: whether to participate in the innovation or not; which activities to undertake; who to ask for information, etc. We do not deal with just one choice at one moment from a restricted number of alternatives, but during the process choices are continually changing, depending upon the decisions already taken as well as upon the changing environment. Starting with some theoretical notions does not mean that a theory, for example rational choice theory, is exclusively valid for the situation under study. It only means that we base ourselves, when confronted with a multitude of alternatives, on an approach that is very general and that has proved to be applicable and successful in other similar scenarios. In this way, we improve the efficiency of our endeavour.

Our (still broad) research questions might be:

- How is the process of innovation proceeding?
- What problems occurred and how did we overcome them?
- Why is this innovation in some organisations implemented quickly and without many problems, while the same innovation triggered a series of problems in other organisations?

The first two research questions are descriptive; the last one requires an explanation. Obviously, in dealing with the last one, it is assumed that we have already solved the earlier descriptive questions.

Reading documents is, of course, the first phase of the fieldwork. It provides us with insight into the roles of certain groups of stakeholders and of key personnel. It can also be useful in unravelling crucial events (hopefully!) and in sorting out problems that emerge during the process. Studying documents, however, is almost never sufficient. In order to amplify and strengthen our knowledge we need information from key people in the organisation. These people are approached for two distinct types of data. The first one is to ask each informant about material and physical conditions and barriers, and about the thoughts, motives, attitudes, behaviours, and so on of a certain group 'on average', at a certain point in time and according to his/her knowledge. Obviously, the informant is asked primarily about the group (s)he belongs to, but we may also inquire about, for instance, the teacher's impression of the perceptions of management and pupils. The second kind of data refers to the informant's personal experiences. We try to get a complete picture of the initial situation and of developments through time – knowledge, expectations, valuations, social contacts with respect to the innovation, attitudes, behaviour, etc. Here we see the specific advantages of a case study: namely, to explain on the level of the individual explicitly and in detail the causes of the individual's behaviour.

4.3.1 Target variables

We notice that the first descriptive problem demands an accurate account of the progress of the innovation process. Now it depends, of course, on the kind of innovation we are dealing with – the innovation of a curriculum, a new teaching method, an additional schooling project, an experiment in parents' participation – that determines which variables can function as markers for the state of affairs. Let us assume that we are dealing with the use of computers for certain teaching purposes by teachers, and that this school's policy aims for the full participation of all teachers. Distinguishing between target variables (the dependent variables) on the one hand, and independent variables on the other hand, we start by discussing the target variables. The final central target variable is, evidently, the percentage of participating teachers. A target variable such as this is often complemented by other, less central, target variables. Examples would include the kind of work one uses the computer for, how many pupils are involved in the teaching; how much time is spent on the computer, and so on. These variables are surely not the ones that would necessitate a case study. All of them are quantifiable; they can be measured reliably at a certain moment after the introduction of the policy.

Target variables, however, have some other important aspects where a case study becomes very useful. Target variables may be well known or they may hardly be known. Perhaps they are only known by a restricted group of actors (e.g. the schools management team), or perhaps they are shared by a larger group. Furthermore, perceptions of goals may differ largely from the officially established goals. Target variables can change in the course of time, for instance when they meet with strong resistance, or when there is a lack of objective opportunities (e.g. lacking knowledge about computers, unvaliable software). Only by monitoring an innovation through time with all groups of relevant actors may one get to grips with the role these targets play in the actual process.

This 'monitoring in time' deserves futher comment. These not only refer to the dependent variables, but to all variables relevant to the study. Our point of departure is that the more points in time the measurement is based on, the more precise and detailed our description can be. The question arises of how many points in time should be involved in the measurement procedure. Regrettably, the number of temporal points is often rather restricted. Researchers and policy-makers generally agree on the necessity of measuring the 'baseline situation'. Also, the importance of measuring the contextual characteristics of the case (such as the presence or absence of an adequate infrastructure) and of the people involved (abilities, motivation, uncertainty) is not debated. The problem is that, owing to financial and practical circumstances, the monitoring process often is restricted to just a few points in time and, in the worst case scenario to only one point, sometimes after the innovation has actually been implemented.

Moreover, it is clear that interviews are held at certain discrete moments, and that book-keeping occurs with reference to a certain discrete moment, although researchers may be inclined to refer to 'continuous monitoring' in a case study. On top of that, contrary to a multi-moment survey, in a case study one cannot refer to 'successive waves'. Respondent A is interviewed at a different moment from respondent B. There is continuity, but it is not systematic with respect to observation and interviewing. However, using retrospective questions in each interview, one can try to cover a certain common period in all interviews (for instance, a specific month or a six month period). This, in principle, creates the opportunity of collecting data from all interviewees that are more or less comparable (e.g. focusing on the original situation, the situation after two months, after four months, after six months). Afterwards *phases* may become recognisable and labelled, such as start, expansion, consolidation, drawback. A distinction, which is afterwards decided upon, is generally linked to certain crucial events (a stimulating course, a sudden enlargement or shrinking of financial resources, the introduction of new material, the withdrawal or replacement of a leader, a decisive meeting, a policy change, or whatever). The link has to be explicitly legitimised. Moments such as these are more readily remembered by the respondent, and questions that are asked about behaviour or opinions at such moments produce more reliable results than questions about behaviour and opinions on 1 March, say, or during, the last two weeks of June, etc.

4.3.2 Procedures of explanation

To solve the general explanatory research question, we should focus on interacting people. The central actors in our school example are the teachers: it is the individual teacher who decides whether or no to use computers in his/her work. Other relevant groups of actors are the management, the board of directors, the administrative staff and the pupils. Thinking about the causes of different levels of success of innovations in organisations, and even why, under certain circumstances, in practice things go far differently than what is expected, we realise that a process of innovation depends on individual people.

- who are to a certain degree prepared; who are to a certain degree prejudiced; who are to a certain degree willing to change; who are to a certain degree forced to change; who partake in specific stakeholders groups; who are provided, to a certain degree, with the physical goods needed in the processof innovation;
- Who, during the process, experience events and who gather certain knowledge and ideas; who have contacts with others who transfer their positive or negative motivation, or from who they learn abilities;
- and who do, or do not, adjust their views, opinions and behaviour.

The final result of all these changes in interactions, opinions and behaviour may be that the end effect concurs or does not concur with the original goals of the innovation, and that the contributions of individual participants to the innovation may differ strongly. Now the question to answer is: how can we predict the outcome of a person's choice? A central place is taken by the idea that a person, who is confronted with a choice, is led by his/her *expectations with respect to the consequences of participation and of non-participation on the short term and in the long run*. Each alternative leads an individual to compare its advantages and disadvantages. The core of rational choice theory is, in general, that people choose the option that offers the most favourable outcome for them.

So, the next question is: expectations in which respects? In our example, we may think of physical costs, such as training costs; loss of leisure time; keeping or losing one's job; improvement of teaching results; keeping or losing one's colleagues' social approval. One may for instance be afraid that participation will lead to loss of social approval from colleagues, while abstaining will not effect this approval. As a result, there will be a tendency not to participate (all other aspects excluded!). But after some time the situation may have changed: as more colleagues do participate (for other reasons), the expectation may take a reverse direction: one may now become afraid of being seen as old-fashioned, and therewith losing social approval by non-participation! These fine details of a social process only become visible by a case study.

There is a complication. People may have different opinions about the relative importance of all these 'aspects', and for one person aspect A is far more important than aspect B, while for another person the balance may be the opposite. So, in order to explain and predict a person's choice, we need information about what is called the *evaluation of these expectations*. In other words: what are the respective *weights* of training costs, loss of leisure time etc. for the person involved? If a certain consequence (let's say: 'loss of leisure time' is of no importance for someone, (s)he may expect that participation in the innovation will cost a lot of leisure time (or almost no time at all), but whatever the expectation, it is not relevant for the attitude and the behaviour of that person.

The attitude of a person is considered to be the result of a summation of the products of expectation and evaluation over all consequences.[4] The idea of 'product' (of two variables, here expectation and evaluation) implies a statistical interaction between expectation and evaluation; hence the 'x' in Figure 4.1, which is the usual notation for a statistical interaction. So, in principle, for each person the expectations (and how (s)he values this expectation) for each of these consequences should be measured; per consequence the expectation and its evaluation are multiplied, and the products are summated into a score for 'attitude'. The model can be simplified by taking only some

---

[4]Empirically, this assumption cannot be tested, because a multiplication requires that expectations as well as evaluations be measured at a ratio scale level, which generally cannot be realised. See for instance Evan, M.G. (1991) and Meiienbergh, GJ. et al. (1990).

general consequences of behaviour into account (usually time, money and social approval), and assuming the evaluations to be equal among persons.

Now there may be a large cleavage between attitude and behaviour. An attitude may be very positive, and still the corresponding behaviour does not take place. In order to explain this discrepancy, we need the very important idea of 'opportunity structure'. Sometimes one can hardly define a situation as a free choice situation, especially when participants in a social system are forced to act in a certain way. Enforcement by the management is an example. Also belonging to this category are material conditions; presence or absence of expertise and help; own abilities. Several social contexts, each with its own regulations and restrictions, may be involved: the school, the union, the municipal council, the state. These circumstances illustrate one of the arguments for doing a case study: the fact that the phenomenon to be studied cannot be isolated from its context(s). The opportunity structure for behaviour according to one's free will may be extremely limited (such as in traffic), or be less limiting, such as the availability of sufficient material for instruction during an organizational innovation; one might acquire the material elsewhere, although this will cost some time.

A distinction, however, has to be made between the objective and the subjective opportunity structure. The subjective opportunities – that is, the objective opportunities as they are seen, perceived, by people – may be different from the objective opportunities. One may have a wrong idea about one's own capacities and abilities, or simply not be informed about the existence of technical assistance, e.g. the presence of a help-desk. In a process analysis the researcher may discover that a discrepancy between objective and subjective opportunities explains why persons may start enthusiastically but gradually become inactive, because they had a wrong perception of their own abilities. Others experience a long period of hesitation before becoming active, because at the start of the process they didn't know about the presence of a help-desk or the willingness of other people involved to help them. Many participants in a social system have a one-sided view on the topic, and even get it completely wrong. The researcher, by being informed from several sides, and on the basis of his/her experience, sometimes easily blows the constructions that people themselves make. It certainly is a topic that stimulates the insight that there are several kinds of 'truth'. Having people talk freely about perceived obstacles and barriers, is one of the most useful assets of field studies.

We conclude that the attitude of people depends on their expectations with respect to the consequences of their behaviour. However, this is only one determining factor of their behaviour. The other factor is the opportunity structure. In Figure 4.1, the essence of what has been said above is pictured in a causal diagram. We designed the model mainly to indicate how the ultimate behaviour (degree of participation) is determined. But we may also distinguish intermediate phases in the behaviour: speaking with others about the innovation; asking for advice; studying documents and other activities that are relevant for reaching or obstructing the final aims of the innovation. The model may be used for each of those phases separately.

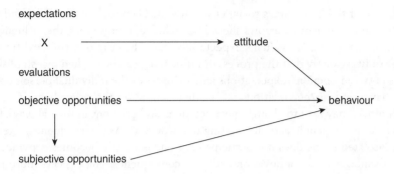

Figure 4.1   A first path diagram

4.3.3 Explanatory models

The model shows that attitudes are determined by an interaction of expectations and evaluations, and that what results is one of the determinants of behaviour. Additionally, behaviour is directly determined by the objective opportunities. But also indirectly: the objective opportunities determine the subjective opportunities which, in turn, determine behaviour.

An additional arrow could be drawn from behaviour back to the expectations. It is perfectly possible that someone starts very motivated and convinced of their own capacities, but that (s)he quickly discovers personal shortcomings, or other unexpected factors. Obviously, this may influence the expectations at a later moment.

On the left side of the model an important component should be added. A complication is that at the start of the implementation some people involved may be largely uncertain about their expectations and they cannot estimate the consequences of their own behaviour. This can provoke resistance towards any change. Therefore, it is important – certainly in the initial phase – to carefully establish whether the informants have a clear idea of what the innovation is going to mean for them, that is, having knowledge with respect to the consequences of the innovation.

Expectations and knowledge about their own abilities are, in turn, influenced by background variables, such as education and prior experiences with innovations such as this. Therefore, a block of *background variables* should be added at the left side of the model. At the base of expectational or attitudinal differences, are differences in background variables: sex, age, number of years in service, education, prior experience and, above all, position in the organisation (in the schools context, a member of the management team, a teacher or administrative and technical staff). Most background variables are 'hard' and can be operationalised at the start of the project without ambiguity. Furthermore, they need only be measured once.

A shortcoming of the model in Figure 4.1 thus far is that it typically represents a model for the determination of individual behaviour; it does not show the influence of the individual's social environment. Therefore, on the left-hand side of the model some more arrows should be included, representing the influence of other actors on the individual's expectations, etc. The crux of a (process-tracing) case study is exactly that the process of influencing can be studied by establishing links between opinions, expectations and attitudes of the individual person on the one hand, and his/her relations with other people on the other hand. Contact with others may lead to changing expectations and opinions in several ways. One perceives more people actually starting to participate. As a consequence, one gets more isolated if one does not participate, or one gradually becomes convinced of the advantages of the innovation and, as a consequence, one expects more positive effects as a result of self-participation. Or one gradually views the objective opportunity structure in a more realistic way, or one picks up, through interactions, some of the skills and abilities that are needed in the process. Managers will probably stimulate social interaction about the innovation, especially the positive effects of an innovation, in the hope that it will become more widely accepted. Social interaction implies not only directly 'helping' individuals, but also the gradual construction of a social context that supports, judges, and serves as a reference group for the individual. Expectations with respect to the approval of others may influence the cost/benefit ratio of their own behaviour. And if one expects that many colleagues will drop out, owing to lack of time or other reasons, it is irrational to continue oneself because of the risk of becoming socially isolated.

The researcher will therefore ask questions such as:

- Who do you interact with?
- Who do you ask for information?
- Who are you influenced by?

Assuming that data on knowledge, expectations, aspirations, etc., are at least measured with some respondents at some points in time, the researcher is able to carry out checks on statements such as: 'at the time I was strongly depending on Joan because she could tell me a lot about it'. If we include these ideas, we can produce the model shown in Figure 4.2.

A problem remains that an adequate completion of a real 'sociomatrix' (a square matrix in which each cell indicates the presence or absence of a specific social relationship between the row-person and the column-person) assumes standardised questioning in terms of 'what are you doing with whom?'. Missing data are difficult to deal with. The exploratory character of an approach, in which the researcher, during the process, finally reaches an adequate formulation (and consequently misses that information from earlier interviewees), cannot be reconciled with this.

One might represent the process of innovation for one person by drawing a long 'time line', on which – at several consecutive points in time – the scores of this person on the crucial variables are indicated. To give a much shortened illustration:

- (low) expectations on t_0
- contacts with the very enthusiastic person X
- (positive) expectations on t_1
- the first (disappointing) own experiences
- (negative) expectations on t_2
- forced to develop own abilities
- (moderately positive expectations on t_2
- renewed behaviour and its evaluation, etc.

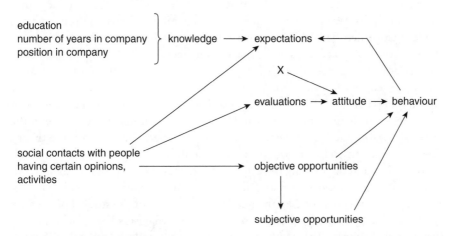

Figure 4.2   An extended path diagram

The causal model in the figure is, as it were, replicated for one person, going from left to right (and from up to down in the enumeration above) a number of times, even if only with a small number of variables.

One of the strong aspects of a case study is the opportunity it offers to focus on (dis-)similarities between the ideas and perceptions of several groups of people involved. We try to explain group-specific ideas and perceptions by establishing links between individual opinions and background characteristics. Sometimes we confront informants with the 'mental models' of others, or with the researchers' explanation. When we deal with 'individual participation' diverging answers can be expected. We may ask people how they evaluate their own behaviour in comparison to that of others. If everyone provides us with an answer, we can study whether the perception of their behaviour is in accordance with reality (as reflected in the opinion of others), and again try to interpret differences. We may question informants about their own explanation of the developing process. Perhaps these explanations concur with each other and with the researcher's explanation. In this context, the term 'debriefing' is used: a researcher regularly puts his/her work (results and procedures) before colleagues to have them evaluate it. The quality of the research can be considerably enhanced by this procedure.

4.3.4 Analytic narratives

In some aspects, the approach followed in this section has common grounds with the so-called 'analytical narratives' development in methodology.[5] At the start of the twenty-first century, this method, originating from political science, economic and historical traditions, tries to put case studies in the frame of rational choice theory and game theory. From the 'narratives' of a case study we can extract the goals and preferences of key actors and the effective rules that influence actors' behaviours. The method also implies that strategic interactions that produce equilibrium of the system are investigated. These interactions constrain some actions and facilitate others. The label 'narrative' refers to the science of history: it pays close attention to stories, accounts and context as it traces the behaviour of particular actors, clarifies sequences, describes structures and explores patterns of interaction. Cases covered vary from the International Coffee Organisation to twelfth-century Genoa (Bates et al. 1998). The approach is characterised by a central concern with institutions, but focuses on choices and decisions. Institutions are effective in the sense of rewards and punishments, and can be analysed as actors in game theory. The label 'analytic' refers to the process of identification of individuals and collective actors, and discovering the actors' preferences and perceptions, their evaluation of alternatives, the information they possess, their expectations and strategies, and the constraints that restrict their actions. Outcomes of the studied process are accounted for by identifying and exploring the mechanisms that generate them (Bates et al. 1998: 10–13). Methodologically, this research approach has more in common with finding a suitable model by a process of iterations than with traditional theory testing. The theory is used as a tool for discovering facts rather than as an immovable structure. The 'analytic narratives' researchers, however, start with descriptions of historical events and often end up with mathematical models. Both features are absent in the methods sketched in sections 4.3.1–4.3.3. Common ground, however, is qualitative descriptions to start with, the application of theories from the beginning, and the use of the 'variable language'.

4.3.5 Discussion

Above, we used a set of central concepts to illustrate which data are to be collected in the first place, within the frame of a case study on innovation implementation. For several reasons, the reader may feel uneasy about this approach. To start with, it seems contradictory to the usual, open character of a case study to try to mould data to a previously constructed theoretical set of concepts. The reply, however, would be that we need theoretical concepts such as these *anyway*, to steer data collection (which variables do we include?) and to bring order into the collected data. It is, of course, possible that some of these concepts prove to be barely relevant,

---

[5]One of the central sources is Bates et al. (1998). See also Rodrik (2003), as well as the special edition of *Social Science History*, 2000, 24 (4).

and that others will need to be considered during the process of collecting and analysing data. Being open to different choices and flexible in approach is a prerequisite for a case researcher. Besides, we can already dispose of a number of the relevant variables about innovations in organizations. In this sense, our example is certainly not typical of a classic exploratory approach. Anyway, we do not yet know why in *this* organisation the innovative process develops in this specific way. The theory is used as a tool for disciplined empirical research.

The process of finding and evaluating evidence in case studies in a disciplined way is sometimes referred to as the *quasi-judicial* method. This label indicates that the emphasis is on eliminating erroneous interpretations. Dennis Bromley (1986: 25–6) describes this procedure by setting out eight formal steps for applying this method to clinical or social science research.[6] These are the following:

1) The initial problems and issues of the case must be clearly stated.
2) Background information should be collected to provide a context in which to understand the problems and issues of the case.
3) Existing or *prima facie* explanations of the case must be evaluated to determine whether they fit the evidence and to discern how they are lacking.
4) A new explanation should be set forth correcting the problems identified in the previously existing explanations.
5) The sources of evidence and the evidence itself used in the new explanation must be evaluated or 'cross-examined'.
6) The internal coherence and logic of the new explanation, including its compatibility with the evidence, should be critically examined.
7) The new explanation's conclusions regarding the case must be presented.
8) The new explanation's implications for comparable cases must be discussed.

These steps clearly illustrate the necessity of making the explanations explicit, including the concepts and theories used, during the research process.

A second critical question would be whether it is useful to apply the concepts in a situation where there are a very low number of informants. A decent data analysis requires equivalent operationalisations, little missing data and a *large number of units*. Only under these conditions would we be able to draw conclusions about the applicability of a theory or about the relevance of variable X compared to variable Y. However, we use the data of our informants to complement our raw causal model, which contains variables such as expectations, evaluations, attitudes and behaviour, and to correct it. How does the process affect this person, or that person? In doing a survey the most we can conclude is that a difference exists between an individual opinion on t_1 and t_2 (t_1 mostly on retrospection!). With a case study, however, we can detect intermediate changes and developments, and even offer explanations for them, even if we are studying only a few people. Changes in goals, accidental contacts, changing opinions are seldom

---

[6]Bromley actually presents ten procedural steps for the 'quasi-judicial' method, which are integrated into eight steps, as mentioned above, by Chima (2005).

detected in a survey, and can lead to much unexplained variance. In a case study we can tackle this unexplained variance. We focus on the details of a complex social interaction.

A third objection to our approach might be that, in a case study such as the one chosen, we need organisational theories in the first place, not some general behavioural concepts such as the ones we used. Yin (2003) seems to tune his classification of theories to the aggregation level of cases dealt with. He mentions

> *individual theories* (for example, theories of individual development, cognitive behaviour, personality, learning and disability, individual perception, and interpersonal interactions); *group theories* (for example, theories of family functioning, informal groups, work teams, supervisor–employee co-ordination, and interpersonal networks); *organisational theories* (for example, theories of bureaucracies, organisational structure and functions, excellence in organisational performance, and inter-organisational partnerships); and *societal theories* (for example, theories of urban development, international behaviour, cultural institutions, technological development, marketplace functions) as well as theories that cut across levels, such as decision-making theory. (Yin 2003: 31)

We fully agree that theories specific to each level and specific to substance, exist and should be applied appropriately. But it is our opinion that in focusing on a case study on people, who interact with each other in specific circumstances and under certain conditions, and who are endowed with certain abilities and are striving for certain goals, we should primarily study variables such as those pictured in Figures. 4.1 and 4.2. Knowledge deduced from specific theories of a higher level of aggregation should be fully used, of course, in complementing our design. But, after all, we study *people.*

4.4 Causality

The debate on the shortcomings of case studies focuses on two aspects: the explanation problem and the generalisation problem. Here, we focus on the assumed impossibility of drawing reliable causal conclusions. Within this context, Campbell and Stanley (1963) commented upon the absolutely insufficient character of the 'one shot case study'.[7] Later this severe judgement was considerably weakened in view of the arguments to be discussed in Chapter 5 (see also Cook & Campbell

---

[7]This is the classic reference source for social scientists reflecting on the possibilities for causal reasoning in non-random situations. This contribution had its predecessors, was afterwards published as a monograph, and was finally replaced by the influential volume by Cook and Campbell (1979). In this standard source, many possibilities for causal argumentation in non-random situations are offered. The introductory chapters on causality and validity are of a high level, and are difficult for many students to follow. Chapters 5 and 6 contain an introduction to time-series analysis for single-subject designs (again, not an easy read). An updated text is Shadish, Cook and Campbell (2002).

1979). In this section, we explore the causality problem a bit further. These paragraphs may serve as a prelude to Chapter 5.

Lieberson (1991, 1994) and Ragin (1987, 2000) discuss the difficulties connected with causal interpretations based on a small number of units. Lieberson reaches a negative conclusion, Ragin is more optimistic. Before explaining the differences, we emphasise that their definition of 'case studies' is very special and does not take into account the richness of information that case studies may have. That is because they exclusively focus on documentary sources. They work with 'hard' variables on the level of the cases only (as political scientists, they predominantly deal with nation-states). They do not deal with organisations and individuals, where triangulation can be applied and usually data is much more rich, flexible and diversified.

To understand their contributions, it is necessary to first discuss the usual arguments with respect to the impossibility of causal analysis in case studies. In *extensive research*, causal analysis is effected on the basis of handling, in an exploratory or a testing mode, causal models. These models are represented by an a priori or a posteriori sketched 'picture' of variables connected by arrows. They suggest the construction of cross-tabulations over a large number of units. Once a correlation has been detected between two variables connected by an arrow, we conclude that at least one of the necessary conditions for a causal influence is present. In case research, in principle nothing prevents sketching, and working with, a causal model (as we actually did in the preceding paragraphs!). But looking at the possibilities for causal analysis, at first sight our endeavour immediately comes to a stop. With *one case*, we see that one high value on dependent variable Y co-exists with a specific value (high or low, to keep it simple) on a possible independent variable X, but that only fills one cell of the cross-classification, and with only one observation (this is the old argument for using the derogatory label 'one-shot case study'). And even if the number of cases is enlarged to eight or ten, the N is far too low to draw a reliable conclusion about a statistical association between X and Y. The central problem in doing case studies is, according to Lieberson, that a researcher may have very inspiring ideas (about the failure of attempts to reach a certain target in evaluation research, for example) but that in the context of one or a few case studies this idea can hardly be tested, *unless data on sub-units are collected*.

Lieberson[8] (1991, 1994), following Skocpol (1979) and Nichols (1986), has illustrated quite fundamentally the impossibility of causal analysis in working with a small number of units in terms of Mill's 'method of difference' and 'method of agreement' (Mill 1872). This is pertinent because researchers using a multiple case study often implicitly or explicitly refer to one of Mill's famous methods to argue

---

[8]For a more extended treatise, see Lieberson (1985). This book does not explicitly cover case study methodology, but it is a must for anyone interested in the possibilities of causal argumentation in social science research, and therefore also in case studies. The author criticises thinking in terms of 'explained variance' and other habits in daily research practice.

that one cause is more important than the other. We agree with Lieberson, that generally it is hardly possible to base such statements on empirical data. All interpretations of data on the basis of a small N presuppose deterministic associations, while in reality probabilistic models should be used.

Mill's classic 'method of difference' implies that if we dispose of two cases that differ on the dependent variable and on one other variable, while they are identical in all other respects, only this one (independent) variable can be the cause of the difference on the dependent variable. Lieberson poses the question of whether it would be possible, in this way, that is to say by a comparison of the situations and behaviour of two drivers, to determine whether 'drunk driving' is the cause of an accident (see Table 4.1).

Assuming a correct dichotomisation of these variables, and neglecting measurement error, we have to conclude from this data that the cause of the collision is

Table 4.1   The problem of the two drivers

Accident	Drunk driving	Car from right-hand direction	Driver speeding	Runs through red light
Yes	Yes	Yes	No	Yes
No	Yes	No	No	Yes

the approaching car from the right-hand side, while drunk driving or neglecting traffic signs have nothing to do with the accident. Both drivers are drunk, but only one of them gets himself involved in a collision. Our error is, of course, that we implicitly assume that the independent variables do not interact; that the impact of cause or condition A is independent of other causes or conditions. With only two cases, there is no way to control this possibility. And if we enlarge the number of cases a little by introducing a case for each of the 16 logical possibilities, we remain with the question of whether all relevant variables have been included, and whether they can be measured without error. In short, the results in Table 4.1 say nothing about the relative influence of such independent, conditional variables.

We continue, with Lieberson, the argument in Table 4.2, in which the scores of the first driver remain as in Table 4.1, but those of the second driver are changed. We are now confronted with Mill's 'method of agreement': if two identical phenomena (now both drivers are involved in an accident) have but one factor in common, that factor is the cause of the phenomenon.

Table 4.2   The problem of the two drivers revisited

Accident	Drunk driving	Car from right-hand direction	Driver speeding	Runs through red light
Yes	Yes	Yes	No	Yes
Yes	Yes	No	Yes	Yes

The only independent variable that changed relative to Table 4.1 is the speed of the second driver. One would therefore expect this variable to be the cause of the accident now. This, however, is not the case: drunken driving and running through a red light now compete as explanations for the collision, whereas they were excluded in Table 4.1. The fact that in the data in Table 4.2 the second driver drives too fast and causes an accident completely changes our interpretation of the cause of the accident for the first driver.

Arguments in situations in which a small number of cases serve as a database are almost always based on Stuart Mill's logic. The example shows how vulnerable the identification of the real causes is. We add that the use of only a few variables, as in the example above, involves a far-reaching simplification of reality, and that dichotomisation and neglect of measurement error are simplifications as well. It will be clear that causal analysis with case studies in the usual variate language on the level of the *cases alone* is almost hopeless.

Lieberson attacks, with the above mentioned analysis, what is called *comparative analysis*, which has a long tradition, especially in political science (see, for instance Tilly, Paige, Barrington Moore, Wallerstein, Smelser, Rokkan). In political science, usually countries or states constitute the units, and the dependent variable refers to the political system of the unit, the origin of peasant revolutions, strikes, military regimes, etc. In the intended explanations a small number of 'hard' variables, which of course differ from one study to the next, are used.

The political scientist Ragin (1987) shows, as Lieberson does, the shortcomings of this approach. However, he reaches an alternative solution that, on first sight, seems to have much in common with Lieberson's. Ragin constructs a table of all logically possible combinations of scores on the independent variables (with three score variables: 'eight rows' with four dichotomous vaiables one would have $2 \times 2 \times 2 \times 2 = 16$), and subsequently establishes which value on the dependent variable empirically occurs in conjunction with each independent scores-pattern. As a next step, Ragin uses Boolean logic to discover under which combination of conditions a phenomenon (score 1 on the dependent variable) occurs. In this way, he tries to frame causal conclusions on the basis of data from only a small number of units (mostly, countries). The frequency of occurrence is neglected. Finally, rewording the formula into the simplest structure leads to the intended result. As an example we present Table 4.3. The phenomena being studied are the conditions for 'successful strikes'; the cases are a small number of studied strikes (Ragin 1987: 96).

In Table 4.3 only four combinations of conditions lead to successful strikes: aBc, ABc, ABC and Abc. The fact that AbC as well as ABC occur, leads us to the conclusion that AC is a sufficient condition. In the same way, the fact that ABc as well as ABC occurs, leads to another sufficient condition: the pattern AB. And the co-occurrence of ABc and aBc leads to a third: Bc. So a first wording of the conclusion reads: S = AC + AB + Bc. This expression is redundant, however, because the element AB implies ABC as well as ABc, and both patterns are already among those implied by the other elements. So, finally, we arrive at the simplest Boolean

Table 4.3 When are strikes successful?

Conditions				
A or a	B or b	C or c	Success(s)	Frequency(f)
A	b	C	no	6
a	B	c	yes	5
A	B	c	yes	2
A	B	C	yes	3
A	b	c	yes	9
a	b	C	no	6
a	B	C	no	3
a	b	c	no	4

A = booming product market   a = no booming market
B = threat of sympathy strikes   b = no threat of sympathy strikes
C = large strike fund   c = low strike fund

expression: $S = AC + Bc$. That is to say, S (successful strikes) occur when there is a booming market for the product manufactured by the workers *and* a large strike fund, *or* when there is a threat of sympathy strikes by workers in associated industries combined with a low strike fund.

In comparing this approach with regression analysis, we conclude that thinking in terms of 'isolated variables' has given way to thinking in terms of 'configurations'. Each unit is represented by a pattern of scores on the relevant variables. In other words, statistical interaction is taken into account. This provides advantages, because often the impact of variable A on variable C may be conditioned by variable B. Ragin uses the general label 'multiple configurational causation'. By introducing interaction terms in a regression equation one may touch this problem, but not solve it.

In his later work (2000) , Ragin considerably extends his thinking on methods. He borrows the notion of 'fuzzy sets' from mathematics and informational computing. Dichotomies like successful/unsuccessful are replaced by, mostly, seven-point scales. These are not to be seen as common ordinal scales. They are ordinal, but at least the first and the last category, as well as some 'midpoint', are to be theoretically interpreted anchor points, and the assignment of units to the verbally labelled categories requires careful consideration. He presents evidence for his finding that many variables are less 'hard' than one might think at first sight, a fact that accentuates the need for more differentiation than membership/non-membership of a category. Instead of a dichotomy such as this, it becomes a matter of degree how a unit belonging to a set is expressed. On the other hand, Ragin thoughtfully comments on the use of (apparently crisp) ratio-level variables and the usual correlation and regression analyses, because of the fact that much of the variation on a variable might be irrelevant (e.g. distinguishing between states that are 400 years old and states that are 200 years old on a variable 'age' that covers the whole domain of nation-states), but, mostly, because regression is based on additive models of variables, while variables actually interact with each other in affecting a dependent variable.

Another important addition in his later work is the introduction of probabilities in the analysis of necessary and sufficient conditions for a dependent variable. It is recognised that missing variables may result in the appearance of empty cells in the cross-tabulations of independent and dependent variables, and measurement errors may be incurred in observations in the 'empty' cells. That is why Ragin establishes some a priori percentages 'that should be obtained', such as 'necessary and/or sufficient in 90% of the cases', while maintaining the principle of necessary and sufficient conditions.

The reader is reminded of the essence of sufficiency and necessity in logic and in causality by the following definitions:

- 'A is a necessary condition for B' implies the impossibility of non-A/B.
- 'A is a sufficient condition for B' implies the impossibility of A/non-B.
- 'A is as necessary and sufficient condition for B' implies the impossibility non-A/B and A/non-B. Hence, in the cross-tabulation of two dichotomous variables, one being the necessary cause of the other, at least one cell is empty. Likewise if it is a sufficient condition; at least two cells are empty if A is a necessary and sufficient condition for B.

Ragin's 'fuzzy-set method' is also used for the analysis of causal relations in a restricted number of cases, while some of the cases' properties may be based on a lower level of aggregation, for instance individual persons. In a study of neighbourhood (dis)satisfaction in 29 European post-war housing estates (ranging over 16 cities), the author applies Ragin's method to detect what patterns of independent variables caused satisfaction or dissatisfaction of the people living in these estates. The dependent variables were based on large-scale surveys as well as some of the independent variables. It was found that the 'social mix' of a neighbourhood did not – contrary to the expectations – affect the satisfaction score, but the combination of ethnic mix and lack of social cohesion has apparent negative effects (Van Gent 2006). It might be interesting to compare results with those of a multi-level analysis of the same original data.

Ragin's point of view with respect to homogeneity might give rise to misunderstandings about the population or domain to study. As, for some part of the population, causal processes may be quite different from those for another part, Ragin (2000) considers the search for a relevant and *homogeneous* population as one of the central aspects of case (or rather case-comparative) studies. A population (= a domain) defined in advance might be too heterogeneous to make sense. In his opinion, '"diversity-oriented" research follows the lead of case-oriented research on problematizing populations and emphasizing their constructed nature. Populations are viewed as no more than working hypotheses and are open to revision in the course of an investigation' (Ragin 2000: 45).

Ragin illustrates his 'search for homogeneous populations' with the example of the influence of the economic gap and political representation on riots.

Calculated over all American states (the cases in his multiple-case study), the correlations are low. But the influence of economic gaps on riots is strong in the Northern states, and the influence of political representation is strong in the Southern states. So, the Northern states seem to constitute a domain that is different from the Southern states with respect to this causal reasoning. In other words, the geographical situation interacts with both independent variables. In statistical terms, Ragin's 'homogeneity of populations' boils down to the absence of interactions between independent and contextual variables. It is generally advisable to be aware of these interactions, but it does not seem to be advisable to take Ragin's striving for homogeneity too rigidly, because this procedure might end up as a series of isolated single cases (no two cases are exactly the same). Our emphasis, in Chapter 3, on delineating the domain or population as strictly as possible at the start of the research, is independent of the rather narrow meaning that Ragin attaches to domain as a function of a causal structure.

Ragin's work on causal analysis, based on some principles of set theory in mathematics and the availability of data on a moderate number of cases (usually N is about 5–50), has found many followers in recent years. Use of his methods is facilitated by the availability of computer programs. In QCA 3.0 (Drass & Ragin 1992), the simple use of dichotomic variables and Boolean operators is applied. In FS/QCA 2.0 (Drass & Ragin 1999), all fuzzy-set procedures are implemented as well as the use of probabilistic criteria. Both programs can be downloaded from the website www.u.arizona.edu/~cragin.

The significance of these procedures is restricted to the availability of data from a multiple-case study, and to specifically causal research questions. As such, it fits perfectly well within the political sciences' interest in the methodology of case studies. The field of applications is, however, already much wider.

Some of the objections against the first set theoretic approaches have more or less disappeared, such as the fact that in dichotomising continuous variables much information is lost, or that frequencies are not taken into account. Still, several simplifications that are needed remain hidden in the background. First is the fact that its use seems to be restricted to the macro-level, where relatively 'hard' variables are used and measurement error is not grave. Second, there is the problem of variation in scores on the dependent variable with units having an identical pattern on the independent variables. Third, we are forced to restrict ourselves to models with only three to five variables, while valid models require a lot more variables. Another argument – mentioned by Ragin himself – refers to the difficulties when some patterns simply do not occur and analysis is very much hindered. Finally, it is not always evident that results in terms of configurations of independent variables can be interpreted theoretically. However, Ragin is probably right in his opinion that the interpretability of results of his configurational approach is better than the results of the usual row of beta-weights resulting from a regression analysis based on isolated variables. Nevertheless, stressing the fact that there are several causal ways that may result in the same outcome is a methodological advance.

From the general methodological point of view that the use of more methods and different approaches (also in the analysis of research data) is better than restricting oneself to one method, and the general idea that Ragin's method could supplement other methods, we recommend experimenting with it.

4.5 Conclusions

The data sources of central importance in case studies are field documents, informants and observation – in this order. In an example, it is indicated that informants may supply information about (part of) the social system they belong to, as well as about their own expectations, values, experiences and behaviour during the period under study. The process of collecting information is always guided by a theory, even if it is a very primitive one – perhaps only consisting of some commonsense ideas of the researcher. We used a path diagram to sketch, on a micro-level, how individuals, in their behaviour with respect to an innovation, are guided by their goals, their (restricting or facilitating) circumstances, and their social relations. In a case study, many individual people, representing different groups of stakeholders, are intensively studied. By detailing their social relations as well as their development, we are able to create a picture of a process in an organisation, and suggest explanations for stagnation or progress.

We paid attention to causality, and to Lieberson's pessimistic view on the possibility of causal analysis using only a few cases. We also discussed Ragin's solutions to causality problems using case study data. Both views are especially relevant to the analysis of 'aggregated level' data, such as in the political sciences. Ragin's methods are not the only way to study causality. As we will see in the next chapter, the opportunities for causal analysis are considerably widened if we think of multiple-level cases studies, and of other ways to enlarge the number of data points. On the level of individual actors *within a case*, serious work with respect to explanations can be done, for instance, testing whether the role or position of individuals is a strong determinant of their motivation, or a reflection of the time they are willing to invest. Within one case we can dispose of data of many individuals, and we can construct cross-tabulations and estimate covariances. Another interesting alternative is to enlarge the number of measurements in time: time series analysis is the obvious example. We have to keep in mind, of course, that we need to satisfy the other necessary conditions for causality: time order and the absence of spurious causality. Moreover, the presumed causal connection should be plausible, that is to say, understandable, and interpretable in order to be accepted.

4.1 Use the monographs selected in Exercise 1.3. Scrutinise all data sources in these studies and answer the following questions. (a) Does the researcher account for his/her steps in collecting data? (b) Is a protocol and/or a diary mentioned? If so, what is the use of these methods? (c) Which key persons are approached? Is this, in your opinion, an adequate selection? Which key persons are omitted?

4.2 Apply the list of theoretical concepts described in section 4.2 to the phenomenon of a merger process between two food distribution chains in your country, in which the research question concerns the problems experienced in the process and how people coped with these.

4.3 With respect to causal conclusions in the monographs of Exercise 1.3, (a) are the labels 'causality', 'causal influence', etc. used by the author? If not, do you think these labels are avoided while they are in fact essential? (b) If causal conclusions are drawn (explicitly or implicitly), do you consider this as justified? Scrutinise the evidence, first, for a conclusion about the correlation between variables, and second, to interpret this correlation as testimony for a causal influence.

KEY TERMS

field documents

informants

respondents

observation

theory

target variables

explanatory models

path diagram

explanation with a few cases

Boolean logic

FIVE

How to Enrich Your Case Study Data?

A fundamental criticism of case studies is that case study data permit many interpretations, theories and models, and we often do not have enough data to select, in a sensible way, one out of many alternatives. To express this in technical language, there are more theories than data. In this chapter, we use the concept of 'degrees of freedom' (section 5.1) to clarify this point. In sections 5.2–5.9 we discuss several ways to enrich our data, that is, to solve the problematic lack of degrees of freedom.

5.1 Introduction: degrees of freedom

To start with, research results might be (partly) random. We know that the variance of a social phenomenon over a number of units is almost always composed of 'systematic variance' (obeying certain regularities, for instance, that manifest in stable correlations with other variables) and unit-specific or random variance. In working with hundreds of cases, as we do in extensive research, these unit-specific and random peculiarities are supposed to add up to zero, and in this way we are able to split the variance into systematic and random variance. If, however, we deal with only a handful of cases, it is almost impossible to break down the total variance into a systematic and a non-systematic component. In practice, this means that an interpretation or explanation we attach to the results can always be attacked (and on good grounds) by somebody who favours another explanation, someone who states, for instance, that our results are based on random fluctuations.

The problem is easiest to understand in the context of searching for a causal explanation of a single central characteristic (e.g. the success or failure of a new therapy or an organisational innovation). We find a certain outcome, and we try to explain this by observation. But we can freely select from roughly all independent variables, and several explanations will be easy to find. This argument lies at the basis of the ancient criticism qualifying the case study as a 'one-shot' approach (in

Cook & Campbell 1979 the argument was substantially weakened). The following quote indicates the idea:

> An observer who notes a single striking characteristic of a culture has available all of the other differences on all other variables to search through in finding an explanation … it is as though he were trying to fit two points of observation with a formula including a thousand adjustable terms, whereas in good science we must have fewer terms in our formula than our data points. (Campbell 1975: 179)

An often-cited example is the problem of explaining the French Revolution. Historians have come up with at least 25 independent explanations for the origins of the French Revolution. Actually, there are 'more explanations than facts'! An acceptable way out would be, of course, to take one of those explanations and to examine whether *other* revolutions can also be explained by it. And then repeat the exercise with the other explanations. Let us take another example. Suppose we desire to determine the effectiveness of computer-assisted instruction in a group of six students. It so happens that with five students our tentative explanation works very well, but with the sixth student it does not. In the search for an explanation of that deviation we may discover that the sixth student's intelligence is below the level of the others, and we know that a certain minimum level is necessary. Or, we discover that the student has an eye problem that makes looking at the monitor very tiring, or the student has a technical phobia, or has slept very badly the night before, etc. Alternatively, we can try to explain why the other students were successful. We may discover that all of them participated in an informal meeting the day before, where they exchanged knowledge and task profit from the know-how of one of them. The number of alternative explanatory theories is almost infinite (Kennedy 1979). It is therefore useful to discuss this problem in terms of degrees of freedom (Campbell 1975). The number of degrees of freedom is, simply defined, the number of unknown quantities minus the number of independent equations concerning the unknowns.

BOX 5.1

The number of degrees of freedom in a set of data indicates how many observations produce independent information. N independent scores possess N degrees of freedom, which is to say that to determine these scores we need N pieces of independent information. If we had already known the mean of the scores, we would have 'used' one degree of freedom already, because if we know the scores of three of the four observations, the last one is completely restricted: no freedom remains to determine that score. 'Knowledge' such as this can also be expressed in terms of restrictions put to the freedom of the data. Examples of restrictions are that some linear combination of the scores should have a certain value, for instance that the sum of the deviations has to equal zero, or that the mean or the variance has a certain value. With four points plus a restriction such as this, it means that we are dealing with only three degrees of freedom.

To summarise, in a case study we seem to have many theories to explain only one research result. In other words, we have more equations than unknowns, or, as it is commonly expressed, 'the number of units is smaller than the number of variables'. As a consequence, the researcher can fit almost any model or theory to the data of the studied case.

As the number of independent data points grows (e.g. by increasing the number of cases), we express this by saying that the set of data possesses 'more degrees of freedom'. Adding a case, or a variable, or the repetition of a measurement, means that an extra demand is put to the theory: this unknown new score should fit the theory as well. The same holds for adding predictions that imply more unknown scores. Actually, we are looking for a configuration of data points that is unique for one theory, and that excludes all other theories. The more data are put into the analysis, the more rapidly the number of potentially relevant theories or models decreases. Ideally, only one fitting theory remains. Hence, the remedy for the supposed lack of degrees of freedom consists of enlarging the number of data points, in one way or another. In this chapter, we discuss:

- increasing the number of measurement points in time
- introducing sub-units
- increasing the number of cases
- increasing the number of predictions
- using several gradations of the independent variables
- diversifying methods of collecting data
- employing several independent observers
- presenting results to participants in the study and using their opinions as extra data.

Most of these methodological modifications only bring about a relative improvement – we may increase reliability and causal interpretations may become a bit firmer. We do not deal with 'wonder methods' that suddenly bring about a qualitative leap forwards. However, two of the suggestions above are often applied because of their effectiveness: increasing the number of measurement points in time and introducing sub-units. Therefore, we start by elaborating these two techniques.

5.2 Increasing the number of measurement points in time

Although a case study researcher generally has only a limited number of informants at his/her disposal, a case study has some natural advantages over the extensive survey that already weaken the 'one-shot' argument. While in a survey the scores on all variables are measured at one and the same point in time, and may be heavily influenced by the specific historical configuration, such as a political happening, a physical disaster in that period, etc., a case study covers at least a certain period of time, and therefore is less dependent on such events. By measuring some individual variables, such as knowledge, opinions, attitudes and behaviour, several times and taking the mean of those measurements, we may at least be in a position to counter the interpretation that our scores are heavily influenced by random variation.

A more basic argument is this. With respect to a causal connection, the dependent variable should co-vary monotonously over time with the independent variable. In a survey, we compare scores on variables over individuals. In a case study, by using many measurement points over time, we can draw, per case, a beautiful diagram in which this covariance, or the lack of it, is demonstrated.

BOX 5.2

It is useful to reflect for a moment on the idea that this *longitudinal approach*, which is characteristic of an intensive case study, actually is to be preferred over the usual approach in transversal, extensive research, in which we construct cross-tabulations over many units, but at one moment in time. In transversal research, our interpretations depend on a *comparison between units*. If unit A scores higher than unit B on an independent variable as well as on a dependent variable, we assume that if unit A's value would change into B's value on the independent variable, it would adopt unit B's value on the dependent variable as well. This untested 'comparability' assumption is avoided in longitudinal research.

It would be too optimistic, however, to think of case studies in terms of designs that, by definition, for each unit provide us with a large number of measurements on the same variables over time. Three or four observations per unit represent the common situation; only two observations is not unusual. But the general principle is that the more observations one can make, the more reliable the explanation will be.

As stated in Chapter 1, in applied science there is a strong tradition known as 'single-subject research'. It is also known as N=1 research and as 'case study research'. This strongly quantitative tradition stands apart from all others in case study research. It is grounded in the health sciences, developmental psychology and psychotherapy. Its special character is represented in the use of multiple observation points, in the order of 50 or more, facilitating the use of the statistical apparatus of time-series analysis. Monitoring a patient or client on some variables over a long period, in which a new medicine or treatment is applied, stopped, again applied, etc., illustrates the core of the business.

Single-subject research has many applications outside the fields where it originated. An example is the study of the impact of a traffic safety regulation system on the number of traffic incidents by collecting data before and after its introduction. In these contexts, we mostly refer to applied science, where the label 'case study' is used because the domain consists of one or a few units (often a country). However, these 'time-series case studies' may also very well harbour a more 'basic scientific' interest in a general phenomenon, such as the general effect of a therapy, the effects of speed limits on the behaviour of people, the impact of a new law on criminal behaviour, housing developments or the influx of immigrants and asylum seekers.

5.3 Introducing sub-units

Another way to increase the number of degrees of freedom in a case study is to introduce a lower aggregation level, with many sub-units that may be measured on several variables. An obvious example is the study of organisations or local settlements. Many social systems contain subsystems of a lower level: schools contain classes, classes contain pupils. When our research question refers to a phenomenon that occurs in school classes, our observations need not be restricted to the class level (such as the size and the location of the class), but we will, to ground our interpretations and explanations, collect data on the level of the individual pupils as well, and we pay attention to the relations between pairs of pupils. It not just is a 'trick' to study the variance within a group of individuals, it is important theoretically as well, because explanations in social science are eventually based on the behaviour of individuals. If the interpretation of an assumed causation deals with units on a lower level, and the characteristics of these units can be measured, we deal with 'nested' or 'embedded' units. This allows the case researcher to apply cross-tabulations and more advanced forms of data analysis. (S)he remains within the boundaries of the original domain of organisations, but within each element of the domain a sub-domain appears.

Take this simple example. To explain the success of an innovation in an organisation, we not only use data from several organisations (the cases), but within each case we collect data from individuals. In the analysis, properties of organisations (such as leadership, communication structure) come together with properties from individuals (such as rank, position, motivation, abilities).

Relevant questions are whether all units of the lower level are included in the study, or whether a sample is drawn. And if a sample is drawn, are units randomly selected (stratified or non-stratified), or is some form of non-random procedure used. Often, decisions such as this, referring to 'selection within the case', are neglected. If we seriously wish to speak about respondents, comparable to a survey, we need to be careful in the selection process. In a case study of one or more organisations it will often be impossible to approach each member of the population by mail, telephone or email. In a large organisation, a (stratified) random sample is most probable. In a small organisation, such as a school, it is not wise to select 'half' of the population or another fraction. It is better to include everyone.

As the number of data points grows, the necessity to quantify – and the possibility of doing so – is larger. A large variety of procedures for multivariate data analysis and statistics, as developed in survey analysis, is available. To start with, simple procedures, such as cross-tabulation, correlation analysis and analysis of variance, are generally sufficient. We do not discuss the traditional quantifying analysis of large numbers of respondents or other sub-units because it is not different here from the usual survey analysis – descriptive and explanatory analysis are standard.

Second, however, we may deal with the so-called 'multilevel' research designs. They are to be considered when studying simultaneously the variance of units on a certain level of aggregation and the variance of (sub-units that are nested within these. Multilevel analysis can be applied when, for instance, we dispose of systematically collected data of respondents within a certain number of cases. In researching only one case, it may be possible to organise systematic data collection with the sub-units, or it may be possible that we dispose of repeated measurements of the same units in time, but here the concept of 'multilevel' designs is irrelevant: *with one case we cannot study variance between cases*. It will also be clear that when the number of cases is very small, say less than 10 (which implies the main body of case research), an analysis of variance on certain variables has little use; the number of units is too small (and the criteria of selection used are too specific) to reliably estimate parameters. With a larger number of cases and suitable data, it is possible, in principle, to carry out multilevel analysis. In this way, we may, for instance, discover that certain correlations at the level of individuals occur in one type of cases but not in another. A discovery like this is still not very interesting if the distinguishing variable has a nominal character: some cases yes, other cases no. It starts to be interesting if we are able to label the variable in question – if we can interpret and understand why that interaction between individual level-variable and case-level variable occurs. During the past decades multilevel analysis has offered many new avenues to analyse data adequately. Well-known programs are HLM 6 (Raudenbusch & Bryk 2002) and MLwiN 2.12 (Goldstein). Some general statistical packages such as SAS and SPSS also contain multilevel analysis procedures.[1] This still doesn't mean that a multilevel model can always be adequately conceptualised and interpreted. In the field of case studies the applications are still rare.

Apart from departments, classes or persons, several other types of sub-units can be considered. In a more general sense, for example, these can be activities, events, meetings, choice situations, social or technological processes, or interactions with the environment. McClintock et al. (1979) use 'planning events' in a case study in the public sector; 'choice situations' in a welfare organisation; and 'tasks' in a university in which the numbers were so large that a quantifying analysis was possible. Even an individual person can be 'split up' in sub-units such as 'roles', 'abilities', etc. In research practice we find applications of the same principle in handling documents. Within a document, paragraphs, sentences or words can be the sub-units, and within a film, systematically chosen fragments can be the sub-units.

---

[1]A useful introduction to the theme is Hox (2002). See also Kreft and De Leeuw (1998), Snijders and Bosker (1999) and Raudenbush and Bryk (2002).

McClintock et al. (1979) introduced the label *case-cluster method* in this frame to clarify the clustering of sub-units within the case.[2] They developed a case-cluster method as a completely autonomous approach. This includes working with several categories of informants. After designing a blank cross-tabulation per category of informant or respondent, information is collected for each cell of the table. We think, however, that McClintock et al.'s case-cluster method scarcely deals with case study research. It refers mostly to a field study in which a (large) number of units are included. The units (planning situations, choice situations, tasks) can be randomly selected because there are so many of them. The case is just a time/spatial framework (McClintock et al. use the expression 'focus-organisation'; more generally, focus-level) for the sampling of sub-units that constitute the actual domain of the research question. McClintock et al. do not seem to be aware of this dilemma – that is, 'what it refers to'. However, the *phenomenon* to be studied of the case study deserves a central place. When we consider the question of whether counter employees choose a formal or an informal approach when dealing with customers, and we study this phenomenon in two post offices, we may call these post offices the cases or 'bearers' of the phenomenon, and label the lower level of 'counter interaction' as a unit of observation. But this then turns the whole matter upside down. The real domain of the research question is constituted by social interactions and the selected post office is the more or less accidental location in which these interactions are studied. The number of social interactions can be multiplied infinitely, and here the term 'case study' is clearly inadequate.

With respect to the selection of an 'umbrella' social system, sometimes there is an argument to select a context in which the sub-units show maximal variance, while the differences between the selected context and other contexts are minimal. The idea is that in the selected context the heterogeneity of the population is maximally reflected. The selection of a higher-level unit as starting point has, however, more relevance for external validity (the generalisability with respect to time, place and social systems) than for the problematic methodology of case studies. Our main attention is obviously focused on relations of the level of the units within that system. Another important problem is related to working with 'special types'

---

[2]From this point of view, McClintock et al.'s 'case-cluster method' (1979) may aptly be called case study methodology, contrary to our earlier remarks. Besides systematic selection, mostly using stratification, of cases, they work with a systematic selection of informants from different groups, called 'stakeholders' in the context under study. In a university, for instance, technical and administrative staff, students, and scientific staff belong to several echelons. Strangely, McClintock et al., in cross-tabulating events (tasks, 'planning events' or other sub-units) against kinds of informants, pretend to present a kind of Multi Trait Multi Method (MTMM) design, while on the other hand they emphasise the importance of the existence of different opinions within different groups of stakeholders. In a MTMM design, the desired result is obviously that differences between methods (informants) are subordinated to differences between objects. Therefore, McClintock et al.'s reference to MTMM is inconsequent. The final aim of MTMM, the comparison of correlations, in order to estimate the reliability and validity of substantive results, becomes obscured (McClintock et al. 1979). See Appendix 3, 'A note on triangulation'.

of sub-units. It deals with demarcation. Demarcation of, for instance, 'tasks' of employees in an organisation is not simple. To prepare a cup of coffee will generally be considered too small as a unit; 'to do research' as too large.

Are there any more procedures we can adopt to increase the number of data points?

5.4 Increasing the number of cases

The more cases are studied, the more independent information becomes available. In a multiple-case study, several questions are raised:

- Do we study and analyse these cases simultaneously or consecutively?
- If consecutively, do we adjust our methods and techniques, such as the wording of questions and the data to collect, to our experiences with the earlier cases?
- Do we compare the results of the cases with each other, and how do we deal with differences and similarities between the cases?
- Do we aggregate the information from different cases?

The answer to the first question is determined mostly by practical considerations, such as available time and whether we can recruit enough researchers to work in the same period. There is also a financial argument: studying cases in parallel generally costs less time than tackling one after the other; in the same time period more cases can be tackled. This is often a strong argument for following a parallel or simultaneous approach. A more basic argument, pointing in the other direction, is that studying cases one after the other offers the opportunity to adjust procedures, for example after stumbling upon an unexpected problem. Frequently, the approach taken in later cases is different from that followed earlier in the study. The answer to the first question, therefore, seems to lead us towards conducting a 'pilot study' with one or a few cases, on the basis of which the definitive approach and questioning is determined. Afterwards, other cases can perhaps be tackled simultaneously.

Following this procedure, however, sometimes confronts the researcher with a dilemma: are the results of the pilot cases to be included in the final result (notwithstanding, for instance, the lack of important data, or less reliable results because a wrong question was included) or should they be 'forgotten' once they have served their purpose in clarifying the cases? Obviously, the last solution is the better one. In practice, the researcher will be strongly tempted to include the pilot results because of the usually small total number of cases. A compromise is perhaps advisable: use some, but not all, results from the pilot studies.

The answer to the other questions is of course related to the arguments for selecting more than one case. When cases are selected because we expect them to be comparable, and consequently to be represented reliably by a common model, we deal with *pure replication* (or as Yin (2003: 47) says 'literal replication'). In this situation we will test the descriptions and explanations developed on the basis of the cases studied earlier, with new cases. If our hypothesis about comparability is not rejected, we possibly aggregate results over several cases. Perhaps, however, we selected certain cases because, on the basis of theoretical considerations, we expected contrasting or at least diverging results – Yin uses the expression 'theoretical replication' when we try to enlarge the boundaries of the domain.

What we start with depends upon our hypothesis regarding the homogeneity of the domain. Assuming the possibility of rather large differences between public and private educational systems, we will allow for separate types within this framework. But this assumes, for instance, after having studied three private and three public schools, that the variance within each type is much smaller than the variance between types.

A comparable situation emerges when we wish to compare cases in an exploratory way, implying that we do not have specific expectations regarding the results. This offers the opportunity to explore the limits of the descriptions and explanations developed on one case, or to formulate hypotheses about the causes of differences between cases. We are dealing now with external validity or generalisability. Here again, several procedures are in use. The first one is that we strive for a model that is common to all cases studied. This procedure is advocated and popularised by Glaser and Strauss (1967). Study one case, design a model, study the next case with this model in hand, adjust the model till both cases fit, go to the third case, etc., until, as is hoped for, all cases fit and no further adaptation is needed (Glaser and Strauss refer to this as 'saturation' and Yin calls it 'explanation building'). An objection to this inductive approach is that it is awkward, in a qualitative approach, to decide clearly what is similar and what is dissimilar. Of course, certain margins have to be accepted, but how wide do we allow them to be? Another objection is that no a priori boundary is set for the complexity of the model. Adding a newly studied case under the wings of an already existing model is often only possible after introducing new specifying conditions in the model. This causes the model to be more complicated. And the more each new case leads to further adjustments of the model, the less parsimonious and the less interesting it threatens to be.

A second variant is that we allow differences between (types of) cases. This alternative is often searched for when the quest for a common model threatens to fail. Now we design types: for certain cases we design model A, for other cases model B. As no two cases are exactly identical, the researcher is likewise confronted with the choice between similar and dissimilar, equivalent or not equivalent. Not infrequently, it is a next best solution. However, from a methodological point of view, a typology is of a lower level than a theory. Therefore, we emphasise that constructing a simple typology (mostly the final result of this approach) is a rather all to easy procedure; a taxonomy or typology is almost always easy to design. Whatever we do, it is at the least necessary to argue why the designed typology is as it is. Hypotheses regarding the causes of the differences should be sought for; differences between cases should be explained and interpreted.

A still cheaper solution is to describe, analyse and report each of the cases separately. It is the least demanding procedure that fits the idiographic tradition quite well. Again, we have to try to formulate hypotheses regarding the differences between the individual cases.

In order to solve explanatory problems, the best way is to try to design one informative theory that is valid for all cases studied.

5.5 Increasing the number of predictions

It is generally advocated – as a kind of ideal – that it is better to work with competing theories in studying one case. This remedy for the problem of the lacking degrees of freedom is, in our opinion, outside the context of formulating a null hypothesis, not of much practical value (besides, in extensive research, time and again research experience shows that the one 'crucial variable' as well as the other 'crucial variable' plays a role, that is to say that no *single* theory explains the results). Campbell (1975) indicated another way to expand the number of degrees of freedom. From each theory, each model, one can deduce a larger or smaller number of predictions, to be tested with the data of the case itself. It is not true that each theory can be applied to a case; it even shows that an experienced researcher, after seriously studying one case, seldom unconditionally accepts a specific theory because always some data seem to refute the theory. Within the limits of the study of one case, often some extra degrees of freedom are already present because several dependent variables are measured. We deal in this respect with the idea of 'pattern-matching' (Yin, 1984, 1994): a complex pattern of scores has to fit a theory. Our point of departure is always that if theory T is true, the consequences or predictions p_A, p_B, p_C ... p_Z are to be true. In dealing with an evaluation of the effects of an intervention (as so often is the case) it is not very informative to state that X (the intervention) co-varies with a certain value on the dependent Y variable. But if scores on some five or six different Y variables show the predicted pattern, there is much less room for uncertainty.

BOX 5.3

In a study on the impact of 'access window' times on retailer distribution costs, Quak and De Koster (2007) used four different variables with respect to distribution costs: number of round trips, number of vehicles, total travel distance and total time. Hence, the number of predictions is multiplied by four. An 'access window' time (applied in many European cities) implies access to the city centre for freight carriers only during specified periods (e.g. 6am–9am), the so-called 'access window'. Many carriers and large retail chains have seen their transportation costs rise as a result of the growing number of cities with these time limits. Problems arise when some hypotheses are confirmed and others are disconfirmed; or when, if within an hypothesis several independent observation statements are included, some

---

predictions concur, and others don't. The use of rules of thumb ('the majority of the hypotheses are confirmed, so we can conclude that the theory is confirmed' or 'if two predictions are refuted, we can conclude that the hypothesis is refuted') is a worse strategy than a continued search for the reasons why certain predictions are confirmed and others are refuted. A case study in which, during the research process, subtleties of this kind can be included, and in which perceptions of participants are also monitored, provides more information than a standardised survey.

If at the start of the analysis one can imagine some competing interpretations, and if one succeeds in moulding these into alternative predictions, one's position is considerably strengthened when some of these predictions are refuted. If we are lucky enough to be able to refute all interpretations except the one based on the intervention, it becomes difficult to describe the data otherwise than as resulting from the intervention. Our position is strengthened still more if we succeed in replicating this result in other cases. Apart from this, the suggestion has its restrictions: we have to keep in mind the famous series of 'alternative interpretations' presented by Cook and Campbell (1979), and only seldom shall we be able to definitely refute all but one of the interpretations. In other words, the guide to follow reads: expand the theory as far as possible; deduce predictions by expanding the number of dependent variables that are expected to be influenced by or, explicitly, not influenced by, the intervention. The more independent predictions are verified, and the more predictions from competing theories are refuted, the stronger our hypothesis regarding the influence of the intervention stands. The absence of a large number of cases can be compensated for by a richness of predictions from our theory. It is another illustration of the principle of increasing the number of measurement/observation points in case studies.

BOX 5.4

Boskma and Herweijer (1988) refer to a study of Heikema van der Kloet (1987) that deals with testing a public policy theory (implicitly) applied by local municipalities to legitimise the expansion of statutes regarding mandates and the delegation of authority. This theory leads to the following expectations:

- after the transfer of authority to civil servants the number of items on the agenda during council meetings decreases
- the engagement and the motivation of chief civil servants increases
- rulings and decisions are given more quickly
- rulings are more often given which later appear not to have the agreement of the manager concerned.

(Continued)

(Continued)

When, in a municipality in which the delegation of authority was recently introduced or extended, these four phenomena occur, enough ground exists to positively evaluate the policy theory. If, moreover, in municipalities in which the delegation of authority was recently submitted to stricter rules, reverse effects are manifested, our position is all the more strengthened. Next, other communities can be selected to replicate the study. The results may also be replicated, or the research design can be adjusted to include some alternative explanations. If these are refuted, we once again feel stronger about our original explanation.

5.6 Using several gradations of the independent variables

Even with a small number of cases scientific progress can be obtained by searching for more differences on the independent variable than the usual dichotomy. The general idea is that the stronger the independent variable, the more, or the faster, change in the dependent variable is to be expected. In a laboratory, our task would be to design a study in which the independent variable is characterised by a series of fine-grained values, and to formulate predictions in accordance with the strength of the independent variable (the relationship between the amount of medication in mg and health improvement is a simplified example). In a case study, we may sometimes dispose of several cases that were or that are subjected to different values on the independent variable in their natural context.

5.7 Diversifying methods of collecting data

Increasing the number of observations can be effected by using several methods of collecting data, for instance observation, interviewing and documentary analysis. Often the term 'triangulation' is used to indicate this practice of using several data sources.[3] The opportunity to compare subjective data with objective data (e.g. with respect to the time budget or the availability of material resources) should be welcomed. In this way, we have an opportunity for control. But it does not work without confronting a dilemma.

With every application of this principle we have to ask for the researcher's expectations and intentions. If sources converge, one is generally inclined to accept this result

---

[3]Some scientists apply this label for other purposes as well, such as using more than one theory ('theory triangulation'), more than one researcher ('researcher triangulation'), or more than one method (Patton 2002). The common idea behind all these procedures is, of course, the enlargement of the set of degrees of freedom. It would be better to restrict the meaning to 'triangulation of sources', and use other labels in a more concise way for the rest (see Appendix 3).

without further questioning. But if different data sources lead to diverging results, how is this to be interpreted? Should we be disappointed about the result because we interpret it as unreliable, or should we accept these diverging results enthusiastically because an easy explanation for the divergence between, let's say, interviewing and observation, or between objective and subjective data, presents itself?

From the minutes of a meeting one may infer that the management of a team continues to support a certain innovation. But when interviewing people, several individuals express their opinion that the management frustrates their efforts. This divergence prompts new research and may lead to discoveries about a lack of communication, or the existence of too many independently acting subgroups. If sources do not converge, it is necessary to continue the study in order to deepen understanding.

The dilemma we are faced with often presents itself in reading case studies based on data from different groups of stakeholders. Sampling ideas and perceptions from different groups of informants is one of the clear advantages of a case study. We often pursue an explanation of differences in opinions and interpretations of different groups of stakeholders. Within this frame, we feel satisfied in actually finding those different opinions. But if the researcher finds a convergence of opinions, (s)he is tempted to change perspective, and interpret this convergence as proof of 'reliable results'. To prevent ambiguity, it is necessary to indicate the interpretations with respect to contrasting results beforehand. With other words, try to be as precise as possible about the use of mixed methods beforehand. If possible, formulate expectations (hypotheses!) about confirming or contrasting results.

Creswell (in Bergman 2008: 72) mentions five ways to address contradictory findings:

1) as a means of uncovering new theories or extending existing theories
2) leading to the collection of additional data
3) leading to the reanalysis of the collected data
4) using data as a springboard for a new inquiry
5) giving priority to one form of data over the other.

With respect to point 5, it does not seem to be a very constructive idea to state a priori that the validity and reliability of one kind of data is better than it is for the other kind.

5.8 Diversifying researchers

Another way of enriching case study data is to have the data collected and/or analysed by several researchers, or even to have the report written by independent researchers. This can be understood in distinct ways. First, it may simply mean that we enlarge our research capacity – that more cases are tackled and that each researcher tackles his/her own cases. Increasing the number of cases strengthens reliability. Comparability of approaches is required. Room for subjective biases is larger than for an interviewer in a standardised survey, or for an experimental researcher in a laboratory. Training and mutual criticism (and a protocol and diary that one has to commit oneself to) are necessary. With a relatively large number of cases, and random distribution among researchers, there is a greates possibility for multilevel analysis. We can study whether researcher A arrives at another picture, based on her cases, than researcher B over his cases, where, in view of random allocation, a similar picture could be expected.

Second, working with several researchers facilitates working with more people per case. In general, this principle is a good idea because a 'lone researcher' not infrequently develops particular biases, that, however, can be repaired in time if there is an opportunity to be corrected by a partner or a team of researchers. This does not mean that everything is done together. Rather, the work, for instance the interviewing, is distributed among researchers, and 'in the evening' the collected material, as well as the interpretations and explanations, can be debated. In another approach, roles can be distributed: A does the interviewing, B analyses documents. The points of view of the distinct researchers may be seen as 'data points' that after ample discussion may be reduced to – hopefully – reliable and valid data. A 'luxurious' variant is putting one researcher apart by excluding him/her from fieldwork obligations and reserving him/her the role of 'sparring partner' or, more precisely, as devil's advocate, to counter the interpretations the field researchers attach to their data.

Concerning the individual researcher's biases, sooner or later each case researcher develops the idea that data converges. New data adds little to the material already collected, and the jigsaw pieces begin to fall together. This is a very general experience that needs to be mistrusted if it emerges relatively early in the research process. General methodological principles, such as 'always try to refute your own ideas' and 'strive for counter-examples', are psychologically difficult to realise for the individual researcher. Critical remarks made by others, or rather competing interpretations put forward by colleagues, can play a very useful role in preventing premature closure. The same holds, of course, for the use of different data sources.

Third, only when researchers do exactly the same work (replication of an interview is impossible, but analysis of a protocol or documents is perfectly possible), and results can be compared, may one view the researchers as each other's replications, comparing different 'measuring rods' measuring the same object. Only then are we able to use strong methods of analysis and draw firm conclusions. Such a luxurious situation is, however, very rare in view of the budgets normally available for case study research.

5.9 Presenting results to participants and using their opinions as extra data

Having the opportunity to present research findings to the informants, and in this way confront them with *their* descriptions and explanations (keeping in mind that the latter are not infallible), provides researchers with the ultimate opportunity to check the validity of their interpretations. In doing so, in an informal way, the number of data points is automatically enlarged. A welcome situation occurs if the researcher, on the basis of preliminary results, is able to phrase predictions for the future. However, the side-effects of involving researched persons in this way should not be underestimated. The researcher is in a vulnerable position. Research results, including the central causal model, have to be worded in very clear language. Informants in general are pleased to co-operate as a research assistant in this way and to be valued as such, although a small financial reward may also help a lot.

There is also a learning opportunity here. A causal model is not infrequently composed of variables that originate from different perspectives, each one of which is supported by different groups of stakeholders. Presenting the composite end result to all participants can have a very healthy influence on biased opinions.

In qualitative research, the presentation of research results to participants, at whatever the stage of the project, is called 'member checking'. Presenting preliminary findings to informants is a subtle form of it. Naturally, there are limitations in doing this. If we do not speak the language of the informants, or if they are too young or too old or do not possess a thorough understanding of the reasons for the study, member checking is practically impossible. In addition, just because researchers give informants an opportunity to comment does not mean 'the members are always right'. The central idea is to establish divergences of opinions – and to interpret them – in different groups of stakeholders. Its purpose is not 'to find one truth'.

BOX 5.5

Miles and Huberman (1994: 165–71) combine the making of predictions with involving participants in their research. They developed a rather subtle procedure in this respect:

During the analysis the researcher formulates some specific predictions about how the social process under study will develop in let's say, six months, time. The researcher also develops arguments that would counter these predictions. The researcher keeps these documents to him/herself.

After six months, several potential informants receive two envelopes. In the first envelope is a form that defines the variable, gives the predictions and asks the informant to judge the adequacy of the prediction. The informant is also asked to write down the most important factors in his/her mind contributing to the (non-)adequacy of the prediction. Only after that, the informant opens the second envelope. It contains the prediction plus the arguments that were formulated earlier by the researchers. The informant is asked to rate the pertinence of each factor in accounting for the actual situation, and to explain the reasoning behind

(Continued)

---

that rating. The motive behind this two-phased questioning is obviously not to influence the informant by an externally generated framework, but to detect whether more contributing factors are at work than had been assumed. This seems to be an excellent, although cumbersome, procedure for validating predictions about future events.

5.10 Conclusions

The concept of degrees of freedom is used to elaborate the well-known criticism of case studies: 'too little data, as a consequence of which the researcher is confronted with a relative abundance of interpretations and applicable theories without being able to select one of these'. In this chapter, we outlined several ways to extend the degrees of freedom and thus enrich our case study research. Some research designs that are explicitly rich in information include a systematic extension of observations over time. Ultimately, this led to the tradition of 'single-subject research'. Others are characterised by embedded designs, that is to say designs that allow an extensive, quantitative study of sub-units. Other procedures were also discussed. Careful research into the possibilities for increasing the richness of data can contribute to the usefulness of case studies within the set of research strategies.

EXERCISES

5.1 With the research question of Exercise 4.2, how can you increase the number of 'data measurement points' (and the number of degrees of freedom) in your study?

KEY TERMS

degrees of freedom
increasing the number of measurement points in time
introducing sub-units
increasing the number of cases
increasing the number of predictions

using several gradations of the independent variables
diversifying methods of collecting data

diversifying independent researchers/observers
presenting results to participants in the system under study

SIX

How to Analyse Your Data?

Having collected the data, we are certainly not yet ready to write the final report. How are these data going to be analysed in order to be used? In this chapter, section 6.1 tackles the differences between data analysis in case studies and data analysis in extensive research. In section 6.2, we discuss five strands that play a major role in case study data analysis: the 'Yin' tradition, 'qualitative' approaches, the 'Miles and Huberman' techniques, time-series analysis and Ragin's logic. In section 6.3 we suggest a possible analysis of the data collected for the example presented in Chapter 4. In section 6.4 a summary and several conclusions are presented.

6.1 Introduction

> The human understanding, from its peculiar nature, easily supposes a greater degree of order and equality in things than it really finds. When any proposition has been laid down, the human understanding forces everything else to add fresh support and confirmation. It is the peculiar and perpetual error of the human understanding to be more moved and excited by affirmatives than by negatives. (Francis Bacon's *First of the Idols of the Tribe*, 1863)[1]

The basic problem of data analysis is the same for all types of research: to reduce a huge amount of data in order to obtain an answer to the research question. In extensive research, data consists of numerical scores on precise, pre-coded, variables. They can be neatly arranged in a data matrix with, generally, variables in the columns and respondents in the rows. In the major part of intensive research, such as a case study, the initial data sources are field documents, interview transcripts and observation protocols. Is it possible to use the general idea of a data matrix for intensive research as well? Yes, but with some important annotations.

First, guided by the research question we have to split the information contained in the data sources and arrange it in parts. These parts refer only to a certain extent

---

[1]Bacon, Francis (1863). *The New Organon*. Boston: Taggard and Thompson. After the Latin edition of 1620, *Novum Organum. I. Pars Contemplative*.

to what one could call variables. Some of them, such as background variables, could of course have been pre-coded at the start. Variables expressing appreciation and activities are often suitable to pre-code as well. But most of the data refers to sentences, abbreviations, quotes, valuations, non-numerical symbols and short verbal notions. Next, these verbal notions are submitted to several rounds of reduction and abstraction. A set of simplifying categories can probably be established by some trial and error. In general, no clear criteria are available beforehand to distribute verbal answers over categories. One should not immediately push verbal answers in a (too) simple coding scheme. By coding qualitative material afterwards, we keep the door open to finally dispose of a system of categories that is as close as possible to reality. But compared to pre-coding we should realise that the problem is only delayed.

Second, most case studies possess a more or less exploratory character, and not all cells of an imaginable data matrix can be filled in a systematic and comparable way. As a consequence of the lack of uniformity in data collection, the data matrix usually contains many missing values.

Finally, contrary to extensive research, data collection and data analysis are not sharply separated in time, but go hand in hand in a permanently changing order. A data matrix in qualitative research has, accordingly, not the clear position of a watershed between data collection and data analysis as it has in quantitative research.

The crucial phase is, of course, the interpretation of the results and drawing conclusions. For a reader who is used to procedures such as scale construction, variance, factor and regression analysis and many other quantitative techniques, the steps taken by an 'intensive researcher' may seem to be rather meagre. Of course, the following principle works just as well for quantitative as for qualitative research: *determine, guided by the research question, the relevant concepts and variables, and reduce the material in such a way that easy-to-handle figures or score patterns result that serve the solution of the research question.* The precision of qualitative data is, however, much less than the precision of quantitative data. The other side of the coin is that the 'intensive researcher' stays closer to the original data, and pays considerably more attention to a valid interpretation of the material than his/ her quantifying colleague generally does.

But researchers should remember that in all types of analysis things that are not equal have to be aggregated into 'equivalence classes'. Written answers, for instance, have to be expressed in a restricted number of response categories or equivalence classes, say five or seven. It would be an illusion, whichever course in analysis is taken, to assume that no details are lost in that process.

6.2 Five traditions

Research literature in the field of case study data analysis is rather diversely oriented, depending on the definition of 'case study'. Roughly, we distinguish five traditions:

1   Analysis of data collected in the field of changing organisations, according to Yin.
2   Analysis of data collected in one of the qualitative traditions, especially the grounded theory approach of Strauss and Corbin.
3   Data analysis and presentation according to the work of Miles and Huberman.
4   Time-series analysis.
5   Data analysis according to Ragin's method, using Boolean logic and fuzzy-set theory.

It would be a misunderstanding to assume that, after designing the research project and collecting data, the researcher is free to select one of the above-mentioned strands of analysis. Actually, the first two as well as the last one are strongly bound to a specific conceptualisation of case studies, as is indicated by attaching the authors' names to each of these strands. There is barely any common ground. Only the presentational techniques recommended by Miles and Huberman can be applied in the context of different kinds of research approaches.

1 Research in the field of changing organisations according to Yin

Case study methodology in this frame is mainly inspired by the work of one author – compare Yin (1984/2003), Yin (1993/2003) and Yin (2004) as well as many of his contributions to scientific journals in the field of organisation theory. Yin's approach fits the empirical-analytical tradition completely. This author is almost exclusively oriented towards applied research. We can be relatively brief about his approach. Yin himself is praiseworthily succinct in his texts – his strength is in confronting the reader with many examples. He emphasises the necessity for the researcher to be quite clear about choosing a theory-oriented general strategy for analysis, or developing a descriptive framework for analysis when there are no theoretical propositions available. Working on the basis of theoretical propositions is, of course, to be preferred. Yin distinguishes five different dominant modes of analysis: *pattern matching, explanation building, time-series analysis, logic models and cross-case synthesis*. We will discuss each one here.

Pattern matching is characteristic of a testing approach. This strategy boils down to comparing an empirically found score pattern on a number of variables with a predicted theory-based pattern: on such-and-such variables the scores have to be such-and-such (when using more cases, an alternative pattern has to be predicted for some variables). Several data points are assumed (scores on dependent and independent variables when dealing with explanatory problems, on 'descriptive variables' when dealing with descriptive problems). Using non-equivalent dependent variables is in fact one of the specific strategies for increasing the number of data points. Pattern matching can, however, be used for eliminating one or more rival explanations, by introducing several independent variables and testing the empirical consequences of each of them. If one wants to apply 'pattern matching' as a technique for analysis, one needs to be aware of this choice beforehand because it has repercussions for the stages of design and data collection (deduce at the start as many relations between variables as possible from the selected model and from rival explanations, and measure those variables). Data analysis as such is standard. The larger the set of variables contained in the predictions on the central model, the more states of the world are excluded, and the more informative the resulting theory or model is, that is if the predictions are not refuted.

Explanation building is, of course, only applicable in studying problems of causality. It is typical of the modern mix of exploration and testing in social research. After adjusting, on the basis of some initial hypotheses, a model or theory to the first case, it is tested and readjusted when applied to subsequent cases. Explanation building is characterised by a series of repetitions. The emphasis may be on testing. Conceived in this way, explanation building is a special form of pattern matching. If, however, the emphasis is on an exploratory approach (the 'generation of theory'), it comes close to Strauss and Corbin's procedures (see below).

Time-series analysis can be applied in a testing or in an exploratory mode. In some research projects, a number of measurement results over time are available, such as with traffic accidents in region R. When at moment M a policy measure (let's say a speed limit) is introduced, the emerging pattern can be inspected to see whether there is an effect of that policy. Different regions or countries can then be compared. In this way, analysis – does the pattern differ from a random fluctuation pattern? – boils down to a form of pattern matching. Several dependent variables may also be used, and predictions specifying different effects of the independent variables can be tested. But time-series analysis is also applicable in another sense. Even with only a few measurements over time it is sometimes possible to establish consecutive phases in a developmental process. Some events must always occur before other events, with the reverse sequence being impossible; or some events will only occur in certain specified conditions; or there is always a time lag between certain events, etc. Results from earlier studies such as this can be formulated beforehand, or can be generated on the first case and then tested and adjusted on other cases. It is one of the great advantages of case studies that cases can be followed up over time.

Logic models refer to the application of pattern matching on a time series of measurement points in evaluation research. In evaluation research, it is useful to specify beforehand the sequence of events and causal links, starting with several measurements before the policy intervention is implemented. In empirical research, this predicted sequence may be compared with the actual sequence of events. Models may be applied to the level of macro-units, organisations or individuals. In this way, a young person can be followed in order to develop a sketch of risk-producing factors and circumstances (risk, for instance, with respect to become a drug-user or a criminal offender) as well as phases in the process of becoming addicted.

Cross-case synthesis. In a multiple-case study, several additional problems and techniques of analysis come to the fore. We already mentioned the alternatives of carrying out the case studies simultaneously or sequentially. The latter approach provides the opportunity to adjust research procedures. But in the case of cross-case synthesis, Yin is thinking of problems relating to combining several independent case studies and perhaps cases spread accoss a period of time. In the world of experimental and survey research the label attached to this kind of very specific studies is meta-analysis (see section 7.4). Of overriding importance is finding a common frame, a common feature or a common central process (the phenomenon) in these scattered case studies, and of course – it goes without saying in the meta analysis of experiments and surveys – the presence of sufficient information on many characteristics of these case studies.

Yin does not offer a cookbook of methods, but he does indicate the main directions to follow in analysing data, while emphasising the correspondence between extensive and intensive approaches in basic methodology. All in all, Yin's digressions prompt us to continuously reflect on some basic distinctions in the design and analysis of research:

• the distinction between research questions of a descriptive and an explanatory character
• the distinction between a testing and an exploratory approach
• the presence or absence of data about nested sub-units
• the presence or absence of repeated measurement data on the same units
• the presence or absence of multiple cases.

2 Several qualitative models of analysis

Within this category we corral together symbolic-interactionist, phenomenological, ethnomethodological and many other approaches. Anthropological field research may also be positioned under this label. Sources for symbolic-interactionist research include Glaser and Strauss (1967) and Strauss and Corbin (1998); for phenomenological research see Taylor and Bogdan (1998) and for the ethnomethodological approach, see Silverman (1993). More generally oriented to field research is Bryman and Burgess (1994). Still broader in its coverage is Bryman and Burgess (1999). Denzin and Lincoln (1994/2000) offer an extensive overview of qualitative research orientations, although these authors do not specifically cover analysis techniques. These techniques should not be considered as the same; there are extensive differences that exist between them. Within ethnomethodology, for instance, conversation analysis is well known. In this tradition, transcriptions of conversations are coded and analysed in a very precise way, using many conventions and rules, including pauses, intonations, etc. Another tradition is protocol analysis, which is often used in educational research and in cognitive psychology (analysis of thinking-aloud protocols).[2] In the symbolic-interactionist tradition, the best known approach is 'grounded theory'.[3] Some of its central characteristics are:

- a rejection of thinking in terms of variables and instead a preference for holism
- data collection and data analysis are not separated in time
- insights develop as a result of a constant comparison between cases
- there is a strong emphasis on an inductive, exploratory approach: researchers start with as little theory as possible and generate, during the research process, a theory that is grounded in the observations[4]
- the assumption that in studying a case, one or a few central concepts 'arise from the data'
- 'theory' refers to the elaboration of aspects and relations of a central concept. No difference is made between concepts and theories in the usual way, and nor is the terminology of independent and dependent variables used
- a higher level of abstraction can be reached by going from 'substantive theories' via the study of different substantive fields to 'formal theories' (also known as 'bottom up' analysis).

Most applications refer to the analysis of transcripts of interviews. Often, areas of research are 'difficult', such as interviews with married couples who cannot have children, or interviews with ethnic immigrants who have no legal status. Alternatively, raw material may consist of 'letters to the editor', newspaper clippings, or angry comments on a television programme, photographs, films, etc. Generally, each piece of information is divided into fragments (often quotations),

---

[2]Conversation analysis is described in Ten Have (1998). For the analysis of thinking-aloud protocols the reader is referred to, for instance, Ericsson and Simon (1984). An overview of modern methods for analysing verbal data is provided by Popping (1999).

[3]Glaser and Strauss (1967) is undoubtedly the most famous and well-known book on qualitative research methods. Chapter 3, on theoretical selection, especially deserves attention in the context of case study research. Strauss and Corbin (1998) provides an updated and elaborated text on many aspects of symbolic-interactionist fieldwork. A wide range of applications is to be found in the companion volume Strauss and Corbin (1997). An introduction to qualitative methods in general is provided by Taylor and Bogdan (1998). In the United Kingdom, Bryman and Burgess (1999) is a four-volume set that brings together all of the major topics and issues in qualitative research, including epistemological, ethical and cultural issues, as well as information on the collection and interpretation of data. Bryman and Burgess (1994) is a general textbook on qualitative data analysis. An extensive survey of qualitative methods is offered by Denzin and Lincoln (1994/2000). In this massive volume, the heterogeneity of the contributions, each elaborating a more or less different approach, is overwhelming. Other texts on qualitative analysis are Weitzman and Miles (1995), Fielding and Lee (1998), Kuckartz (2001), Richards (2005), Bazeley (2007), Lewins and Silver (2007) and Gibbs (2007). The older texts are becoming rapidly outdated.

[4]Most authors rather naïvely share this tradition. Only sporadically is reference made to the footnote (Glaser & Strauss 1976), in which it is explicitly denied that the researcher confronts reality as a *tabula rasa*.

and each fragment is given a code (and sometimes more than one code) a process which is called 'open coding'. The aim of the code is to capture the meaning of the fragment. These initial codes may be 'in vivo', that is to say, for instance, simply giving the label 'mother' where the word 'mother' is used in the quotation, or they may be a little more abstract, such as 'youth friend', or 'perception of the quality of parental care'. In the next phase, called 'axial coding', the initial codes are collected, mutually related and ordered into an analytical framework. The aims are to reduce the number of codes, to find overarching codes, to relate codes to each other by developing a 'coding tree', and if necessary to add new codes. The codes are applied to new material to test whether the developed system is adequate. Analysis by a computer program provides many possibilities for recoding, combining codes, counting codes, subsuming codes under more general codes, and so on. Finally, in a process called 'selective coding', the aim is to find a name for the category that seems to have a central position in the network of relations, such as 'coping with infertility', or 'adjustment strategies'. It is usually called a substantive theory. Generalising over different substantial fields may lead to a more general, formal, theory. Applying the label 'theory' where a type or a typology, a process, an aspect or variable is concerned, is typical for most qualitative research.

There is, however, a lack of standardisation in software. One reason, of course, is that computer analysis is much more complex than in quantitative research because results of data collection are not expressed in numbers, or in easy and unambiguous nominal categories. It is a procedure that is vulnerable to subjective biases, and it is time-consuming to group words, expressions, non-numeric symbols, pictures and so on into homogeneous categories (the next step, assigning a code to each category, is less demanding). Furthermore, qualitative research itself is far from homogeneous. Many different strands can fall under the label of qualitative research, such as symbolic-interactionism, ethnography, phenomenology, ethnomethodology, conversation analysis, parts of content analysis, and many others. Most of these traditions use computer programs for analysis that are sometimes adequate for one specific tradition, but are less suitable for others. Finally, the field is developing fast and in unpredictable directions, a consequence of which is that there is still a need for codification of procedures and computer programs.

The lack of standardisation may lead to the good but impractical advice to use more than one program in your research, because while program A is very good in function X, it does not perform function Y, which can however be done by program B. Potential users invariably need a consumer guide to find their way around the maze of program packages. Within the scope of this book, it is not possible to provide the reader with a comparative overview. Besides, it would not be very useful because of the fast developments in the field. We often see that in a university faculty, for one reason or another, a specific program is available and that all qualitative data analysis takes place with the help of this specific program, while in another faculty a different program is used for comparable data. Prices generally prohibit the individual user from acquiring a copy for private use, and licence contracts, such as those of SPSS and SAS, are very rare.

English language packages (we mention the latest versions known in mid 2009) are, for instance, QSR Nvivo 8.0, ATLAS.ti 6.0, MAXQDA, The Ethnograph 6.0 and C-I-SAID. A well-known Dutch program is KWALITAN 5.0 (for information, see www.kwalitan.net). The ATLAS and KWALITAN programs are grounded in the symbolic-interactionism tradition. Almost all programs are data-driven, and in this sense inductive. Statements in advertising material such as 'relating text fragments leads you to the discovery of the texture of the data'; 'visual theory building with the semantic network editor allows you to make relationships between emerging concepts visible' describe the authors' intentions. Qualitative data analysis is primarily exploratory. All these programs use, as a primary database, texts such as interview and observation protocols. Some of them handle text data as well as graphical, geographical, audio and video data. Applications are found in many disciplines. As an illustration, we mention in the health sciences the analysis of X-ray images, tomograms and microscoped samples, and in criminology the combined use of letters, fingerprints and photographs for analysis.

What are the salient features of most of these programs?

1 Primary documents are scanned and entered. Primary documents would be interview protocols, articles, books, films, observation protocols, and so on.
2 Each document split into sections. A section can be a paragraph, a sentence, part of a sentence or a word.
3 Each section is assigned one or more codes. Normally, a code is a label, or a central idea that characterises, or can be found in, the section.
4 Codes are memorised and collected in what one might call a codebook, which is entered in the project file as well.
5 Steps 1–3 are repeated for all primary documents.
6 During the process the investigator can write so-called 'memos'. A memo is an account of procedures used, sudden insights, theoretical interpretations, methodological consid- erations, etc.
7 The primary documents, as well as the assigned codes and memos, together constitute the project file.

The 'easy' analysis can now start. Frequency tables for the codes can be made; documents can be compared on the frequency of codes; tabulations can be con- structed for the frequency of combinations of codes; these analyses can be done for one special section or for a subset of sections, for the complete group of respondents or for the females only, and so on.

All this may seem simple, but two significant problems may have already occurred to the reader:

1 How to 'segment' or 'divide' your primary document into segments?
2 How to code segments?

Regarding the first point, no general point can be made about segmenting. It depends entirely on the raw material and the research question. It will be easier to demarcate topics in the case of interview reports, for example, as the topics constituting the segments will seem obvious.

Regarding the second point, coding is rather complicated because it serves several functions. To start with, by assigning a code, a segment can be identified. Identifying segments by means of a 'source tag' serves the purpose of efficiently storing and retrieving the original material. Second, depending on the research question, codes are assigned that characterise the segment in terms of content, presence or absence of a word or an idea, and so on. Sometimes this is easy (e.g. mentioning or not mentioning financial motives in an interview referring to the choice of an academic study). Sometimes it requires the gradual construction, during the initial stages of coding, of a dictionary or a thesaurus. Essentially, the function of this type of program is comparable to the use of foreign language thesauri and lists of synonyms in word processors. In interviews on political attitudes, the researcher might wish to replace all the interviewee's negative qualifications of politics on a certain topic by the label 'rejects politics'. In a case such as this, one needs to read at least a few dozen interview reports in order to compose a more or less complete list of negative qualifications. After adding a new word, the computer automatically codes all consecutive primary documents containing this word. In some research institutes, for example in the field of communication research, there are existing dictionaries or thesauri. The coding process sometimes requires careful reading and comparing (e.g. whether, in segments of observation protocols of playing children, a child expresses 'caring for others' in his/her behaviour). With respect to this second function of coding, we are already halfway towards more advanced types of analysis.

However, coding may serve a third function, which leads us into the field of advanced analysis. The content of a segment is often initially expressed in a code at a low level of abstraction, and may gradually be replaced, or complemented, by a code at a higher level of abstraction. For example: rain/precipitation/weather/climate. This way of coding allows us to make connections between codes on different levels of abstraction; to develop higher-order classifications and categories; to formulate propositions or statements, implying a conceptual structure that fits the data, and/or to test such propositions to determine whether they apply. This process of abstraction is instrumental in constructing (grounded) theories, that is to say theories that are grounded in the observations, especially in the programs, inspired by the 'grounded theory approach'.

Results of qualitative data analysis may be expressed in frequency counts, displaying words in their contexts, but also in graphic displays of networks containing the developed concepts (labels, codes) and their mutual relations. The relationships may portray several types: 'belongs to', 'leads to', 'is a kind of', 'follows', and so on. It is very important to be precise in this respect, especially as the use of labels for 'variables', 'values', 'causality' and 'correlation' in some strands of qualitative research strongly differs from the usual labels in quantitative (mainstream) research.

Nowadays, analysing data more or less according to the principles of 'grounded theory' is by far the most popular method in social research in dealing with a restricted number of open or semi-structured interviews, let's say between five and 50. The analysis is *not* focused on the description and explanation of each of a number of cases (the interviewed persons). One of the key concepts of grounded theory is called 'constant comparison', indicating that its methods are focused on the development of a cases-overarching (grounded) theory.

Whatever one may think of an approach such as this, it clearly has an exploratory character. One of the main objections of the procedure is that is does not reveal the researcher's subjective ideas and pre-theoretical notions when applying codes. Another shortcoming is intrinsically related to an exclusively exploratory approach: what is the relation to many extant social and behavioural theories, developed in 'mainstream research'? Strauss and Corbin (1997) undoubtedly start, as all researchers, with some theoretical notions in mind, but they try to be as open as possible to what they observe in the field, and to let 'emerging' theoretical networks develop. The theory is 'grounded' in the data. As such, this tradition has undoubtedly enhanced existing analytical techniques. However, research into the range of the results, or research into what is known already, and which precise hypotheses are still to be tested, is almost completely lacking in this tradition. By applying what has been said in this section to case studies, one should not forget that it is only part of the data that are analysed with these techniques and programs – and mostly written data at that. Collecting and analysing audio and video materials is possible sometimes. In principle, it can be analysed according to the same principles and techniques. But the real assets of a case study – using, combining and analysing different types of longitudinal data (sources) in order to answer the research questions – generally are not exploited in sufficient depth when applying some 'qualitative data analysis program' alone.

3 Miles and Huberman's approach (1984, 1994)

This approach focuses on representational *techniques*, not on strategies for analysis, or on a general methodology in the classic European tradition. Miles and Huberman's *Qualitative Data Analysis* (1994) is the most frequently cited source in dealing with the analysis of case study data. These authors, who designate themselves as 'soft-nosed logical positivists' in the first edition of their book, adopt an approach that cannot be subsumed under one of the other existing traditions, but constitutes a tradition in itself. Characteristically, they transfer thinking in terms of matrices, graphic representations and tables, as used in quantitative research, to the analysis and reporting of qualitative data. They suggest that all data collected within the frame of a case study (by way of several sources, such as documents, informants, observation) is laid down – in principle – in a temporary 'monster-matrix'. The cells in this matrix are not filled with numbers, however, but with written notions of various kinds: quotations, abbreviations, acronyms, etc. Inevitably, this matrix comprises an impossible format – Miles and Huberman recommend making use of a large wall or floor! For these authors, analysis consists of summarising parts of the monster-matrix into clear *representations* (called 'displays'), in which, however, still no numerical scores are used, but rather words or other short written symbols. To this end, they use two kinds of representations:

- *Tables*. The entries to the tables are formed by informants (mostly as rows, and often already arranged in groups, for instance according to their position in the organisation studied), by topics or variables, by points in time, by cases (if more than one case is being dealt with), by events or critical incidents, by pairs of interacting persons, or by whatever other set is deemed relevant to represent. In one or more steps these tables can be turned, mirrored, compressed, etc.
- *Networks of squares, rectangles, circles, etc.*, connected to each other by one- or double-sided arrows or by common straight or curved lines. The usual plans of organisations, but also causal models, flowcharts, networks of persons or institutes, decision trees, etc. are included in this category.

How is all of this is going to be put into practice? By copying of parts of the monster-matrix, and by subsequent cut-and-paste work? Evidently, since the start of computer age, better alternatives exist. Yet, it should not be forgotten that a monitor screen shows us only a very small part, and 'paper' matrices are still to be preferred for overviewing a large and complex amount of data. On the other hand, the same demand for clarity prompts us to emphasise the necessity of transforming written information into information that can be more easily handled, that is to say into clear variables and numerical, at least simple symbolic, scores. Miles and Huberman offer hundreds of examples of data matrices, tables and diagrams. On first sight, it seems to be curious that in such a large publication on 'data analysis' the emphasis exclusively focuses on the construction of 'well-arranged representations' as the core of data analysis. Also, in quantitative research, reducing the initial data matrix and compressing the representation of information is the core of the matter. The difference with qualitative data is that, because of the lack of the infinite possibilities that numeric language allows, it is very difficult to present an overview of techniques of data analysis in a systematic way. We can therefore criticise Miles and Huberman in that, although they descibe the many avenues of data analysis that are available, they focus exclusively on the 'aim of representation' instead of finding a 'solution of the research problem'. In doing so, they create the wrong impression that case study data analysis, by definition, is at most exploratory – one can do X, but also Y, or even Z – and that the end result is often quite different from the original research aim.

4 Time-series analysis

The analysis of data based on repeated measurements of a small number of precise variables originates in the health sciences and psychology. Studying the effects of a medication or intervention by monitoring a patient or a client on some important health variables in a experimental setting is the core of this type of research. In earlier times it was labelled 'N=1 studies'. The procedures that are followed are of a highly statistical nature. Applications of statistical models are widespread nowadays in the technical sciences, as well as in business, economics and in many other fields. As discussed in Chapter 1, in this book we do not focus on this specific interpretation of the term 'case studies'. It is mentioned here only for the sake of completeness. A classic text is Box and Jenkins (1976). Other textbooks on this subject include Kratochwill (1978), MacLeary and Hay (1980), Gottman (1981), Chatfield (1996), and Brockwell and Davis (2003).

5 Ragin's approach

This approach was briefly discussed in Chapter 4, so we do not elaborate on this topic in this chapter. Applications are mostly in the political sciences – its field of origin. However, there are no special reasons why implementation in other fields would not be possible. But one should keep in mind that the number of cases should not fall below a certain minimum. The exact nature of this minimum depends on the number of variables to be included in the search for causality. One should not overlook the fact that Ragin's approaches are restricted to problems of explanation – they are immaterial in descriptive research questions.

6.3 Analysis

In the large majority of case study research reports reference is made to Yin, *or* to one of the qualitative traditions, *or* to Ragin, *or* to Miles and Huberman. Although in research reports of case studies attention is paid to recommended procedures of analysis, it is often immediately clear which of the above-mentioned research traditions functioned as the source of inspiration for the investigator. However, researchers invariably do not discuss why they make the choices they do. As a consequence, the character of case study data analysis generally remains obfuscated.

For our purposes, it is not very useful to investigate thoroughly all of the traditions mentioned above. Yin's texts with respect to data analysis are brief and general in nature. They have little to teach the researcher who already has a basic knowledge of quantitative analysis. Methods of analysis in the qualitative traditions, such as symbolic interactionism, conversation analysis and protocol analysis, are rather specific and very diversified. For a general text on case study data analysis they are hardly relevant. Besides, within each of the traditons excellent textbooks are available. We have to be very keen, however, in remembering some central ideas behind these approaches, in particular their focus on meanings, perceptions and social relations. The 'Miles and Huberman' approach offers more starting-points for a methodological text on case studies. We agree with these authors in their emphasis on the use of the language of variables to enhance the precision of research results. The transparency striven for by Miles and Huberman in their tables and graphic representations is very important for the researcher as well as for the reader of the report, who may be interested in a written text, but who cannot help asking 'how is this relevant to me?'

BOX 6.1   An example

A modest little technique to reach case-transcending conclusions after the collection of data is to have two cases compared, to detect similarities and dissimilarities. A still more elegant variant of this finds its origin in the 'repertory grid technique'. Select three cases, indicate in which respect two of them are similar, and the third one is the deviant. Techniques such as these are, however, only possible after having constructed a small data matrix, in which a restricted number of variables and scores is represented. If we only had written portraits of cases at our disposal, a comparison such as this, and a distribution over types, is much more difficult.[5]

Although Miles and Huberman have done a very good job in emphasising the importance of schematised representations of data, we do not follow these authors in presenting and discussing a great many tables and matrices. It is our opinion that it is possible for such representations of reduced data to be 'invented' by the researcher her/himself. Many of Miles and Huberman's diagrams and illustrations are remarkably self-evident. Instead, we are strongly inspired by theories or theoretical concepts. This does not mean that we restrict ourselves to testing research. In that case we would cover only a very small part of the total research endeavour in case studies. But, as discussed in Chapter 4, even when using an exploratory approach, we always need a theoretical foundation from which to begin.

Furthermore, it would be a mistake to discuss a lengthy list of specific procedures for data analysis. It is more appropriate to concentrate on a few well-known concepts and principles of analysis, and to reflect on well-known criteria for data quality, such as reliability and validity. For instance, we have to keep in mind that it is not the aim of the researcher to produce a detailed 'portrait' of each case, describing a multitude of relevant and irrelevant properties, but rather the aim is to solve the problem that the case set out to address as precisely as possible.

In Chapter 4 we looked at what data to collect within the scope of a research project investigating the introduction of a new process in an organisation, with

---

[5]Fransella and Bannister (2003).

special reference to educational organisations. In the light of our research questions, the problem at hand is: how best to present the data we collected? In what follows, we point out some important distinctions and provide some ideas about how to do this. It is not a comprehensive account. We do not strive for completeness. We only offer some examples of how a researcher, armed with a research question and some theoretical ideas, can handle case study data.

Sketching out the theory

The tentative theory should be represented in the usual way, with a model consisting of a set of points and arrows (compare Figures 4.1 and 4.2). Don't forget to include possible alternative theories. These should be handled in the same way, assuming of course that you have measured all relevant variables. The following rules might be followed:

- label each variable with an appropriate acronym (e.g. attitude towards the innovation by ATTINN, etc.)
- list the assumed causes on the left-hand side of the paper and the consequences on the right-hand side
- represent a causal influence using a one-sided arrow from cause to effect
- if two variables are correlated, and it is assumed that they influence each other or that both are influenced by an exogenous variable (a variable outside of the model), represent this correlation using a double-sided curved arrow between both variables
- represent a statistical interaction using an x-sign that links the interacting causes.

When we are dealing with case studies, and certainly in using an exploratory approach, a model such as this is only partly complete; there will still be question marks here and there. In the simplest case, it consists of an inventory of target variables, and a list of possible conditions and causes. With an exploratory approach, the model is continuously being adjusted and supplemented as new elements come to the fore during the research process. But for the researcher it is important to establish the parameters within which (s)he works, as these form the basis for the next procedural steps. Besides, this forces the researcher to concentrate on simplicity. Otherwise, a researcher could easily be tempted to sketch a causal mini-model for each studied person. A certain cause often seems to work for the one, and not for the other. Such differences threaten to draw the reseacher's attention away from the essential picture. In the following, we examine several elements in the model, starting with the dependent or target variables.

The target variables: aggregated behaviour

The first step is simple and has little to do with the specific character of a case study. We need to sketch the progress of the innovation process in terms of the number of teachers involved. A time line (with measurement points on the horizontal axis and percentage of teachers involved on the vertical axis) provides an adequate solution (we deal here with so-called growth curves). If the horizontal line comprises (objectively equal) time intervals, we can add to certain points on the line crucial events, policy interventions, contextual changes. This teaching can reveal sudden interruptions or problems, for instance the departure of an inspiring leader or the withdrawal of funds. Comparing such growth curves for other indicators of the main target (e.g. the percentage of teaching time in which computers are used; the number of pupils who received computer-based instruction) may show whether these subsidiary targets are occurring at the same rate, or whether one occurs faster than the other. Exactly because we want to explain the developments with respect to the target variables, one of our first requirements is to gauge the development of each of these variables.

The interpretation of sudden changes in development, or differences between the growth curves of several indicators, is not always easy. In such cases, an informant's personal experience may become crucial. How does the teacher explain his/her behaviour with respect to the innovation? And how does the informant see the whole process in terms of the major problems and the role of other participants? Of course, by recognising hidden problems we acquire insight into the way people justify their behaviour and overcome difficulties. We usually call the complex of ideas, opinions, perceptions and attitudes of an actor, the 'cognitive map' or the 'mental map' of the actor. Our aim is to detect whether the researcher overlooks important factors in the process. How we analyse 'stories' serves to complement or correct the theoretical path diagrams, such as in Figures 4.1 and 4.2. The ultimate aim is to understand and explain the behaviour of an individual in view of his/her background characteristics, social relations and experiences; it is not about counting frequencies.

Other variables: properties of the 'unit' and of several contexts

To start with, for our own orientation as well as for the readers of our report, it is important not only to describe the outward appearance of the researched organisation (i.e. its size, type, location, material resources, relations with other organisations, etc.) but also to account for its internal structure. Such core data are of special importance when we include more than one organisation in our study. And of course, it is possible that different developments in several cases can be explained by organisational variables.

A comment that will be repeated below, however, needs to be made here. If three of the studied schools are large and two are medium-sized, and if we discover that in the large schools the spread of the innovation is slow and in the medium-sized schools high, we are tempted (even though the empirical base is too weak!) to conclude that the success of the innovation is co-determined by the size of the school. Concurring evidence would be obtained by interviewing the participants in the system. For instance, if the teachers frequently remark that certain obstacles are typical of such large organisations. Thus, a valid interpretation in a case study often rests on 'evidence from many sources'.

We can optimally portray some of our core data in diagrams, such as an organogram, that is an overview of the hierarchy and of the roles people play in the organisation, perhaps supplemented with the names of individuals. In some cases it is even possible that a special organisational structure is created in favour of a certain innovation. Sketching out such a structure may be very useful because it can then be juxtaposed with the 'real picture' of the implementation of the innovation. Comparing the 'pictures' may highlight obstacles in the process of implementation. On the basis of this, conclusions may then be drawn with respect to the absence of leaders, for example, perhaps necessitating changes in the hierarchy of the organisation. If we want to explain developments on the target variables in an organisation, we may think, in the first place, of the conditions that may have changed and of events at the school level or even at higher levels. A school has to deal with municipal rules and laws, with school inspectors, and with legislation and rules on the state level. Such data on these contexts have a partly objective character (such as financial support for special aims) and can be obtained from documentary sources; partly they are less hard because they refer to supporting or countervailing forces executed by individual persons. Data are only partly obtainable via documents; partly they are brought to the attention of the researcher by the informants. Some conditions are constant during the whole process of the innovation, others change systematically or haphazardly. Events at the school level, for instance, can be the absence or presence of material resources (books, hardware and software, classrooms), the appearance or disappearance of new management or even the departure of one strong supporter of the innovation who influences all others. Other projects in the organisation may also interfere, and this can have a restricting or facilitating influence on the implementation of the innovation, for example staff meetings or decisions taken in meetings referring to the way the innovation shall be pursued.

Obviously, a useful way to proceed would be to construct a large table with 'temporal points' as columns and several relevant topics on the different levels of aggregations as rows. In the cells, relevant events may be indicated with words, acronyms or other codes. A comparison with the earlier constructed growth curves of the target variables may provide us with an impression of the association between the pace of the innovation and other events and decisions.

Other variables: some characteristics and abilities of individuals

The personal attributes of the teachers and other relevant groups also need to be considered. Depending on the numbers, data collection by means of a survey seems to be an appropriate approach. In other words, this would be a systematic data collection on *a lower level of aggregation* than the school itself. A survey would be an effective method of gathering in a reliable way the thoughts, motives, attitudes, and so on of larger groups. This could be a full survey of the whole population or a random sample of that population. Subsequently, with the help of usual standards and procedures of quantitative research, correlations can be established. An approach like this, however, is certainly not the main focus of a case study! We work on the *case level*, primarily with informants, not respondents. As already mentioned, we use these informants in the real sense of the word: to obtain more or less 'distantiated' knowledge about the process and its institutional embeddedness, and by focusing on the personal history and experiences of the informant. In this last sense, we can compile a data matrix for several individual informants.

The next question concerns the technical ways a matrix such as this (one row for each informant) can be simplified. A first simplification would be to construct a time line for each informant, on which relevant events and changes in the behaviour are indicated. This sort of graph is common in research on school and professional careers. For each individual, specific significant events (often called 'critical incidents') occur. Further simplification can be achieved if each topic is attributed a raw ordinal variable (i.e. '+' for a favourable and a '–' for an unfavourable development) with respect to the innovation. If the researcher is confident in her/his coding capacities, (s)he can even work with a five-point scale to score the answers and remarks of the informants.

Next, we can show how each individual develops (indicated by a pattern of pluses and minuses) on each of the relevant variables. Such an analysis may reveal, for example, that informants who began with low expectations and modest knowledge may take some time to exhibit the desired behaviour, but when they do, they persevere with it, while those people who started with high expectations and quickly adopted the desired behaviour invariably lose interest and can end up rejecting the innovation.

Other possible 'discoveries' could be:

- the existence of factually wrong expectations and the effects these have an individual
- the existence of discrepancies between subjective perceptions and objective conditions (e.g. one is unaware of the fact that a good user's guide is available)
- a lack of knowledge and expertise with the result that people do not know where to start
- the wish to abstain from participation because the innovation is advocated by a disliked member of staff, with whom the individual does not want to identify, and so on.

In this way, it is possible to focus clearly on behavioural explanations that may be specific for each informant. To reach more general conclusions we have to, of course, compare and combine the patterns of different informants. This only seems to be possible when patterns are reasonably similar. Of course, we may obtain several 'types' of explanations or perhaps even one general explanation for the success or failure of an innovation. Everything depends on the uniformity of the processes that develop with different people. In other words, it depends on the between-informants variance. We will return to this point.

Other variables: properties of pairs of individuals

One of the most appealing advantages of the case study as a method of research is that in enables us to study persons not as isolated individuals, but in their social relations. A case study offers us the opportunity to detect and follow the process by which the distinct characteristics of a person (such as thoughts, perceptions, attitudes, behaviour) are influenced by others within the study.

Representations of one or more relations between persons on one variable can be constructed in several ways. Let us take, as an example, the variable 'help', or 'support'. This variable is important because the implementation of an innovation often occurs by means of personal contacts, and certain people are gradually going to occupy a key position because others call on them for help. Because 'people requesting help' may eventually become 'providers of help to others', it is necessary to review observations after some time. If the number of persons is limited (say, 20 or so at most), we would normally sketch out a network of these persons, in which each person is represented by a small rectangle with his/her name in it. A 'supportive relationship' may be represented by a single-headed arrow and, in the case where mutual assistance is exhibited, by a double-headed arrow. The thickness of the arrow can also be used to demonstrate the intensity of the supportive relationship. Other data can be added to such a diagram, for instance someone's position in the organisation, or the official role they have with respect to implementing the innovation. We have to be careful, however, not to include too many things in one picture diagram. If diagrams become too complex, they can obfuscate rather than clarify the picture.

Other sociometric properties used for constructing matrices refer to general communication levels between participants; the perceived professionalism or influence of others; factual instruction; control; perceived pressure; and offering help/support/encouragement/solutions.

6.4 Limits of tabulations on qualitative data

We advocate reporting qualitative data collected from informants in tables, but the researcher needs to be aware of its limitations.

1 The number of entries

The target is overshot if the selected representation is not lucid. Miles and Huberman (1994) sometimes present tables with five or six entries (= sets of units and/or variables). Representations such as these are inspired by the wish to represent

Table 6.1   An attempt to represent several causes in a data matrix

	Sex	Education	Formal position		Ability	Attitude	Innovative behaviour
Marion	F	High	Senior		++	+	Early adoption
Natasha	F	High	Senior		+	++	Early adoption
Sabina	F	Middle	Junior		?	+	Late adoption
Wendy	F	Middle	Junior		–	#	Early adoption
Kenneth	M	High	Senior		+	–	Middle adoption
Steve	M	Middle	Junior		–	++	Early adoption
Bill	M	Middle	Junior		+	#	Late adoption
Al	M	Low	Senior		++	++	No adoption
Muhamet	M	Middle	Junior		#	+	Late adoption
Sam	M	Low	Junior		–	–	Late adoption

simultaneously several probable causes in a cross-tabulation. However, under-standability and clarity can suffer a lot. By arranging the row-elements according to a certain variable, after which a second organising principle is applied (for instance position in the enterprise and duration of the job) two variables, in an efficient way, find a representation in a table. Table 6.1 clearly represents more than the maximum possible in terms of a clear and readable tabulation.

2 The number of rows and/or columns

If the number of rows remains low (maximally between 15 and 20), the essence of a data matrix may be grasped immediately (this is called 'eye-balling'). If the number of rows increases, especially in a table filled with words in the cells, this become more difficult. The conclusion is that as the number of informants grows, or if several data sources are used, a data matrix becomes an ineffective method of presentation. Alternatively, we can break it down into steps, for instance by reducing informants' data per group into descriptive central measures (medians, means) per subgroup, and including these, together with more qualitative information, in a table. We can do the same with columns. However, on a practical note, words require more space in a cell than numbers, which puts greater restrictions on the number of columns.

3 Missing data

As a more exploratory approach is used, and informants' responses no longer fit into neatly comparable units, working with tables becomes less effective. Directly comparable data only works when standard, uniform questions have been asked. If interviews follow a more unstructured path it is impossible to compare data. Using tables to present finding in these circumstances will result in much missing data and unreliable conclusions.

The central question to be posed within the framework of using tables in the analysis of case study data is whether they allow unambiguous conclusions. The answer is, evidently, that this depends on the character of the data, but that several problems arise. Anyone who has seen a table based on data from different sources – for instance, a table based on answers from 15 informants – knows that a table like that cries out for a *summary*.

Summarising is necessary per subgroup of informants (e.g. in educational research, teachers from junior levels versus teachers from senior levels) to compare the scores of the groups. Summarising per case is necessary if we want to compare cases in a multiple case study. Assuming we deal with three functional groups of each five to eight persons, and in each cell we have an utterance from each person in each cell. The question we have to solve is whether the three groups differ systematically from each other. Obviously, we need to reduce the information, for instance towards a simple ordinal arrangement. Inequalities (almost no two utterances are literally identical) have to be aggregated into equivalence classes. To proceed from 'unique answers from unique persons' we have to decide which answers are comparable, and which not. Is an aggregation like this allowed, or rather, does it produce useful information? Here we are confronted with a specific problem in qualitative data, a problem that is not explicitly discussed by Miles and Huberman. One could even say that these authors rather thoughtlessly neglect it – depending on the form of the matrix they merrily aggregate and disaggregate. We may distinguish three aspects: numbers, precision and variance.

With respect to the number of informants: despite a situation in which they work with very limited numbers of informants, researchers show a tendency to draw conclusions about differences between categories of informants. The numbers of interviewed persons are, however, far too small to reach reliable results. When researchers, on the basis of a table with, for instance, 11 rows (five members of the Board of Governors and six teachers) draw conclusions about differences between those two groups with respect to worries, opinions, attitudes, behaviours, involvement, etc., it is hard to attach much importance to these conclusions.

It is important to realise that we cannot expect frequencies from a case study to be counted, that is to say as long as a serious systematic collection of data in a clearly demarcated group of respondents is absent. One is tempted – and Miles and Huberman offer many examples – to report results when only a few data points are available. Statements are used such as: 'the majority is in favour of ...', or 'lower secondary school teachers are more positive with respect to the innovation than higher secondary school teachers...'. Evidently, in view of the low number of informants, as well as the fact that the selected case need not be representative for the targeted domain, conclusions like these are of little value.

There is no defence in stating that the multitude of tables presented by Miles and Huberman only serve as illustrations and could be compressed into one page (the reason why the number of rows always remains below 15 or 20). Miles and Huberman state very clearly that they regard such tables as the quintessence of data analysis. With larger numbers, these tables would soon become completely unwieldy, and consequently their value would be even less. On the other hand, because of the richness of the data (the researcher often disposes of, for instance, eight or ten indicators for the attitude towards the innovation), conclusions can be quite firm, that is when they converge. This is an example of the application of the idea of increasing the number of degrees of freedom. Evidently, this sort of analysis is strongly dependent on the researcher's scrutiny and continuous monitoring of his/her own subjectivity.

With respect to precision: much can be said in favour of working with detailed data on the individual level for as long as possible, but in order to draw some comparative and final conclusions, the subtlety of the individual answers should be left behind and aggregation should be the objective. Generally, we do not have hard criteria to justify aggregation of individual, unequal and diversified, words or sentences. The question of whether aggregating individual-level data to some central measure on the group level (or even on a case level, if cases are to be compared) is justified with quantitative as well as qualitative data, but is more difficult to answer with qualitative data. The difference is that in quantitative studies, as a consequence of pre-coding, the *respondent* is forced to select one of the answering categories, while in qualitative research it is the *researcher* who is obliged to aggregate different answers into equivalent classifications classes.

With respect to variance: tackling the question of whether diverging answers can be aggregated into an equivalent classification not only depends on numbers and precision, but also on the variance and on the comparison of variances. Aggregating informants' data within a case into a 'case score' generally is only useful when the *within-case variance* is smaller than the *between-case variance*, and the same goes for aggregating informants to functional groups or another aggregated-level variable. The usefulness depends on the relation between *within-case variance* and *between-case variance*. Only in the exceptional situation where the opinions of, for instance, the Board of Governors are homogeneous and diametrically opposed to the also homogeneous opinions of a group of teachers, can such conclusions be more or less trusted. In reality, the frequency distributions almost always overlap. Sometimes a previously agreed a priori rule is applied: if the majority (let's say 80% or whatever the agreed norm is) of a category of people is positive, then this category of people is scored as positive. Evidently, when the homogeneity *within* the group is high, as well as the differences *between* the groups, it makes sense to simplify individual opinions to become group opinions. In the analysis of quantitative data, we dispose of technical means (variance measures and analysis of variance, the core of it being that the within-group variance is compared to the between-group variances and is statistically tested) to legitimate decisions. In qualitative research this is much more difficult and is much more liable to subjective biases.

Analyses of data provided by informants are exploratory: the analysis of data leads us to hypotheses that should be tested by way of extensive, large-scale surveying. They shouldn't be used to draw definite conclusions about differences between categories of people.

To digress for a moment, sometimes it may be more relevant to calculate scores that are not based on a central tendency but on variation of opinions, attitudes or perceptions. On which matters is a functional group largely divided on time t_1, and does this situation change on the next points in time?

6.5 Conclusions

In this chapter, we discussed three (groups of) orientations towards the analysis of case study data: Yin's 'applied organisational research' approach; a heterogeneous set of 'qualitative' or 'fieldwork' approaches; and Miles and Huberman's emphasis on representational techniques. We briefly discussed two other traditions: time-series analysis and Ragin's 'political sciences' approaches (Ragin's approach having been summarily sketched in Chapter 4).

Contrary to the situation in extensive research, a small and handy set of principles to neatly arrange a diversity of methods of analysis doesn't exist in intensive research. There are many good sources for the reader to consult, however, within the different sub-paradigms. That is why we put an emphasis on similarities between intensive and extensive research, and on general principles of methodology. We emphasised problems such as the limitations of presenting data in tables, and the eternal problem of 'comparing incomparables'.

Finally, we underlined that methods based on data that are heterogeneous, multi-sourced and multifaceted, which are generally collected in case studies, allow us to generate very interesting and inspiring hypotheses. However, these hypotheses are clearly tentative. In analysing case study data the researcher should be guided by the research question, and at the same time be aware of the specific assets case studies provide. We think primarily in terms of filling in the gaps in relations between variables regarding subjective motives, attitudes, perceived hindrances and social support during a certain period. The researcher has to be aware of avoiding the pitfall of focusing on frequency distributions. Actually, frequency distributions are not emphasised in case study research. With respect to the final report – the end product of analysis – the interpretations given by the author, and some indications that (s)he has been aware of the limited scope of these conclusions, are more important than the character of the selected representation, which only has to be as transparent as possible.

EXERCISES

6.1 In the case studies selected in exercise 1.3, read carefully the chapters on data analysis. Can the methods be identified as one of the main approaches we distinguished in this book?

Analyse the timing of the research steps. Was the data collection completed before analysis started?

Were distinct sources of data used to confirm each other, or to show that different perspectives can be juxtaposed?

Did the authors attribute opinions or attitudes to stakeholder groups or other categories of people, while only some representatives of these groups were interviewed? Identify the properties of individuals, the properties of groups and of the other sets. Prepare sketches of the theories used. Were rival theories taken seriously? Are there any threats to the validity of causal reasoning? What are they?

KEY TERMS

pattern matching

explanation building

time series analysis

program logic models

grounded theory approach

cross-case synthesis

SEVEN

Assets and Opportunities

The structure of this final chapter differs from that of the other chapters. It covers some more or less separate remaining topics. The main ones are

- Styles of reporting (7.1)
- Combining intensive and extensive approaches (7.2)
- Generalizing from the user's perspective (7.3)
- Meta-analysis (7.4).

The chapter concludes with a few remarks about the efficiency of case studies, and an epilogue that underlines what attracts researchers to carry out or to participate in a case study. This chapter contains no exercises, as the texts on the covered topics only serve as introduction to the subject matters

7.1 Styles of reporting

In reporting case study results, we usually differentiate between a logical and a rhetorical style. The rhetoric style is embodied in the presentation. We try to find appealing ways to illustrate a point, to convince the reader of our argument, and to empathise with our subject. We also try to tell our story well. Case studies appeal to people because they have what might be termed 'face validity' or credibility. They provide evidence or illustrations with which some readers can easily identify. Although this quality is effective in strengthening the reader's interest, it is also a dangerous quality.

In the preceding chapter we suggested that generally an exclusively verbal, narrative research report is not sufficiently transparent. A verbal description of a case does not allow us to be precise. Neither does it offer the possibility to study simultaneously interrelated aspects. Moreover, in a verbal story it is difficult to separate case-specific aspects from case-transcending aspects. Tables and diagrams, however, force us towards a simplification of a very detailed and complex set of data, to focus on the things that really matter. The status of examples in case reports is often obscure: is it evidence, or do they only offer an illustration of something that has already been proven or shown earlier? Finally, where policy-making is at stake, people seldom have time to read long reports. Charts, diagrams, illustrations and overviews are much easier to digest.

Stake (1978: 5), on the contrary, states that the kind of knowledge documented in case reports is more useful and more appealing to the reader because it is 'epistemologically in harmony with the reader's experience and thus to that person a natural basis for generalisation'. He apparently refers to the fact that a case study as research strategy, and a case report that is formulated in terms of concrete phenomena, that avoids methodical-technical or theoretical terms and arguments, fits the concepts and life world of the reader better.[1] Stake's quotation is typical for a kind of holistic thinking in which the general and the specific are not distinguished, in which *Verstehen* experiences a renaissance at the cost of explanation, and in which finally science progresses by 'naturalistic generalisation, arrived at by recognising the similarities of objects and issues in and out of context and by sensing the natural covariations of happenings' (Stake 1980: 69).

Although points of view of this kind are easily ridiculed, it cannot be denied that a well-written case report forms easy reading and, in general, many prefer it to the report of a quantitative research project. Galle (1986: 11) is right in pointing out that policy-makers love case reports:

> They consider such descriptions as an extension of their lay knowledge. In particular when it concerns policymaking and implementation by politicians and high employees. It is all based on profiting from successes and failures of others, and as such it is similar to their way of gathering information in corridors and meetings. A study about the realisation of a handful of different governmental policy measures, or a research report about governmental crisis management, takes its charm from this. Sometimes the description of a case did appeal so strongly to an employee that it fulfils the role of a beloved anecdote to be told over and over again if the opportunity arises.

On the other hand, such use evidently is not envisaged by the researcher in the first place. Moreover, it occurs very selectively, and only if it fits into the frame of reference of the employee. Finally, there is a general complaint about the 'real' use of case studies. In this respect, a multitude of explanations is offered:

- case studies have an aura of subjectivity, unreliability, impressionism
- the status of the instruments is low, 'one need not be a specialist', the high-status statistical apparatus is lacking
- generalisability is estimated to be low as well
- conclusions based on a case study seem to be self-evident and, as such, are more directly based on lay knowledge or prejudices than on empirical data
- through the concreteness of its formulations, it is evident more quickly than with survey results, in which direction policy suggestions point. As a consequence of this, the use or non-use of the results strongly depends on whether they fall in fertile soil. If yes, then policy-makers will cite the report frequently, but selectively; if no, then the report will generally be ignored.

---

[1]See also Sandelowski, M. (2008). The challenges of writing and reading mixed methods studies, in Plano Clark and Creswell (Eds.) and Ellet (2006).

Whatever happens, the conclusion that verbal stories should be avoided and cross-classifications and network diagrams propagated is far too simplistic. Moreover, other forms of reporting exist and are often used in reality. One needs only to remember television films such as *Seven Up*, which revealed the relationship between social inequality and the development of school and professional careers by interviewing, observing in their daily surroundings and tracing the lives of a small group of children every seven years.

Evidently, each form of reporting can be applied in a good or a bad way. Texts that are full of statistics, tables and formulas are far too complicated and, to say the least, not very clear. Using a personal story to portray a case can, on the contrary, be very illuminative. An adequate realisation of the rhetorical function can, in this way, be part of the logical function. It would not do justice to the rhetorical function to view the logical function as the only right one.

Specific rules for reporting case studies are virtually non-existent. Of course it is important to offer the reader as clear and as complete a picture as possible, demonstrating the researcher's procedures, including data selection, analysis and interpretations. It is not enough to present only illustrations or illustrative quotes. The reader should be able to establish how or why such illustrations were selected and to ascertain the evidential basis for the case study researcher's conclusions.

Obviously, one should always have the audience in mind. In a report that will only be read by colleague-researchers, the emphasis should be on giving a full account of earlier case studies in this field that fit in the relevant scientific tradition, as well as on the theories and methods used and the researcher's reasoning for selecting this approach and not another. In a report that is to be read by policy-makers and other actors in the field, the emphasis should be on the details of the case and the results. However, this doesn't mean that the other aspects should be omitted in either case.

Having different audiences in mind, the next question is of course whether different reports should be composed for different audiences. Writing several reports is not an efficient use of resources, so it may be better to compose one report but with clearly recognisable parts, containing all the necessary information for each audience. It is less important what form such a report will take. Whether you start with a summary description of your work and a concise description of the results, possibly combined with some policy advice, and continue with a full description of all methodological details, or whether you start with traditional chapters on research questions, theories, design, techniques of data collection and analysis and finish with a summary, is largely a matter of personal preference. The main point is to clearly address each audience and indicate to them where they can find the information they need.

Reporting a multiple case study, however, confronts us with more problems. Here also, the choice between whether an extensive report about each case should be included (in the main text or as appendices) followed by an integrative and interpretative chapter, or whether the emphasis should be on an integrative text where the separate cases only serve as illustrations, is up to the researcher. This second solution often leaves the reader with a feeling of insufficient insight into the character of each case, while the first solution will rapidly annoy many readers who are not interested in the specifics of each case. For the rest, the report of a multiple case study might profit from a specific 'question-and-answer format' in which each case is described by way of a series of identical questions. The essence is that the researcher compares and combines the information of the distinct cases and, in a multi-method approach, relates the case study results to the results of other parts of the research endeavour. Don't imagine that a description of a case 'speaks for itself'!

The idea of anonymity can create another problem for case study researchers. In an ideal world, transparency is best achieved if the subject of the case study can be named in the report. But frequently, to protect the organisation and individual informants, and preserve their confidentially, the details of the case need to be anonymised. This is a matter of research ethics. The same is valid for the duty of the researcher not to speak to informants about what other informants have told them if there is any chance that the informants might detect the source. Of course complete anonymity is impossible to achieve – the researchers themselves, the management team of the organisation being researched and the individual informants naturally know the real identities.

7.2 Combining intensive and extensive approaches

In asking ourselves questions about combining case studies with other research designs, we almost automatically arrive at literature about 'mixed method research'. Specifically, these sources relate to the mixing of quantitative and qualitative methods. Quantitative methods are experiments, surveys, quantitative content analysis, observation checklists, charts, audits – in short, all methods that use numerals. Qualitative methods relate to studies based on field observation, open interviewing, qualitative documentary analysis, focus groups and others. These methods use words where the quantitative methods use numbers. In several fields, such as nursing, public health, policy evaluation and education, mixing of methods has become fashionable when designing a research project. The position of case studies is open to question, but in scientific discourses case studies are almost always positioned on the qualitative side.

However, differences between intensive and extensive research do not completely coincide with the qualitative/quantitative distinction, which is, in principle at least, based on the difference between kinds of data (numerals or words). Most case studies contain some quantitative elements. This already more or less mixed character of one strategy in itself is not an exclusive property of case studies. Many standardised surveys, for instance, contain some open questions that cannot be analysed quantitatively. More generally, it should be noted that, in contrasting the two research approaches, controversies are likely to be exaggerated. And conceptual differences between research *designs and approaches* on the one hand, and *kinds of data* or *methods of analysis* on the other hand are likely to be obscured by a simplistic polarisation.

However, it is interesting to browse some of the important literature sources[2] on mixed methods. The general idea with respect to the mixing of methods is that a survey component is used to study the phenomenon 'in its width' (i.e. to estimate univariate and multivariate frequency distributions), while case studies are used to approach the phenomenon 'in its depth, by studying language, perspectives, interpretations and the behaviour of the people interacting among themselves. One could say that the first approach is primarily guided by the criterion of external validity (degree of generalisability), and the second by internal validity (can the causal explanations be trusted?). Until recently, most of the literature has been strongly focused on *types of combination*. The usual criteria that are applied are time order and importance:

- Are the quantitative and qualitative components of the research project applied at the same time (simultaneously) or one after the other (sequentially)? If one after the other, then which one is first?
- Are the components more or less of the same significance, or is one component more dominant?

Combining these criteria leads to a typology of mixed methods designs. In practice, the most frequently used designs are the following:

- *The 'qual' part precedes the 'quant' part* in order to explore the field and to study the language used by potential respondents, and in this way to construct a strong and valid foundation for consecutive standardised questioning. This order indeed reflects the classic idea that a qualitative approach functions as an exploratory pilot study for consecutive testing in a quantitative phase. Most qualitative researchers strongly oppose forcing the qualitative component into a subservient help-role. However, if we have little knowledge beforehand, starting with a qualitative stage (i.e. an exploratory and intensive phase) is advisable in order to delineate relevant variables.
- *The 'quant' part precedes the 'qual' part.* Alternatively, we start with a survey to establish frequencies and calculate statistical relations. This has the advantage of providing an overview of the width of the phenomenon and of its variance. The 'qual' part is used to improve the interpretation of the data and to provide a helping hand in explaining the phenomenon under study. A model resulting from quantitative research can profit from

---

[2]Bergman (2008); Creswell and Plano Clark (2007); Plano Clark and Creswell, (2008); Tashakkori and Teddlie (1998). Since the late 1990s, the idea of 'mixed methods' is presented by some authors as a synthesis of the 'quantitative strand' and the 'qualitative strand' and as the natural end to the 'paradigm wars' in social and behavioural research. Bergman (2003) entails some more sober contributions. Most publications focus on descriptive characterisations of mixed methods approaches, and on arguing about the 'necessary' merging of methods in all phases of a research project. Up until now, little attention has been paid to concrete examples of the qualitative components of a quantitative research project, or vice versa, or the distinct contributions of the diverse components to the research results in their totality.

additional information about causal processes, filling in gaps in our knowledge. The perceptions and ideas of stakeholders are introduced and studied, for instance with respect to problems people encounter and how they overcome them. Sometimes deviant cases are used to extend the theory. This specific order is often argued on the basis of Lazarsfeld's old idea of 'deviant case analysis'.

- *In a dominantly 'quant' approach, especially in evaluation research, a 'qual' sub-project is embedded* in order to monitor the process of implementation of a policy measure. Case studies are often used nowadays in the context of evaluation research such as this, especially in process or formative evaluation. A first argument for this use is that some causal links are too complicated to discover, describe and explain using a survey or an experiment. A second argument is that it may be fruitful to describe the 'real-life context' of the implementation of an intervention; mainly, the ways in which the actual intervention differs from the planned blueprint. Third, a case study may serve to explore why in certain cases, and when and how, a failure occurs. The alternative, less frequent, design, concerns a quantitative sub-project, for instance a local survey, 'nested in' an otherwise qualitative study.
- *'Quant' and 'qual' parts, with about the same importance,* are carried out simultaneously, and contribute equally to the results. 'Simultaneously' should not be taken in a very strict sense. The parts are probably carried out more or less at the same time, but the central property of this mixed method is the independent character of each of the parts. A consequence is, of course, that results of one approach cannot be used for improving the design or fine-tuning of the other, with the danger that results are solely presented alongside each other instead of being integrated.
- *Designs need not be restricted to one 'quant' and one 'qual' part.* Sometimes an exploratory approach is followed by a survey, which leads to another qualitative phase of interviewing. Taking this idea a bit further, we might start with some cases that are studied in an extensive way in order not to spend too much time on them. We get a first impression of the width and variance of the phenomenon, and some ideas about the relevance of certain factors for the phenomenon to be researched. They may also provide a basis for constructing a questionnaire. Possibly, more than one data collection method is used: documentary sources, interviews and focus groups come into the picture. With the larger national survey agencies, focus groups are used to test the questions by interviewing people after they filled out preliminary 'test' versions of the questionnaire. Then a survey is carried out. Finally, several well-chosen case studies are undertaken to deepen our understanding of the issue and solve some problems that remain after the first phases.

Nowadays we often see, at least in policy research, a combination of cases and survey (in both orders), followed by a workshop or a conference of panel members representing the different groups of stakeholders. This last element serves different purposes, such as widening public support for the research project, but it mainly serves to check whether, when confronted with the personal experiences and views of representatives from the field, aspects of reality or interpretations of the state of the matter are not partly or completely overlooked in the research as carried out. Such meetings can play a role in replacing a second series of case studies.

Padgett's (2004) study recounts how a team of researchers returned to their original database for more insights after contradictory findings emerged. This occurred during the Harlem Mammogram Study, which was funded by the National Cancer Institute to examine factors that influenced delayed responses to abnormal mammograms among African-American women living in New York City. The research team had collected both structured quantitative data and open-ended interview data. After data analyses, the team concluded that the women's decisions to delay were not driven by factors in their quantitative model. The researchers then turned to their qualitative data, highlighted two qualitative themes, and re-examined their quantitative database for support for the themes. To their surprise, the quantitative data confirmed what the participants had said. This new information, in turn, led to a further exploration of the literature, in which they found some confirmation for the new findings. Used in this way, the researchers could also view the contradiction as a springboard for new directions of inquiry.

An example from our research practice may serve to illustrate this combination of approaches. In Dutch educational research an abundance of extensive, descriptive research has been done on school careers of rude descriptive categories of pupils, mostly on the basis of cohorts that are monitored in time. For instance, percentages of school leavers, with or without qualifications differentiated according to gender, ethnicity etc., are well known. The question arises whether, by following a restricted number of pupils during their school career, more insight can be gained into determining factors such as support or lack of support from the parental home; the role of peers, the development of motivation, and whether pupils have insight into their own capabilities and future prospects, etc.

A possible design for intensive research might be as follows. A cross-classification of sex and ethnicity prompts us to include four groups: Moroccan boys and girls, and Dutch boys and girls. Within each of these four categories, eight pupils are selected from the 11 year-olds, as well as eight pupils from the 13 year-olds on the basis of a large cohort study. Pupils are matched, as far as possible, with respect to the socio-economic status of their parents, age and (start level) intelligence. Each of the 64 pupils ($4 \times 8 \times 2 = 64$) is intensively interviewed at two points in time. Furthermore, test data with respect to school topics is available, teachers are interviewed and a larger group of pupils is asked to write an essay on a well-chosen, related topic. What can and cannot be achieved with a (not completely fictitious) design such as this? Although the design seems to be inspired by principles of analysis of variance, a traditional causal analysis with sex and ethnicity as predictors of a number of dependent variables (e.g. motivation at moment t; self-deciding versus parentally guided) is hardly promising. Matching will not be simple, and will leave ample space for remaining influencing variables; the numbers in each cell are so small that only strong effects will be significant; measurement error may play a destructive role. Furthermore, an analysis of variance would maximally lead to the discovery of differences, and owing to the fact that we already know that Moroccan pupils differ strongly from the Dutch in their school careers, knowledge of this kind is hardly interesting.

The value of this type of research is determined by the expected success of efforts to: (a) detect a multitude of variables related to social contact, motivation, experienced rewards and punishments and image building, as a result of intensive interviewing; (b) detect changes in these variables during the school career on an individual level; and (c) formulate hypotheses about crucial moments and events in the determination of a school career. The subjective ideas of the respondents themselves are relevant. It is an example of exploratory research, where the use of (matched) groups on (exogenous) variables only serves to enable us to formulate tentative hypotheses, not to test them. Evidently, it is difficult to view an individual Moroccan girl as representative of her group if we only include a research group of eight girls, while we know that these eight in many respects differ from each other. Finally, it has to be remarked that this energy-consuming research design is still not extremely intensive: there are only two interviews and some limited data from other sources. Participatory observation is hard to realise. Supplementing the data with additional information from sociometric studies could be useful: is it possible to detect small groups of interacting pupils that are relatively homogeneous with respect to motivation or behaviour?

Of course, mixed methods research is based on the assumption that it generates additional knowledge. Many superlatives are used in addressing the topic of mixed methods:

> Mixed methods are utilized in order to gain complementary views about the same phenomenon ... they are utilized in order to make sure a complete picture of the phenomenon is obtained ... they are used in order to explain the understanding obtained in a previous strand of study ... to assess the credibility of inferences ... to compensate for the weaknesses of one approach by utilizing the other. (Tashakkori & Teddlie, in Bergman, 2008: 103)

The fact that additional and sometimes correcting knowledge can be obtained requires little arguing. If comparable results are obtained with several methods, there is seldom a debate about interpretations. The results are generally regarded as evidence for the reliability and validity of our methods. But there is ambiguity with respect to the handling of contrasting results. 'Sometimes contrasting results are expected: ...mixed methods are used with the hope of obtaining divergent pictures of the same phenomenon. These divergent findings would ideally be compared and contrasted' (Tashakkori & Teddlie, in Bergman, 2008: 103). The ubiquitous concept of triangulation is often used in this context. But do contrasting results mean that we have a problem of validity or reliability in one kind of data or the other, or in both? Or are they to be welcomed as understandably different constructions of reality by different individuals or groups of stakeholders? We mentioned this problem already in section 5.7; and it is elaborated further in Appendix 3.

It has nowadays more or less become a fad to apply mixed methods research. But bearing in mind that *research questions* are decisive with respect to selecting a research design, it is not at all evident that mixed methods should always be applied. Therefore, the 'why' question about mixed methods deserves more consideration than it often receives in many texts on methodology. If mixed methods are applied, their relationship should be carefully considered. This demands, in the first place, that research questions fitting into each of the approaches are explicitly elaborated. Second, that the results of a survey report are counter posed with the results of the case studies, and vice versa. Third, that we actively look for contradictions and seek to interpret differences, etc. The most common failure is reporting independently, without considering whether the results confirm or contradict the research question. Contradictions should be discussed and possible solutions offered. Relating intensive and extensive approaches is not the same as 'integrating results' into something like a 'mean score'. After all, research questions were different as from the beginning. It can also mean offering an acceptable and theoretically based interpretation of differences, or evidence that a first interpretation was wrong.

Special attention in a mixed project should be given to the researchers' qualifications. The most frequently occurring situation is one in which researchers with special qualifications, in quantitative *or* qualitative research techniques, work more or less independently from each other, while in the end results are reported. This creates the danger of postponing differences between scientific ideas to the end of the project, and a Solomon's decision (of an outsider?) with respect to discongruencies of research results. Often, researchers who are one-sidedly of one tradition are very hesitant in participating in debates with colleagues 'on the other side of the fence'. A better solution is that researchers are trained to carry out both surveys and case studies rather independently, without being related to each other. Or at the least, that researchers have a basic training and expertise in both quantitative and qualitative methods and insight about their additional value. In this way, they may be far better equipped to combine insights from different approaches.

BOX 7.2

An example of a fertile colloboration of an intensive and an extensive approach is Kops (1993) *Flexible Starters*, a research project about the transition of young-sters to adulthood in an uncertain work situation. On the basis of 'qualitative interviews' with 21 youngsters, she constructed a questionnaire that was to be presented to 812 youngsters. In *both* approaches, the theoretical starting point was a variant of the theory of cognitive dissonance: the theory of mental

---

incongruity. The survey set out to establish whether the findings from the qualitative component could be generalised to a larger group, and to study whether the discovered patterns could be related to socio-structural variables. In the final report, each of the initial 21 case reports is represented in some 400–1,000 words, in which the most important events are interpreted and explained in terms of the theory used. After a chapter containing a typology of 'development trajectories' on the basis of the qualitative interviews, the results of the survey are reported.

The qualitative component of this project is, between parentheses, on the margin of our definition of case studies. If some additional tens of interviews were done, we still would be inclined to call it qualitative research, but we would probably be less inclined to think in terms of case studies. Moreover, this study was not aimed at specific individual persons. The phenomenon the researcher was interested in was 'the first encounter with the labour market' for a specific social and educational group. The number of interviewees chosen indicates already that a typology was aimed for, each type to be represented by several individuals. But above all, the individual interviews were used to examine the perceptions, images of the future, norms, expectations, and personal life events with respect to the transition to adulthood in order to reach a satisfying explanation of what finally happened. Furthermore, the same respondents were interviewed twice because they were also included in the survey. In this way, developments on the individual level could also be detected. In typifying the initial interviews as a 'qualitative pilot study as a try-out for the main study' one would do injustice to the case study part: research results are mainly found in these case studies.

BOX 7.3

Many other examples can be found of a successful application of mixed methods. In a study about 'choices in child care', the research project could begin by interviewing some 10–20 parents about their preferences and the process of decision-making in order to find some clues about the important variables. After that, a random sample of parents with young children could be asked about their preferences for, and actual use of, one of three types of non-parental child care, for instance care by professionals, care by paid babysitters and care by members of their own social network. Another example is research on 'teenager sex'. The use of questionnaires and a random sample could be combined with interviews with some 20 teenagers and some observational studies. Research

(Continued)

(Continued)

projects among unemployed people are also likely to contain qualitative and a quantitative parts. In a context where it is impossible to draw random samples, the qualitative part often has the upper hand, as in research on the development on drugs use, or research on the survival strategies and techniques of illegal immigrants. Especially on the level of organisations, a mix of methods tends to shift to the 'case study' side. The study of palliative care in nursing homes is only fruitful if it takes place as a case study in one or two nursing homes. An extensive study among a large sample of nursing homes would only add rather superficial knowledge.

7.3 Generalising from the user's perspective

Traditionally, two well-known forms of generalisation are distinguished: the 'sample-to-population generalisation' and the 'theoretical (or analytical or logical) generalisation'. In the early 1990s, the American educational scientist Firestone advocated a third kind of generalisation: case-to-case transfer. Firestone defines this as 'whenever a person in one setting considers adopting a program or idea from another one' (Firestone 1993: 17; see also Kennedy 1979). This approach originates from the user's perspective. For a user of case study results, the central question is not 'towards which population am I allowed to generalise?', or 'towards which theory can I generalise?', but rather *'am I allowed to generalise these results to my situation?'* Firestone's type of generalisation is related to one of the quality criteria proposed by Lincoln and Guba (1985): transferability. For these authors, the concept of transferability replaces the criterion of external validity or generalisability as used in mainstream research. Transferability is very close to usability (Swanborn, 1996a). This seems to be a rather vague criterion, but it indicates the essential quality of applied research – that results should be usable for the client.

Firestone grounds his approach on Kennedy's elaboration of examples from the medical and legal professions (Kennedy 1979). Kennedy argues from the perspective of the user: if someone is in search for an article of law, a policy measure or a remedy for a specific 'illness', and if there is ample documentation covering different situations leading to different measures, how is this person going to select the best strategy? One starts, of course, by looking for 'the most similar' situation.

The arguments of the potential user concern the degree of similarity between the researched cases and his/her own case. The potential user, apparently, has ideas in mind about the relevance of criteria X, and the irrelevance of criteria Y. (S)he works with a primitive theory or model. The only difference with theoretical generalisation is that the theory mostly stays implicit. A necessary condition for case-to-case arguing is that the descriptive characteristics of the case are clearly indicated. Firestone cites Stake (1978: 7): 'the demands for typicality and representativeness yield to needs for assurance that the target case is properly described. As readers recognise essential similarities to cases of interest to them, they establish the basis for naturalistic generalisation'. 'Thick description', however, is not sufficient to enable the user to compare cases. Evidently, many details are irrelevant, and potential users as well as other researchers need more information than just descriptives. Consequently, we do not agree with Firestone where he, following Kennedy, assumes that 'the researcher's theories about the conditions that affect the applicability of study conclusions are less important than those of the reader' (Firestone 1993: 18). On the contrary, it is very important that the researcher formulates his/her theory explicitly (why certain variables are considered relevant and others are left out of the model; why variable X affects variable Y, or why Z conditions the influence of X on Y), including the conditions that determine the domain of the theory. A researcher possibly uses partly false assumptions, but delineating the rude theoretical structure as well as the empirical reference of the research results, is part of the responsibility of the researcher, so that colleagues can start with one or more hypothesis. If the theory is not explicitly formulated, successors are saddled with unnecessary work, and science with an accumulation of dispersed, incoherent results. This point of view is all the more evident if the original researcher used a general theory accompanied by bridge assumptions to accommodate the theory to the specific situation. Making a distinction between the general theory and field-specific theories enables succeeding researchers to be more efficient in their approach. Are there any possibilities to enlarge the plausibility of the theory used by the researcher, apart from applying it to new situations? The plausibility can be enlarged by exposing the consequences of the claimed generalisability of the theory to attempts to refute them by the 'forum of scientists'. Workshops and post-research conferences where opponents from opposing sides debate with each other may very well lead to hypotheses about the domain to become more firmly built on research results. Whether, for instance, the perspectives of teachers or those of students are described, or whether classroom interactions are explained, it is always useful to test the results by challenging them with the criticism of colleague-researchers or methodologists.

It is important, however, to realise that the user may have a different theory (or perceives other variables as important) from the forum of scientists. It is for that reason that Firestone considers the researcher's theory as of less importance than 'the user's theory'. This peculiar directional change towards the user's perspective fits perfectly into the Cronbach tradition, which contrasts so strongly in American policy research traditions with Campbell's ideas. For Cronbach et al. (1980), generalisability or external validity is a much more highly valued criterion than internal or causal interpretation validity, the all-deciding criterion emphasised by Campbell (Cook & Campbell 1979).

We must not ascribe characteristics to qualitative research that it isn't entitled to. A strict procedure to generalise on the basis of a handful of cases does not exist.

Case-to-case transfer (in so far as it may be regarded as a research procedure) cannot be opposed to theoretical generalisation. Both are only possible after procedures and products, as well as the theories used, are made explicit. And the argument that decision-makers in politics, and parents and teachers in the case of school research, prefer something like case-to-case transfer is rather primitive. As is well known, a specific person cannot predict with absolute success the future behaviour of his/her partner or the suitability of a school for his/her children on the basis of the aggregated scores from a number of studies. But it is not a bad thing to advise people on the basis of such aggregate scores. A school director who wants to read research results about the relationship between class size and output level gains more from an aggregate, even international study, based on research in many schools, than from a research report on the same topic in a school that in some respects is like his/hers. On other characteristics the specific researched school may be very different from his or her own, apart from the fact that one may have to search a long time before finding a school that seems to show enough similarity on the surface.

7.4 Meta-analysis

Decades ago, Lucas (1974) (see also Yin & Heald 1975; Larsson 1993) was already in search for a method to combine and aggregate results of a large number of existing case studies about a certain phenomenon. Evidently, the need for aggregation appears when the number of available studies is growing so fast that potential users refrain from trying to read them. This situation is becoming more and more pertinent, especially in the field of evaluation (of traffic regulations, drug addiction policies, mental health therapies, juvenile help services, information campaigns, etc.). At the start of the 1970s hundreds of case studies about the effects of decentralisation already existed, all of them reporting about the effects on information streams, the attitudes of employees and clients, the quality of the services, and suchlike phenomena. Lucas developed what he called the *case-survey*. His approach boils down to scoring each case study report on a completely standardised questionnaire, including background variables of researcher and case(s), design of the project, and results. In addition, the 'surveyor' indicates with each question his/her certainty about the given score. Consequently, it is possible to study the reliability of the score in a subtle way (two coders, and data split on 'both certain', 'one of the two certain' and 'both uncertain'), and to get rid of those cases that deliver too many uncertain results.

Larsson (1993), two decades later, made an inventory of eight cases in the field of organisational research. The N's in these studies covered an interval of 25 up to 215; the number of variables from two to 197! The author distinguishes a list of 12 steps that are to be taken in a case survey. Subsequently, these refer to (1) the development of the research question as a basis for (2) the establishment of criteria for the selection of cases, and (3) the actual selection, (4) designing the coding scheme, (5) coding by several persons (Larsson suggests the use of three coders) as well as, where possible, (6) the participation of the original authors because 'missing data' may be minimised in this way and validity maximised, (7) the establishment of intercoder reliability, (8) solution of differences between coders, (9) the establishment of the validity of the coding results, (10) the establishment of the influence of certain specific method effects on the final conclusions, (11) analysis of the complete dataset, and (12) reporting the case survey results.

Point 10, in particular, seems to be important: to what degree can it be shown that the number or the types of informant, the presence or the length of participatory observation, the application of member's checks or many other peculiarities of the method did affect the substantive results of a case study? Research into this aspect – even when there are enough case studies to be found – is not overly simple. In one of Larsson's case surveys about mergers and take-overs in industry, some methodical characteristics – such as the extensiveness of the dataset per case – proved to correlate with the merger's success. The evident interpretation is that merging companies that are successful gets more publicity, and consequently produces more data, than companies remaining rather independent after a merger, and where nothing much can be said about the merger. The causality direction is probably the reverse of the one that was conceived by the author at the start of his study.

It will be evident that an approach like this one primarily aims at detecting gross total effects over a number of comparable studies, rather than being interested in details, or in comparative studies of differences in social processes. The case surveys Larsson wrote about included, among others, urban renewal processes, profit participatory schemes, and the effects of mergers and take-overs. Evaluation studies are easier to aggregate than case-specific descriptions. It should not surprise us that the need for aggregation finds its origins in the context of evaluation research.

Nowadays the term 'meta-analysis'[3] has come into use. Meta-analyses demand an identical object and a high degree of explicitness of the methods used and results obtained. Techniques were developed to aggregate results of studies statistically, in which the contributions of the separate, primary cases are weighted. This results in an effect size measure (ES). This is indeed an astonishing development in science. For decades, the randomised control treatment (RCT) was, and still is, the gold standard in evaluation research. Many applied sciences struggled to come as close to this standard as possible, but were forced to keep to single case studies, as randomisation was excluded and even comparative cases were difficult to find. The birth of meta-analysis was a breakthrough as it facilitated the combination of results of many single-case studies. Meta-analysis finds its origin in the world of the health sciences. The need for meta-analyses in itself stimulates the necessity of

---

[3] A simple first introduction is Wolf (1986). See also Cook, Cooper and Cordray (1994) and Cooper and Hedges (1994). The best practical guide is Lipsey and Wilson (2001).

extensively and carefully documenting circumstances, diagnoses and treatments of each patient or client, the 'cases' in order to attain guidelines for an 'evidence-based practice' (EBP) and 'evidence-supported treatments' Evidence-based practice is one of the most frequently used expressions nowadays to qualify the character of these applied sciences, and is even used to typify the basis of educational curricula in, for example, nursing sciences. And EBP is almost per definition grounded on meta-analyses. Useful examples of this approach can be found in the free accessible e-journal, *Pragmatic Case Studies in Psychotherapy*. Clement (2007), for instance, presents an extended story of the treatment of OCD (obsessive compulsive disorder). He carefully documented the treatment of a 30 year-old woman in 103 psychotherapeutic sessions during two and a half years. His article is followed by two comments of Kazdin (1982) and Barlow. The latter are well known for their place at the very beginning of the development of evidence-based practice. In this context one may want to consult also the contribution of the APA Presidential Task Force (2006).

7.5 The efficiency of case studies

One aspect that deserves more attention concerns the efficiency of case studies. In most countries little attention is paid to the relative costs of surveys and case studies in relation to their benefits. Scrupulous reflection would force us to estimate in advance the respective contributions of intensive and extensive approaches to the final report, and would probably lead us to work more efficiently within a case study. It is our opinion that in this way more time would become available for prior theoretical reflection as well as for consultation of peers, and less time for orientation and exploration during the fieldwork itself. Biemans (1991: 159) identifies what is, in his opinion, the largest disadvantage of case studies: their time-consuming character:

> Each separate interview should be prepared in advance, an appointment should be made, the interview has to be conducted, the notes taken have to be transferred in a concise report that contains the essence of it; the report should be sent to the interviewee and be discussed with him or her, and finally the end version should be composed and approved by the interviewee. To give an idea, the total time for a two-hour interview is estimated at eight hours. Added to this, regular telephone calls are made for clarification and to obtain additional information. And we didn't mention the time needed for data analysis...

Another aspect that needs attention are the organisational skills that are required when dealing the large piles of data that end up on the researcher's desk, especially with multiple case studies, and particularly when several cases are studied simultaneously. It is no simple task to organise, categorise, file and administer so much material within the process of data collection.

The use of computers for the analysis of case study data is another aspect that requires careful consideration. With a restricted number of interviews, say ten or even 20, it is not at all evident that the raw material has to be cut into pieces, and each piece coded, submitted to axial coding after the open coding, etc. This process takes a lot of time and an experienced researcher might obtain comparable results by glancing at and browsing the interview protocols. Novice researchers, however, should ask advice from their senior colleagues. And remember, every researcher has his/her specific preferences…

7.6 Epilogue

In the preceding chapters reference is made sometimes to extreme points of view – ideas that may boil down to the complete incomparability of case studies and surveys, or even that case studies are the only avenue to valid knowledge of the social world around us. In some European countries the tendency towards polarising intensive and extensive research is not as decisive as it used to be, for instance, in the United States. Moreover, the integration of social and behavioural research in society is now widely accepted in public opinion as well as in policy-making. In much applied research, intensive and extensive approaches form part of one and the same research project. Yet, we rarely find an adequate design in which the parts complement each other in an ideal way. Research proposals remain obfuscated with respect to the possible contributions of each of the parts; in the one part sometimes completely different rules seem to govern the game, and in the final report the results are often not sufficiently confronted with each other. This is probably caused by the fact that most researchers are knowledgeable in quantitative methods and not in qualitative methods, or vice versa.

This book is inspired by the idea that modern social research is in many respects very valuable, but that the emphasis has gradually shifted in the direction of quantitative research and, to be still more exact, to the statistical analysis of survey data. Paying greater attention to the strategy of the case study provides an opportunity to correct this one-sidedness. The case study is not the exclusive domain of the enthusiastic, but methodologically naïve, amateur in participatory observation who works in some marginal corner of society. The case study also belongs to the domain of the multi-versed, methodologically highly skilled researcher, who feels the necessity to add to the value of descriptions based on extensive datasets by systematically paying attention to the often contradictory ideas, thoughts, perceptions, interactions and meanings of the people and groups it is all about.

Here lies the unique contribution of case studies to the solution of many research questions of a descriptive, explanatory or predictive character in social science. Gathering detailed information of many kinds offers an opportunity to come to grips with social processes in a far more subtle way than when one is exclusively restricted to survey data. For the rest, that multi-versed, methodologically skilled researcher should also be, of course, enthusiastic. But that is easier to achieve because case studies are fun! And it is with this statement that we end: it is a final reason why case studies should receive more attention![4]

A case description is vivid. For instance, in doing educational research, the reader feels him/herself back in the classroom. Citations and observation reports reinforce this impression. 'There is no substitute for being on the scene.' A study into organisational ineffectiveness via participatory observation produces a much more readable report than a quantitative analysis of production data.

A case description is picturesque. The researcher portrays a hospital. Healthcare phenomena, for example, have a greater richness and complexity than can be illustrated with regression-analyses!

A case description can be breathtaking. The researcher can become embroiled in role conflicts and then attempt to get out of them. A researcher working with the uniformed police, for example, may expect to be asked to do some little odd jobs, such as entering a pub a uniformed officer wants to avoid to see whether a certain person is present.

A case description is complex. Researchers develop relationships with many people and groups involved in the research project. Some of them would normally never belong in his/her social world. (S)he engages in situations and events that will never be experienced again.

A case description is, finally, illuminating. Researchers may observe, describe and interpret things that an 'extensive researcher' wouldn't perceive at all and that are missed by a layperson. A case researcher forces him/herself to continuously look for alternative and tentative interpretations – to understand 'what it is all about!'

KEY TERMS

Logical function of reporting
Rhetorical function of reporting
Mixed methods research
Several ways to combine qualitative and quantitative research
Sample-to population generalisation

Theoretical generalisation
Case-to-case generalisation
Meta-analysis
Effect size measures

---

[4]These remarks are mainly taken from Reijnders (1984).

Appendix 1

Selected Literature on Case Studies

An overview of book literature on case study methodology includes the following sources. Publications which we consider of special interest to the reader who wants to deepen an understanding are indicated with one or more asterisk(*). The reader will find complete references in the bibliography, but as a quick guide we provide most titles with a brief synopsis.

Abramson (1992).   A peculiar mix of a Yiddish diary of a Jewish-Russian immigrant to the USA (the author's grandfather) and a critical interpretation of it by his grandson, a psychology professor at UCLA. From a Popperian perspective, many questions are raised in connection with quotations from the diary, and alternative interpretations are offered.

Adelman, Jenkins & Kemmis (1984).   A brief definition and an analysis of the advantages of the case study, combined with practical tips about how to do a case study. The article is also included in Simons (1980).

*Bergman (2008).   An interesting collection of contributions on mixed method research, covering about the whole spectrum of opinions.

Biemans (1989).   The author starts with five and later adds 17 case studies to describe designing, adapting and marketing medical-technical apparatus. The attention is focused on networks of firms, research laboratories and users. Data is mainly collected via a restricted number of interviews per case. Biemans presents some practical tips for designing case studies such as this in organisations, gaining access to the field, etc.

Diesing (1972).   One of the first extensive treatises based on an holistic point of view in social science, and a discussion of the case study within this framework.

Feagin, Orum & Sjoberg (eds) (1991).   This reader is of a typical sociological character and contains a number of essays on the background and procedures followed in several famous case studies (among others 'Middletown III'). It also contains a plea for holistic, engaged, qualitative research as an alternative to the scientific method in sociology.

Fishman (1999). An important text for everyone interested in developments in the field of case studies in clinical psychology.

*George & Bennett (2005). One of the best publications on (comparative) case study research in the tradition of the political sciences.

*Gerring (2006). A lucid and almost complete handbook on case study research in the political sciences tradition, more or less in the footsteps of George & Bennett (2005).

* Glaser & Strauss (1967). This is the most well-known text on grounded theory research, a strand of qualitative research in the symbolic-interactionist tradition. It is one of the first methodology books that focuses on the relation between meaning and social interaction. As such, it is one of the inspiring sources for our approach of the role of case studies in social research.

*Gomm, Hammersley & Foster (eds) (2000). This book contains ten earlier publications, some of them (very) old, others more recent, by authors such as Eckstein, Robinson, Mitchell, Stake, and Lincoln and Guba. Additionally, two 'commenting' and summarising contributions by the editors of this debate-stimulating book focus on generalisation and the use of theory in case studies.

Goode & Hatt (1952). This title is mentioned here for the sole reason that it is one of the oldest and most well-known defences of qualitative case studies. After more than half a century of social scientific research, it is, of course, largely outdated now.

Gummesson (1991). Argues the case for participatory 'action research' in organisations and for combining the researcher's and the consultant's role. Gummesson is a protagonist of engaged, qualitative research. The chapter on 'Case Study Research', contains few new methodological insights for readers who are acquainted with this type of research, but it offers much information of an anecdotal nature. Many insights have value, but they are consistently presented from a one-dimensional point of view.

Hamel, Dufour & Fortin (1993). This booklet in Sage's 'Qualitative Research Methods Series' is of French-Canadian origin. It addresses some of the early sociological and anthropological studies, such as Le Play's work. The case study is defined as a qualitative strategy. The book's main value lies mostly in its very extensive, but rather heterogeneous, bibliography.

Kazdin (1980). A short introduction into the clinical case study and its use, presenting some historical examples.

*King, Keohane & Verba (1994).   This book focuses on the design and analysis of case studies in political science. The authors intend to build a bridge between qualitative (i.e. case studies) and quantitative research, but this effort only partly succeeds because of the statistical language used. The book is aimed at a high level, and many parts will be very interesting for qualitative researchers, if they can follow the argument! The publication has received much attention. For examples, see the review series in the *American Political Science Review*, 1995, 89 (2): 454–481.

Kolodner (1993).   At first sight, this book on a specific approach in the field of Artificial Intelligence has nothing to do with case study research. However, the ways in which small differences between comparable situations are classified as less important, and the ways in which these situations are put together as one type, while other differences lead to different types, are very instructive for everyone interested in how to handle differences and similarities between cases.

Merriam (1988).   A simple, sometimes superficial, introduction to qualitative case studies, with relatively little attention paid to methodology but a great deal on data collection. The author defines a case study as 'particularistic, descriptive, holistic and inductive'. All examples are taken from educational research. This book can also be read as a handbook for field studies. It contains many references to other authors.

Merriam (1998).   An updated and elaborated version of Merriam (1988).

*Miles & Huberman (1984/1994).   A well-known and massive volume that covers qualitative data analysis. The authors offer a multitude of suggestions for the construction of tables, networks and other data displays. Its most significant disadvantage is that it is extremely voluminous, and very impractical if the reader tries to use it as a 'cookbook'. Many of its 'techniques of analysis' are largely trivial, in the sense that an intelligent researcher can think of them him/herself, but for a student who has lots of time at his/her disposal, there are many useful suggestions, applications, examples and hints to be found in this 'sourcebook'. References made to 'Miles and Huberman' are often regarded as a 'must' in research proposals defending a 'qualitative' approach. It is, in that context, regrettably almost never stated which specific approach, covered by Miles and Huberman, is meant.

Ragin (2000).   This book is a must for anyone interested in fuzzy-set theory.

*Ragin & Becker (eds) (1992).   The booklet comprises an interesting collection of contributions from a heterogeneous group of authors, among others Stanley Lieberman's 'Small N's and big conclusions'.

Rose (1991). A brief introduction consisting mainly of descriptions of organisational examples and comments. Its preoccupation is with qualitative, feminist and Marxist research.

Rothney (1968). A handy, practical booklet (though outdated now) in which data collection and reporting about 'children as cases' is described. It is useful for educational scientists and pedagogues.

Shontz (1965). A short plea for case studies, with examples from clinical psychology, and an analysis of different uses of case study research.

*Simons (ed.) (1980). This reader contains a number of high-level contributions in the field of theory of knowledge. Case studies are posited in the qualitative, holistic tradition. Problems about values and ethics, as well as some more practical aspects such as the education of researchers, are not avoided.

Stake (1994). For Stake, 'a case' is what we have called 'the bearer' of the phenomenon. In this rather philosophical essay, the author, from a constructivist point of view, focuses on learning about 'the specifics' in a case.

Stake (1995). A rather opportunistic small book based on seminars with, among others, Swedish students. It focuses more on technical aspects of classic field research than on methodology in a general sense.

Strauss & Corbin (1998). As the successor of Glaser and Strauss's *Discovery of Grounded Theory* (1967), this book is a much more detailed and advanced study, containing many practical suggestions for qualitative research in this tradition.

*Yin (1984/1994/2003). This is perhaps the best direct source for anyone interested in doing a case study in one or more organisations. It is a brief, very clear introduction to case study methodology, obviously inspired by applied, organisational research. In the reviewed edition of 1989 some pages are added on the use of theory in case study research. In the second edition (1994) and the third edition (2003) a few topics are further expanded and updated.

Yin (1993/2003). This text offers many applications of case study research, and addresses the problem to be solved and the research design. Most chapters refer to case studies in evaluation research. Although this booklet shows a lot of internal overlap, as several chapters are based on earlier articles, it is a useful addition to Yin's earlier book. The author also tackles the topic of 'ethnographic research' and 'the grounded theory approach', comparing them with his own preferred procedures (Yin 1993: 46, 57).

Appendix 2

The Political Science Debate on Case Studies

Lijphart (1971), in a study that became a classic, distinguished six types of case studies. The first type refers to the antique, descriptive, idiographic case studies. He uses the label 'atheoretical case studies' in referring to this set of studies. Cases are used as distinct examples; there are no attempts at generalisation. Also, there is no room for theory development, or for testing. 'Interpretative case study' theories are used, but again, they are not developed or tested, and there are no generalisations either. A theory is used to pinpoint of variables and to interpret results. Often a case study is used as an illustration of a certain theory that the researcher is addicted to. We frequently find this approach in symbolic-interactionist research (Swanborn & van Zijl 1984).

If theories are used for developing or testing purposes, Lijphart distinguishes between:

- hypothesis-generating case studies
- theory-confirming case studies
- theory-infirming case studies and
- deviant case studies.

The nature of these types of case study in obvious from their labels. Hypothesis-generating case studies are characteristic of an exploratory approach, resulting in hypotheses or theory. The next two are characteristic of a testing approach. The distinction between confirming and disconfirming (or deviant) case studies, which can only be made after the research is completed, is surprising: both types can be taken together under the label 'testing research'. Lijphart emphasises that the significance is not that important. Confirmation of a theory that already rests on a firm empirical base is not very interesting, and when such a theory is discredited by one case we are not immediately inclined to throw the theory in the waste paper basket. 'Deviant case analysis' serves the special purpose of studying the limits of a theory: what falls within it? Which conditions or cases fall outside the domain of the theory? Why does this case deviate? Do we have to specify a theory in order to include the deviating cases as well? In Lijphart's opinion, the most important types are the hypothesis-generating case studies and deviant case analysis, especially when the latter takes the form of a strict testing of the theory by means of using extreme cases.

Eckstein's typology (1975) (see also George 1979; Mitchell 1983), runs parallel to Lijphart's. The similarity is illustrated in the following outline:

Lijphart (1971)	Eckstein (1975)	Standard term
A-theoretical	Configurative-idiographic	Non-theoretical
Interpretative	Disciplined-configurative	Theory-application
Hypothesis-generating	Heuristic	Exploration
—	Plausibility probes	'Preliminary testing'
Theory confirming	Crucial case studies	Testing
Theory infirming	Crucial case studies	Testing
Deviant cases	—	A form of exploration

Eckstein (1975) is one of the classics in political science literature on case studies. The author defends the legitimate role of case studies in theory-guided, testing research, and challenges the use of comparative research designs that were popular in the 1970s. He discusses several central methodological concepts, such as 'degrees of freedom', often without using the terminology as it is used today. Eckstein owes his expression 'configurative-idiographic' to Verba. The enumeration is based on his contribution to the discussion on the role of case studies in comparative research: from upper to lower in the presented table, the importance of case studies grows. Eckstein identifies himself strongly with the point of view that 'everything can be done' in a case study, and that its value is especially located in the latter two applications. 'Plausibility probes' is a mixed form, a first validation of a theory, when costs of a real testing approach are prohibitive or not yet known. In fact, the schemes of Lijphart and Eckstein run a parallel course, as George (1979) already stated. Contrary to Eckstein, George softens the distinction between studying one case and 'comparative research' in his argument for a 'structured, focused comparison'. George addresses the question of how case studies are to be used systematically, but in an exploratory way, to develop theories.

These debates are a source of inspiration for the political scientists King, Keohane and Verba (1994). Their book is a plea for the use of qualitative as well as quantitative methods in political science, starting from some general methodological principles. The type of qualitative or case study they have in mind is, however, limited to the study of large political systems using a database of a restricted number of 'hard' variables. It has little in common with our emphasis on 'interacting individuals' and their values, opinions, attitudes and processes of meaning. A handful of extensive reviews are collected in the *American Political Science Review*, 1995, 89 (2): 454–81. An overview of current ideas about these topics can be found in George and Bennett (2005), and in Gerring (2006).

From a theory of science point of view, the follow-up of these debates is very interesting. Historians, and case study-oriented political scientists tend to follow a process-tracing approach, more or less as indicated in this book, or they focus on necessary and/or sufficient conditions in the analysis of causation. The last approach is strongly connected to Ragin's use of Boolean algebra, fuzzy-set analysis and modifications of the traditional idea of necessary and sufficient conditions: they are formulated in probabilistic terminology, such as 'necessary and/or sufficient in 90% of the cases', and the deterministic dichotomy is replaced by the absence or presence of a particular range of values of a continuously coded variable. What almost all researchers have in common is that they ask questions about the causes of major outcomes in particular cases, for instance whether different kinds of welfare states in advanced capitalist countries lead to different effects. Historical analysts are centrally concerned with the temporal dimensions of political explanation. They attach great weight to duration, pacing and timing of events. Finally, they emphasise the deep understanding achieved through a mastery of secundary and/or primary source material (Mahoney & Villegas 2006).The generally used label for this strand of approaches is 'comparative politics'.

Appendix 3

A Note on Triangulation

The label 'triangulation' was introduced to the social sciences by Campbell,[1] Webb et al. (1966) and Denzin (1970). It became a popular concept in almost all handbooks on social science methodology.

'Triangulation' is based on the geodetic technique to determine the distance to a third point if the distance between two points is known together with the angles that are formed by the line that connects the two points and the lines to the third point. There is more 'hope' than 'wisdom' in the application of this principle to social science. There are few parallels between the distance between two points and the use of two researchers or two instruments, let alone between the angles of lines and whatever corresponds to that in social research. Another essential criticism is that in geometry knowledge of both angles is *necessary* in order to locate the third point. There is no parallel for this requirement in the social sciences. In short, the use of the term 'triangulation' in social science is far from ideal, but one cannot ignore the fact that the label is frequently used.

Much has been written about triangulation, and many different types have been distinguished in the course of time, such as theoretical triangulation, data triangulation and researcher triangulation. But the core question remains the reaction of the researcher if, let's say, two instruments produce *identical* results, and what the reaction is if *different* results are produced. Often reference is made to a classic article by Campbell and Fiske (1959). These authors aimed at making a reliable distinction between 'the trait to measure' and irrelevant characteristics of the used methods. Overall, this reference is not appropriate because the aim of social science researchers in using triangulation generally is to detect whether the perceptions of meanings of different people are really different. Validation is not the goal! The aim is to describe and explain an object from different perspectives, and in this way to attain a more complete result. If, in qualitative research, researchers obtain different results, their (happy) reaction is probably: look, these different groups of actors each have their own perspective. But if the results are equal or at least comparable, the interpretation is often: look, our measurement instruments are reliable! Most researchers are not aware of this peculiar ambiguity.

---

[1]Campbell and Fiske (1959). The label is only mentioned in this article in the *Psychological Bulletin* (p. 101), but Campbell refers to publications of his dating back to 1953 and 1956.

What we have to understand, of course, is why one applies triangulation. What does one expect from this technique? Is, for example, checking the validity of a measurement what is needed, or is one aiming at combining several partial scores into a total score, that is combining the different perspectives into one 'overarching' perspective? There is still another postmodern variant of triangulation: one does not combine different scores, but interprets each score in its own right. The argument here is that because of their different epistemological base, they cannot and should not be combined.

Moreover, one should not use the label 'triangulation' for very different things. Using several theories alongside each other to explain results is an old, wise, frequently applied and often necessary approach to take in solving a problem. One does not need to use the label 'triangulation of theories'. The same holds for using several observers, several samples, several techniques for the analysis of data, and for other facets of research where the label 'triangulation' is used. If it has to be applied, our advice would be to restrict its application to specific kinds of data or data sources, such as interviewing + observation, or observation + documentary evidence.

Appendix 4

A Note on Contamination

The term 'contamination' can be placed in a long-standing methodological tradition. A well-known application, not mentioned in Chapter 5, is the shift from independent variables towards dependent variables in order to improve predictability. Some authors extend the concept of contamination in several directions. 'Cognitive-intellectual contamination' is used to indicate that a researcher might exclusively use a perspective linked to his/her own culture to study cases outside that culture. The researcher's specific frame of reference limits the extent of his/her conclusions and gradually dominates his/her observations. Another type of contamination occurs when, in a multiple case study, the same researcher, using the same instruments, is subject to expectation bias. The result might be that the cases look more alike than they are in reality. A final manifestation of contamination might be that cases can no longer be conceived as independent when stakeholders gradually learn from earlier cases. An example would be the behaviour of police officers in handling riots. This last form, however, does not refer to select the researcher's thought process or selection of data, but refers to the changing reality. Although in this context very interesting questions can be raised, for instance why policy officess apparently learn from some cases and not from others, the use of the term 'contamination' for all these different phenomena is confusing. In the end, one cannot avoid the conclusion that reality itself is contaminated. whereas we usually assume that the studied social systems are independent, if this assumption turns out to be false in a research project, then we need to include certain variables (such as learning from earlier experiences) in the model. It is, in a way, a typical example of the argumentation of some researchers: 'look, the variable language doesn't work; we need an holistic approach'.

Bibliography

Abramson, P.R. (1992). *A case for case studies: an immigrant's journal*. London: Sage.

Adelman, C., Jenkins, D. & Kemmis, S. (1984). Rethinking case study, pp. 93–102 in J. Bell et al. (eds), *Conducting small-scale investigations in educational measurement*. London: Harper & Row.

Ajzen, I. & Fishbein, M. (1980). *Understanding attitudes and predicting social behaviour*. Englewood Cliffs, NJ: Prentice-Hall.

Alemann, H. von & Ortlieb, P. (1975). *Die Einzelfallstudie*, pp. 157–177 in J. van Koolwijk & M. Wieken-Mayser (eds), *Techniken der empirischen Sozialforschung* (vol. 2). Munich: Oldenbourg.

Allison, G.T. (1971). *Essence of decision: explaining the Cuban Missile Crisis*. Boston: Little, Brown. A second edition (1999) is co-authored by G.T. Allison and P. Zelikow. New York: Addison Wesley Longman.

APA Presidential Task Force (2006). Evidence-base practice in psychology. *American Psychologist*, 61: 271–285.

Arnold, D.O. (1970). Dimensional sampling: an approach for studying a small number of cases. *American Sociologist*, 5: 147–150.

Bachor, D.G. (2000, May). Rethinking case study research methodology. Paper presented at the Special Education National Research Forum, Helsinki, Finland.

Bachor, D.G. & Baer, M.B. (2000, May). An examination of pre-service teachers' portfolio diaries. Paper presented at the annual meeting of the Canadian Society for the Study of Education, University of Alberta, Canada.

Barlow, D.H. & Hersen, M. (1984). *Single case experimental designs: strategies for studying behavior change*. New York: Pergamon.

Barton, A. & Lazarsfeld, P.F. (1955). Some functions of qualitative analysis in social research. *Sociologica*, 1(24): 321–361.

Bass, R.F. (1987). The generality, analysis and assessment of single-subject data. *Psychology in the Schools*, 97–104.

Bassey, M. (1999). *Case study research in educational settings*. Buckingham: Open University Press.

Bates, R.H., Greif, A., Levi, M., Rosenthal, J.-L. & Weingast, B. (1998). *Analytic narratives*. Princeton, NJ: Princeton University Press.

Bazeley, P. (2007). *Qualitative data analysis with NVivo* (2nd edn). London: Sage.

Becker, H. (1958). Problems of inference and proof in participant observation. *American Sociological Review*, 23: 652–660.

Becker, H.S. (1968). Social observation and case studies, pp. 232–238 in D. Sills (ed.), *International encyclopaedia of the social sciences* (vol. 11). New York: Macmillan and Free Press.

Becker, H.S. (1990). Generalizing from case studies, pp. 233–42 in E.W. Eisner & A. Peshkin (eds), *Qualitative inquiry in education: the continuing debate*. New York: Teachers College Press.

Becker, H.S. (1992). Cases, causes, conjunctures, stories and imagery, pp. 205–216 in C.C. Ragin & H.W. Becker (eds), *What is a case? Exploring the foundations of social inquiry.* New York: Cambridge University Press. Also included in R. Gomm, M. Hammersley & P. Foster (eds) (2000). *Case study method: key issues, key texts.* London: Sage.

Becker, H.S., Geer, B., Hughes, E.C. & Strauss, A.L. (1961). *Boys in white: student culture in medical school.* Chicago: University of Chicago Press.

Behling, J.H. & Mewes, E.S. (1984). *The practice of clinical research: the single case method.* Lanham, MD: University Press of America.

Bennett, A. (1997). *Lost in the translation: big (N) misinterpretations of case study research.* Paper presented at the 38th Annual Convention of the International Studies Association, Toronto. 1997.

Bennis, W.G. (1968). The case study. *The Journal of Applied Behavioral Science,* 4: 227–231.

Bergman, M.M. (ed.) (2008). *Advances in mixed method research.* Los Angeles, CA: Sage.

Bernstein, C. & Woodward, B. (1974). *All the president's men.* New York: Simon & Schuster.

Beveridge, W.I.B. (1950). *The art of scientific investigation.* London: Heinemann.

Biemans, W.G. (1989). *Developing innovations within networks – with an application to the Dutch medical industry.* PhD thesis, University of Eindhoven, Eindhoven (NL).

Biemans, W.G. (1991). Case research als onderzoeksmethode bij organisatieonderzoek ten behoevern van marketing (Case research as a method of organizational research in marketing), pp. 149–168 in *Jaarboek van de Nederlandse Vereniging van Marktonderzoekers '90–'91.* Haarlem: de Vrieseborch.

Binneberg, K. (1985). Grundlagen der Pädagogischen Kasuistik, *Zeitschrift für Paedagogik,* (31): 773–788.

Blaikie, P. (1993). *Approaches to social enquiry.* Cambridge: Polity Press.

Blalock, H.M. (1964). *Causal inferences in non-experimental research.* Chapel Hill, NC: University of North Carolina Press.

Blau, P.M. (1955). *The dynamics of bureaucracy.* Chicago: University of Chicago Press.

Bogdan, R. & Taylor, S.J. (1975). *Introduction to qualitative research methods.* New York: Wiley.

Boix, C. & Stokes, S.C. (eds) (2006). *The Oxford handbook on comparative politics.* Oxford: Oxford University Press.

Bolgar, H. (1965). The case study method, pp. 28–38 in B.B.Wolman (ed.), *The handbook of clinical psychology.* New York: McGraw-Hill.

Bonoma, Th.V. (1985). Case research in marketing: opportunities, problems and a process. *Journal of Marketing Research,* 22: 199–208.

Boskma, A.F. & Herweijer, M. (1988). Beleidseffectiviteit en case studies: een vergelijking van verschillende onderzoeksontwerpen (Social policy effectiveness and case studies: a comparison of several research designs). *Beleidswetenschap,* pp. 6–9.

Bovenkerk, F. (1977). Geen woorden maar daden, pp. 127–143 in L. Brunt (ed.), *Anders bekeken.* Amsterdam: Boom.

Box, G.E.P. & Jenkins, G.M. (1976). *Time series analysis: forecasting and control.* Oakland, CA: Holden-Day.

Bradshaw, Y. & Wallace, M. (1991). Informing generality and explaining uniqueness. *International Journal for Comparative Sociology,* 32: 154–171.

Brockwell, P.J. & Davis, R.A. (2003). *Introduction to time series and forecasting.* New York: Springer.

Bromley, D.B. (1986). *The case-study method in psychology and related disciplines*. Chicester: Wiley.

Bryman, A. (1996, 1988). *Quantity and quality in social research*. London: Routledge.

Bryman, A. & Burgess, R.G. (eds) (1994). *Analysing qualitative data*. London: Routledge.

Bryman, A. & Burgess, R.G. (eds.) (1999). *Qualitative research*. London: Sage.

Bulmer, M. (1979). Concepts in the analysis of qualitative data. *Sociological Review*, 27(4): 651–677.

Bunge, M. (1967). *Scientific research*. Berlin: Springer. Reissued (1998) as *Philosophy of Science*. New Brunswick, NJ: Transaction Publishers.

Burgess, R.G. (ed.) (1984). *The research process in educational settings: ten case studies*. London: Falmer.

Campbell, D.T. (1975). Degrees of freedom and the case-study. *Comparative Political Studies*, 8: 178–193.

Campbell, D.T. & Fiske, D.W. (1959). Convergent and discriminant validation by the multitrait-multimethod matrix. *Psychological Bulletin*, 56: 81–105.

Campbell, D.T. & Stanley, J.C. (1963). Experimental and quasi-experimental designs for research on teaching, pp. 171–246 in N.L. Gage (ed.), *Handbook of research on teaching*. Chicago: Rand McNally.

Chatfield, C. (1996). *The analysis of time series: an introduction*. London: Chapman and Hall.

Chima, J.S. (2005). *What's the utility of the case-study method for social science research?* American Political Science Association.

Clement, P.C. (2007). The story of 'Hope': successful treatment of OCD (Obsessive Compulsive Disorder). *Pragmatic Case Studies in Psychotherapy*, 3(4): 1–36.

Cline Seal, G.G., Gobo, G. & Silverman, D. (eds) (1999). *Qualitative research practice*. London: Sage.

Cook, T.D. & Campbell, D.T. (1979). *Quasi-experimentation: design and analysis issues for field settings*. Chicago: Rand McNally.

Cook, Th.D. Cooper, H. & Cordray, D. (1994). *Toward explanatory meta-analysis*. New York: Russell Sage Fundation.

Cooper, H. & Hedges, L.V. (1994). *The handbook of research synthesis*. New York: Russell Sage Foundation.

Cressey, P.G. (1932). *The taxi dance hall*. Chicago: University of Chicago Press.

Creswell, J.W. (1994; 2nd edn 2003). *Research design: qualitative, quantitative and mixed method approaches*. Thousand Oaks, CA: Sage.

Creswell, J.W. (1998). *Qualitative inquiry and research design: choosing among five traditions*. Thousand Oaks, CA: Sage.

Creswell, J.W. & Plano Clark, V.L. (2007). *Designing and conducting mixed method research*. Thousand Oaks, CA: Sage.

Creswell, J.W., Plano Clark, V.L., Guttman, M. & Hanson, W. (2003). Advanced mixed methods research designs, pp. 209–240 in A. Tashakkori & C. Teddlie (eds), *Handbook on mixed methods in the behavioral and social sciences*. Thousand Oaks, CA: Sage.

Cronbach, L.J. (1975). Beyond the two disciplines of scientific psychology. *American Psychologist*, 30 (2): 116–127.

Cronbach, L.J. et al. (1980). *Toward reform of program evaluation*. San Francisco: Jossey-Bass.

Davis, T.M. & Bachor, D.G. (1999, June). Case studies as a research tool in evaluating student achievement. Paper presented at the Canadian Society for Studies in Education Conference, Sherbrooke, Quebec.

Denzin, N.K. (1970). *The research act*. Chicago: Aldine.

Denzin, N.K. & Lincoln, Y.S. (eds) (1994). *Handbook of qualitative research* (3rd edn 2000). Thousand Oaks, CA: Sage.

Diesing, P. (1972). *Patterns of discovery in the social sciences*. London: Routledge & Kegan Paul.

Drass, K. & Ragin, C.C. (1992). *QCA: qualitative comparative analysis*. Evanston, IL: Institute for Policy Research, Northwestern University.

Drass, K. & Ragin, C.C. (1999). *QC/FSA: qualitative comparative/fuzzy-set analysis*. Evanston, IL: Institute for Policy Research, Northwestern University.

Dukes, W.F. (1965). N = 1. *Psychological Bulletin*, 64: 74–79.

Dul, J. & Hak, T. (2008). *Case study methodology in business research*. Oxford: Butterworth-Heinemann.

Dyer, W.G. & Wilkins, A.L. (1991). Better stories, not better constructs, to generate better theory: a rejoinder to Eisenhardt. *Academy of Management Review*, 16: 613–619.

Easton, G. (1992). *Learning from case studies* (2nd edn). New York: Prentice-Hall.

Eckstein, H. (1975). Case study and theory in political science, pp. 79–137 in F.I. Greenstein & N.W. Polsby (eds), *The handbook of political science: strategies of inquiry*. Reading, MA: Addison-Wesley. This article is also included in H. Eckstein (1992). *Regarding politics: essays on political theory, stability and change*. Berkeley, CA: University of California Press, as well as (abridged) in R. Gomm, M. Hammersley & P. Foster (eds) (2000). *Case study method: key issues, key texts*. London: Sage.

Eisenhardt, K.M. (1989). Building theories from case study research. *Academy of Management Review*, 14: 532–550.

Eisenhardt, K.M. (1991). Better stories and better constructs: the case for rigor and comparative logic. *Academy of Management Review*, 16: 620–627.

Ellet, W. (2006). *The case study handbook: how to read, discuss and write persuasively about cases*. Boston, MA: Harvard Business School Press.

Ericsson, K.A. & Simon, H.A. (1984). *Protocol analysis: verbal reports as data*. Cambridge, MA: MIT Press.

Evan, M.G. (1991). The problem of analyzing multiplicative composites: interactions revisited. *American Psychologist*, January: 6–15.

Feagin, J., Orum, A. & Sjoberg, G. (eds) (1991). *A case for the case study*. Chapel Hill, NC: University of North Carolina Press.

Festinger, L., Riecken Jr., H.W. & Schachter, S. (1956). *When prophecy fails*. Minneapolis, MN: University of Minnesota Press.

Fielding, N.G. & Lee, R.M. (1998). *Computer analysis and qualitative research*. London: Sage.

Fienberg, S.E. (1977). The collection and analysis of ethnographic data in educational research. *Anthropology and Education Quarterly*, 8: 50–57.

Firestone, W.A. (1993). Alternative arguments for generalizing from data as applied to qualitative research. *Educational Researcher*, 22 (4): 16–23.

Fishman, D.B. (1999). *The case for pragmatic psychology*. New York: New York University Press.

Flyvbjerg, B. (2003). Five misunderstandings about case study research, pp. 420–434 in G.G. Clive Seale, G. Gobo & D. Silverman (eds), *Qualitative research practice*. London: Sage.

Foreman, P.B. (1948). The theory of case studies, *Social Forces*, 26 (4): 408–419. Also included in B.J. Franklin & H.W. Osborne (eds), *Research methods: issues and insights*. Belmont, CA: Wadsworth. pp. 187–204.

Fransella, F. & Bannister, D. (2003) *A manual for repertory grid techniques* (2nd rev. edn). New York: Wiley.

Galle, M.M.A. (1986). Case-studie en beleidsontwerp (Case study and policy design). *Sociodrome*, 4: 11–13.

George, A.L. (1979). Case studies and theory development: the method of structured, focused comparison, pp. 43–68 in P.G. Lauren (ed.), *Diplomacy: new approaches in history, theory and policy.* New York: Free Press.

George, A.L. & Bennett, A. (2005). *Case studies and theory development in the social sciences.* Cambridge, MA: MIT Press.

Gerring, J. (2007). *Case study research: principles and practices.* Cambridge: Cambridge University Press.

Gibbs, G.R. (2007). *Analyzing qualitative data.* London: Sage.

Glaser, B.G. & Strauss, A.L. (1965). *Awareness of dying.* Chicago: Aldine.

Glaser, B.G. & Strauss, A.L. (1967). *The discovery of grounded theory.* Chicago: Aldine.

Gluckman, M. (1961). Ethnographic data in British social anthropology. *Sociological Review*, 9: 5–17.

Goertz, G. & Mahoney, J. (2005). Two level theories and fuzzy-set analysis. *Sociological Methods and Research*, 33: 497–538.

Goertz, G. & Starr, H. (eds) (2003). *Necessary conditions: theory, methodology and applications.* Lanham, MD: Rowham and Littlefield.

Goetz, J.P. & LeCompte, M.D. (1984). *Ethnography and qualitative design in educational research.* New York: Academic Press.

Gomm, R., Hammersley, M. & Foster, P. (eds) (2000). *Case study method: key issues, key texts.* London: Sage.

Goode, W.J. & Hatt, P.H. (1952). *Methods in social research.* New York: McGraw-Hill.

Gordon, J. & Shontz, F. (1990). Representative case research. *Journal of Counseling and Development*, 69: 62–66.

Gottman, J.M. (1981). *Times series-analysis: a comprehensive introduction for social scientists.* Cambridge, MA : Harvard University Press.

Greenwood, G.E. & Parkay, F.W. (1989). *Case studies for teacher decision making.* New York: Random House.

Guba, E.G. (1981). Criteria for assessing the trustworthiness of naturalistic inquiries. *Educational Communication and Technology Journal*, 29: 75–92.

Guba, E.G. & Lincoln,Y.S. (1994). Competing paradigms in qualitative research, pp. 105–117 in N.K. Denzin & Y.S. Lincoln (eds), *Handbook of qualitative research.* Thousand Oaks: Sage.

Gummesson, E. (1991). *Qualitative methods in management research.* Newbury Park: Sage.

Hamel, J., Dufour, S. & Fortin, D. (1993). *Case study methods.* Newbury Park: Sage.

Hamilton, D. (1980). Some contrasting assumptions about case study research and survey analysis, in H. Simons (ed.), *Towards a science of the singular: essays about case study in educational research and evaluation* (CARE Occasional Publications No. 10). Norwich: Norwich Centre for Applied Research in Education, University of East Anglia.

Hammersley, M. (1992). So, what are case studies? pp. 183–200 in M. Hammersley, *What's wrong with ethnography?* London: Routledge.

Harré, R. (1979). *Social being.* Oxford: Blackwell.

Hartley, J.F. (1994). Case studies in organizational research, pp. 208–229 in C. Cassell & G. Symon (eds), *Qualitative methods in organizational research.* London: Sage.

Heikema van der Kloet, H.R. (1987). Overdracht van bevoegdheden: een terreinverkenning (Transfer of legal rights: an exploration). *Bondsblad*, 84 (15): 4–5 and 9–11.

Herriott, R.E. & Firestone, W.A. (1983). Multisite qualitative policy research: optimizing description and generalizability. *Educational Researcher*, 12: 14–19.

Hertog, F. Den (2002). Blending words and numbers. Maastricht: University of Maastricht (NL), unpubl.

Hox, J.J. (2002). *Multilevel analysis: techniques and applications*. Englewood Cliffs, NJ: Erlbaum.

Huber, H.P. (1984). Entwicklungstendenzen in der Einzelfallstatistik: eine Standort-bestimmung. *Psychologische Beiträge*, 26: 348–362.

Imai, K., King, G. & Nall, C. (2008). The essential role of pair matching in cluster-randomized experiments, with application to the Mexican Health Insurance Evaluation. Available at: imai.princeton.edu (accessed 22/02/2010).

Ives, K.H. (1986). Case study methods: an essay review of the state of the art, as found in five recent sources. *Case analysis*, 2: 137–160.

Kahn, W.A. (1993). Facilitating and undermining organizational change: a case study. *The Journal of applied behavioral science*, 29: 32–55.

Kalleberg, A.L., Knoke, D., Marsden, P.V. and Spaeth, T. (1994). The national organization study: an introduction and overview. *American Behavioral Scientist*, 37: 860–871.

Kazdin, A.E. (1980). *Research designs in clinical psychology*. New York: Harper & Row.

Kazdin, A.E. (1982). *Single-case research designs: methods for clinical and applied settings*. New York: Oxford University Press.

Kennedy, M.M. (1979). Generalizing from single case studies. *Evaluation Quarterly*, 3: 661–678.

Kent, R. (2009). Case centred methods and quantitative analysis, pp. 184–207 in D. Byrne & C. Ragin (eds), *Handbook of case-based methods*. Thousand Oaks, CA: Sage.

King, G., Keohane, R.O. & Verba, S. (1994). *Designing social inquiry: scientific inference in qualitative research*. Princeton, NJ: Princeton University Press.

Kolodner, J. (1993). *Case-based reasoning*. San Mateo, CA: Morgan Kaufmann.

Kops, Y. (1993). Flexibele starters. PhD thesis, University of Utrecht, Utrecht (NL).

Kratochwill, T.R. (ed.) (1978). *Single subject research*. New York: Academic Press.

Kratochwill, T.R. & Levin, J.R. (eds) (1992). *Single case research design and analysis*. Hillsdale, NJ: Erlbaum.

Kreft, I.G.G. & De Leeuw, J. (1998). *Introducing multilevel modelling*. Newbury Park, CA: Sage.

Kuckartz, U. (2001). *An introduction to the computer analysis of qualitative data*. London: Sage.

Kuzel, A.J. (1999). Sampling, in B.F. Crabtree & W.L. Miller (eds), *Doing qualitative research* (2nd edn). Newbury Park, CA: Sage.

Larsson, R. (1993). Case survey methodology: quantitative analysis of patterns across case studies. *Academy of Management Journal*, 36 (6): 1515–1546.

Lee, Y.S. (1983). Public management and case study methods. *Teaching Political Science*, 11: 6–14.

Lewins, C. & Silver, C. (2007). *Using software in qualitative research: a step-by-step guide*. London: Sage.

Lieberson, S. (1985). *Making it count*. Berkeley, CA: University of California Press.

Lieberson, S. (1991). Small N's and big conclusions: an examination of the reasoning in comparative studies based on a small number of cases. *Social Forces*, 70: 307–320. Also included in C.C. Ragin & H.W. Becker (eds) (1992). *What is a case? Exploring the foundations of social inquiry*. New York: Cambridge University Press, and in R. Gomm, M. Hammersley & P. Foster (eds) (2000). *Case study methods: key issues, key texts*. London: Sage.

Lieberson, S. (1994). More on the uneasy case for using Mill-type methods in small-N comparative studies. *Social Forces*, 72: 1225–1237.

Lijphart, A. (1971). Comparative politics and the comparative method. *The American Political Sciences Review*, 65: 682–693.

Lijphart, A. (1975). The comparable-cases strategy in comparative research. *Comparative Political Studies*, 8: 158–177.

Lincoln, Y.S. & Guba, E.G. (1985). *Naturalistic inquiry*. Beverly Hills, CA: Sage.

Lipset, S.M., Trow, M. & Coleman, J. (1956). *Union democracy: the inside politics of the International Typographical Union*. New York: Free Press.

Lipsey, M.W. & Wilson, D.B. (2001). *Practical meta-analysis*. London: Sage.

Louis, K.S. (1982). Multisite/multimethod studies. *American Behavioral Scientist*, 26: 6–22.

Lucas, W.A. (1974). *The case survey method: aggregating case experience*. R-1515-RC. Santa Monica, CA: Rand Corporation.

Lynd, R.S. & Lynd, H. (1929/1956). *Middletown: a study in American culture*. New York: Harcourt, Brace.

MacLeary, R.T. & Hay, R.A. (1980). *Applied time–series analysis for the social sciences*. Beverley Hills, CA: Sage.

McCall, G.J. & Simmons, J.L. (1969). *Issues in participant observation*. Reading, MA: Addison-Wesley.

McClintock, C.C., Brannon, D. and Maynard-Moony, S. (1979). Applying the logic of sample surveys to qualitative case studies: the case cluster method. *Administrative Science Quarterly*, 24: 612–629.

Mahoney, J. & Villegas, C. (2006) Historical inquiry and comparative politics, pp. 73–89. in C. Boix and S.C. Stokes (eds), *The Oxford handbook on comparative politics.* Oxford: Oxford University Press.

Meehl, P. (1965). Clinical versus statistical prediction. *Journal of Experimental Research in Personality*, 81–97.

Mellenbergh, G.J., Molen dijk, C., de Haas, W. and Gunter/Morst. G. (1990). The sum-of products variable reconsidered. *Methodika*, 4: 37–46.

Merriam, S.B. (1988). *Case study research in education: a qualitative approach*. San Francisco: Jossey Bass.

Merriam, S.B. (1998). *Qualitative research and case study applications in education*. San Francisco: Jossey Bass.

Merton, R.K. (1945). Sociological theory. *The American Journal of Sociology*, 26: 50: 469.

Merton, R.K. and Barber, E. (2004). *The travels and adventures of serendipity: a study in sociological semantics and the sociology of science*. Princeton, NJ: Princeton University Press.

Miles, M.B. (1982). A mini-cross site analysis. *American Behavioral Scientist*, 26: 121–132.

Miles, M.B. & Huberman, A.M. (1984). Drawing valid meaning from qualitative data: toward a shared craft. *Educational Researcher*, 3 (5): 20–30.

Miles, M.B. & Huberman, A.M. (1994). *Qualitative data analysis: an expanded source-book* (2nd edn). Thousand Oaks, CA: Sage.

Mill, J.S. (1872). *A system of logic* (vol. 2) (8th edn). London: Longmans, Green, Reader & Dyer.

Mintzberg, H. (1979). An emerging strategy of 'direct' research, *Administrative Science Quarterly*, 24: 580–589.

Mitchell, J.C. (1983). Case and situation analysis. *Sociological Review*, 187–211. Also included in R. Gomm, M. Hammersley & P. Foster (eds) (2000). *Case study method: key issues, key texts.* London: Sage.

Moore, Barrington Jr. (1966). *The social origins of dictatorship and democracy: lord and peasant in the making of the modern world*. Boston, MA: Beacon.

Moore, W.E. (1967). *The conduct of the corporation*. New York: Random House.

Mulhauser, F. (1975). Ethnography and policy-making: the case of education. *Human Organization*, 311–315.

Nichols, E. (1986). Skocpol and revolution: comparative analysis vs. historical conjecture. *Comparative Social Research*, 9: 163–186.

Niederkofler, M. (1991). The influence of strategic alliances: opportunities for managerial influence. *Journal of Business Venturing*, 6: 237–257.

Nisbet, J. & Watt, J. (1984). Case study, pp. 79–92 in J. Bell et al. (eds), *Conducting small-scale investigations in educational management*. London: Harper & Row.

Oskamp, S. (1965). Overconfidence in case study judgments. *Journal of Counseling Psychology*, 261–265.

Padgett, D.K. (2004). *The qualitative research experience*. Belmont, CA: Wadsworth.

Paige, J. (1975). *Agrarian revolution: social movement and export agriculture in the underdeveloped world*. New York: Free Press.

Patton, M.Q. (2002). *Qualitative research and evaluation methods* (3rd edn). Newbury Park, CA: Sage.

Petermann, F. & Hehl, F.-J. (Hrsg.) (1979). *Einzelfallanalyse*. Munich: Urban & Schwarzenberg.

Pion, G.M., Cordray, D.S. & Anderson, S. (1993). Drawing the line between conjecture and evidence about the use and benefit of practice methodologies. *Professional Psychology: Research and Practice*, 24: 245–249.

Plano Clark, V.C. & Cresswell, J.W. (2008) *The mixed methods reader*. Thousand Oaks: Sage.

Platt, J. (1988). What can case studies do? *Studies in Qualitative Methodology*, 5: 1–23.

Platt, J. (1992). 'Case study' in American methodological thought. *Current Sociology*, 40. Special issue. Trend Report: The Case Method in Sociology. pp. 17–48.

Popper, K.R. (1963). *Conjectures and refutations*. London: Routledge & Kegan Paul.

Popping, R. (1999). *Computer-assisted text analysis*. London: Sage.

Quak, H.J. & de Koster, M.B.M. (2007). Exploring retailers' sensitivity to local sustainability policies. *Journal of Operations Management*, 25: 1103–1122.

Ragin, C.C. (1987). *The comparative method: moving beyond qualitative and quantitative strategies*. Berkeley, CA: University of California Press.

Ragin, C.C. (2000). *Fuzzy-set social science*. Chicago: University of Chicago Press.

Ragin, C.C. (2008). *Redesiging social inquiry: set relations in social research*. Chicago: Chicago University Press.

Ragin, C.C. & Becker, H.W. (eds) (1992). *What is a case? Exploring the foundations of social inquiry*. New York: Cambridge University Press.

Raudenbush, S.W. & Bryk, A.S. (2002). *Hierarchical linear models: applications and data analysis methods*. Newbury Park, CA: Sage.

Reijnders, M.I. (1984). De waarde van de case-study voor het proces van beleidsvoorbereiding (The value of a case study in preparing for policy), pp. 47–57 in S.J.C. van Eijndhoven & J.M.G. Leune (eds), *Voorbereiding van onderwijsbeleid*. The Hague: SVO.

Richards, L. (2005). *Handling qualitative data: a practical guide*. London: Sage.

Rihoux, B. & Grimm, H. (2006). *Innovative comparative methods for policy analysis: beyond the quantitative–qualitative debate*. New York: Springer Kluwer.

Rihoux, B. & Ragin, C.C. (eds) (2008). *Configurational comparative methods: qualitative comparative analysis (QCA) and related techniques*. London: Sage.

Rodrick, D. (ed.) (2003). *In search of prosperity: analytic narratives on economic growth*. Princeton, NJ: Princeton University Press.

Rokkan, S. (1966). Comparative cross-national research: the context of current efforts, pp. 3–26 in R. Merritt & S. Rokkan (eds), *Comparing Nations*. New Haven, CT: Yale University Press.

Rose, H. (1991). Case studies, pp. 189–202 in G. Allan & C. Skinner (eds), *Handbook for research students in the social sciences*. London: Falmer/Taylor.

Rothney, J.M. (1968). *Methods of studying the individual child: the psychological case study*. Waltham, MA: Ginn-Blaisdell.

Runyan, W.M. (1982a). In defense of the case study method. *American Journal of Orthopsychiatry*, 52: 440–446.

Runyan, W.M. (1982b). *Life histories and psychobiography: explorations in theory and method*. New York: Oxford University Press.

Sandelowski, M. (2008) Tables or tableaux? The challenges of writing and reading mixed methods studies, pp. 301–338 in Plano Clark and Cresswell, J.W. *The mixed methods reader*. Thousand Oaks: SAge.

Schatzmann, L. & Strauss, A.L. (1973). *Field research*. Englewood Cliffs, NJ: Prentice-Hall.

Scholz, R.W. & Tietje, O. (2002). *Embedded case study methods: integrating quantitative and qualitative knowledge*. London: Sage.

Shadish, W., Cook, T. & Campbell, D. (2002). *Experimental and quasi-experimental designs for generalised causal inference*. Boston, MA: Houghton-Mifflin.

Shaw, C. (1966). *The Jack Roller* (2nd edn). Chicago: University of Chicago Press.

Shaw, C.R. (1931). Case study method. *Publications of the American Sociological Society*, 21: 149–157.

Shontz, F.C. (1965). *Research methods in personality*. New York: Appleton-Century-Crofts.

Silverman, D. (1993). *Interpreting qualitative data: methods for analysing talk, text and interaction*. London: Sage.

Simons, H. (ed.) (1980). *Towards a science of the singular: essays about case study in educational research and evaluation*. Norwich: Centre for Applied Research in Education, University of East Anglia.

Simons, H. (1996). The paradox of case study. *Cambridge Journal of Education*, 26: 225–240.

Skocpol, T. (1979). *States and social revolutions: a comparative analysis of France, Russia and China*. Cambridge: Cambridge University Press.

Smelser, N. (1973). The methodology of comparative analysis, pp. 45–52 in Warwick, D. & Osherson, S. (eds) *Comparative Research Methods*. Englewood Cliffs: Prentice-Hall.

Snijders, T.A.B. & Bosker, R.J. (1999). *Multilevel analysis: an introduction to basic and advanced multilevel modelling*. Newbury Park, CA: Sage.

Social Science History (2000) 24(4). Symposium on Robert H. Bates, Auner Great, Margaret Levi, and Barry R. Weingast's *Analytic Narratives*.

Stake, R.E. (1978). The case study method in social inquiry. *Educational Researcher*, 7 (2): 5–9. Also included in R. Gomm, M. Hammersley & P. Foster (eds) (2000), *Case study methods: key issues, key texts*. London: Sage.

Stake, R.E. (1980). The case study method in social inquiry, pp. 62–75 in H. Simons (ed.), *Towards a science of the singular: essays about case study in educational research and evaluation*. Norwich: Centre for Applied Research in Education, University of East Anglia.

Stake, R.E. (1981). Case study methodology: an epistemological advocacy, in W.W. Welsh (ed.), *Case study methodology in educational evaluation*. Minneapolis, MN: Minnesota Research and Evaluation Center.

Stake, R.E. (1994). Case studies, pp. 236–247 in N.K. Denzin & Y.S. Lincoln (eds), *Handbook of qualitative research*. Thousand Oaks, CA: Sage.

Stake, R.E. (1995). *The art of case study research*. Thousand Oaks, CA: Sage.

Stake, R.E. & Trumbull, D. (1982). Naturalistic generalizations. *Review Journal of philosophy and social science*, 7 (1): 1–12.

Stein, H. (1952). Case method and the analysis of public administration, pp. xx–xxvi in H. Stein (ed.), *Public administration and policy development*. New York: Harcourt, Brace, Jovanovich.

Stenhouse, L. (1978). Case study and case records: towards a contemporary history of education. *British Education Research Journal*, 4 (2): 21–39.

Stenhouse, L. (1980). The study of samples and the study of cases. *British Educational Research Journal*, 6: 1–6.

Stenhouse, L. (1984) Library access, library use and user education, pp. 211–233 in R.G. Burgess (ed.) Norwich: Falmer.

Stenhouse, L. (1988). Case study methods, pp. 49–53 in J.P. Keeves (ed.), *Educational research, methodology and measurement: an international handbook*. Sydney: Pergamon Press.

Stoecker, R. (1991). Evaluating and rethinking the case study. *The Sociological Review*, 39: 88–112.

Stouffer, A.S. (1941). Notes of the case study and the unique case. *Sociometry*, 4: 349–357.

Strauss, J.L. & Corbin, J.M. (eds) (1997). *Grounded theory in practice*. Thousand Oaks, CA: Sage.

Strauss, A.L. & Corbin, J. (1998). *Basics of qualitative research techniques and procedures for developing grounded theories* (2nd edn). London: Sage.

Sturman, A. (1999). Case study methods, pp. 103–112 in J.P. Keeves & G. Lakomski (eds), *Issues in educational research*. Oxford: Elsevier.

Swanborn, P.G. (1996a). A common base for quality control criteria in quantitative and qualitative research. *Quality and Quantity*, 30: 19–35.

Swanborn, P.G. (1996b). De Fishbein/Ajzen theorie in de kritiek (Critical remarks about the Fishbein/Ajzen theory). *Nederlands Tijdschrift voor de Psychologie*, 51: 35–46 (in Dutch).

Swanborn, P.G. & van Zijl, P. (1984) Interactionists do it only symbolically. *Mens en Maatschappij*, 59: 152–164 (despite its title, the article is in Dutch!).

Taylor, S.J. & Bogdan, R. (1998) *Introduction to qualitative research methods* (3rd edn) New York: Wiley.

Tashakkori, A. & Teddlie, C. (1998). *Mixed methodology: combining qualitative and quantitative Approaches*. Thousand Oaks, CA: Sage.

Tashakkori, S.J. & Teddlie, C. (eds) (2003). *Handbook of mixed methods in social and behavioural research*. Thousand Oaks, CA: Sage.

Ten Have, P. (1998). *Doing conversation analysis: a practical guide*. London: Sage.

Thyer, B.A. & Thyer, K.B. (1992). Single-system research designs in social work practice: a bibliography from 1965 to 1990. *Research on Social Work Practice*, 2: 99–116.

Tilly, C. (1975). *The formation of national states in Western Europe*. Princeton, NJ: Princeton University Press.

Toalmin, S. (1958) *The uses of argument* (2nd edn 2003). Cambridge: Cambridge University Press.

Towl, A.R. (1969). *To study administration by cases*. Boston, MA: Harvard University Business School.

Travers, M. (2001). *Qualitative research through case studies*. London: Sage.

Tripp, D.H. (1985). Case study generalization: an agenda for action. *British Educational Research Journal*, 11: 33–43.

Van den Berg, H., Denolf, L. & Van der Veer, K. (1997). *Het kleine verschil: slaag- en faalfactoren bij de trajectbemiddeling van allochtonen* (The small difference: success- and failure factors in the trajectory of job intermediacy for allochtonous people). Amsterdam: Jan Mets.

Van Gent, W.P.C. (2006). The conditions for neighbourhood (dis-) satisfaction: 29 European post-war housing estates compared. Paper presented at the European Network for Housing Research conference 'Housing in Expanding Europe', Ljubljana, Slovenia.

Velsen, J. van (1967). The extended-case method and situational analysis, pp. 129–149 in A.L. Epstein (ed.), *The craft of social anthropology*. London: Tavistock.

Vidich, A.J. & Bensman, J. (1958). *Small town in mass society: class, power and religion in a rural community*. Princeton, NJ: Princeton University Press.

Wallerstein, I. (1974). *The modern world system: capitalist agriculture and the origins of the European world economy in the sixteenth century*. New York: Academic Press.

Warwick, D. & Osherson, S. (1973). *Comparative research methods*. Englewood Cliffs, NJ: Prentice-Hall.

Webb, E.J., Campbell, D.T., Schwarz, R.D., Sechrest, L. & Grove, J.B. (1981). *Nonreactive measures in the social sciences*. Boston, MA: Houghton Mifflin. (First published under the title 'Unobtrusive measures' in 1966.)

Weitzman, E.A. & Miles, M.B. (1995). *Computer programs for qualitative data analysis*. London: Sage.

Whyte, W.F. (1941). *Street corner society: the social structure of an Italian slum*. Chicago: University of Chicago Press.

Wilson, S. (1979). Explorations of the usefulness of case study evaluations. *Evaluation Quarterly*, 3: 446–459.

Wilson, S.M. & Gudmundsdottir, S. (1987). What is this a case of? Exploring some conceptual issues in case study research. *Education and Urban Society*, 20: 42–55.

Windsor, D. & Greanias, G. (1983). The public policy and management program for case/course development. *Public Administration Review*, 26: 370–378.

Winegardner, K.E. (2007). *The case study method of scholarly research*. The Graduate School of America. Available at: www.arasite.org/anniefcritan.html (accessed 22/02/10).

Wolf, F.M. (1986). *Meta-analysis: quantitative methods for research synthesis*. Beverley Hills, CA: Sage.

Wolf, G.K. (1986). Single case evaluation: basic assumptions and consequences for the applications. *Psychologische Beiträge*, 28: 265–278.

Yin, R.K. (1993). *Applications of case study research* (2nd edn 2003), Newbury Park, CA: Sage. (First published 1993)

Yin, R.K. (1994). *Case study research: design and methods* (2nd edn). London: Sage. (First published 1984; 3rd edn 2003)

Yin, R.K. (2004). *The case study anthology*. London: Sage.

Yin, R.K., Bateman, P.G. & Moore, G.B. (1983). *Case studies and organizational innovation: strenghtening the connection*. Knowledge: Creation, Diffusion, Utilization, 1985b (3), 249–260.

Yin, R.K., Bingham, E. & Heald, K.A. (1976). The difference that quality makes. *Sociological Methods and Research*, 5: 139–156.

Yin, R.K. & Gwaltney, M.K. (1981). Knowledge utilization as a networking process. *Knowledge, Creation, Diffusion, Utilization*, 2: 555–580.

Yin, R.K. & Heald, K.A. (1975). Using the case survey method to analyze policy studies. *Administrative Science Quarterly*, 20: 371–381.

Author Index

Harré, R. 1
Hay, R.A. 124
Hatt, P.H. 18
Heald, K.A. 148
Hedges, L.V. 149
Heikema van der Kloet, H.R. 107
Hersen, M. 7
Herweijer, M. 107
Hox, J.J. 102
Huberman, A.M. 10, 15, 53,77, 111,
    115, 122–125, 130

Imai, K.

Jenkins 124, 59

Kazdin, A.E. 7, 150
Kennedy, M.M. 27, 98, 146
Keohane, R.O. 57
King, G. 17, 57, 59
Kops, Y. 144
Kratochwill, T.R. 7, 124
Kreft, I. 102
Kuzel, A.J. 53
Kuckartz, U. 118

Larsson, R. 148, 149
Lecompte, M.D. 50, 53
Lee, Y.S. 11, 118
Levin, J.R. 7
Lewis, C. 118
Lieberson, S. 89-91, 95
Lijphart, A. 14
Lincoln, Y. 19, 36, 117
Lipsey, M.W. 149
Lipset, S.M. 39, 60
Lucas, W.A. 148
Lynd, R.S. and H. 38

MacLeary, R.T. 124
McClintock, C.C. 103
Mellenbergh, G.M. 81
Merton, R.K. 17
Miles, M.B. 10,15, 53, 77,111, 115, 118,
    122–125, 130
Mill, J.S. 89, 90
Mintzberg, H. 27

Moore, Barrington Jr. 91
Moore, W.E. 38

Nall, C. 59
Nichols, E. 89
Niederkofler, M. 66

Padgett, D.K. 142
Paige, J. 91
Patton , M.Q. 53, 70, 108
Plano Clark, V.L. 137, 140
Platt, J. 10
Popper, K.R. 62

Quak, H.J. 106

Ragin, C.C. 15, 19,
    89–95, 134
Raudenbusch , S.W. 102
Richards, L. 118
Rodrik, D. 86
Rokkan, S. 91

Sandelowski, M. 137
Skocpol, T. 89
Shadish, W. 88
Shaw, C. 11
Shontz, F.C. 19
Simon, H.A. 118
Smelser, N. 91
Snijders, T. A. B. 102
Strauss, J.L. 10, 19, 31, 38, 39, 53, 54,
    72, 105, 117, 118, 122
Stein, H. 11
Silver, C. 118
Stake, R.E. 10, 38, 137, 147
Stenhouse, L. 10
Stoecker, R. 18
Swanborn, P.G. 37, 55, 77

Tashakori, A. 140, 143
Taylor, S.J. 117
Teddlie, C. 140, 143
Ten Have, P. 118
Tilly, C. 91
Towl, A.R. 11
Trow, M. 39, 60

Van den Berg, H. 65
Van Gent, W.P.C. 93
Van der Veer, K. 65
Verba, S. 15, 57
Vidich, A.J. 38

Wallerstein, I. 91
Weitzman, E.A. 118
Whyte, W.F. 11

Wilson, D.B. 149
Windsor, D. 11
Wolf, F.M. 149
Woodward, B. 9, 38

Yin, R.K. 9, 10, 12, 13, 15, 34, 41, 46,
    50, 55, 66, 75, 77, 88, 104, 105,
    106, 115, 148

Subject Index

quantitative vs. qualitative research 11, 21
quasi-judicial method 87

random selection 51
rarity of the phenomenon 34
research questions 25–29
revelatory case 51
rhetorical function of reporting 137

selection of cases 45–72
single- and multiple-case studies 15, 21
single-subject research 7
selection on pragmatic grounds 52
selection on substantive criteria 52
selecion on the independent
    variables 54–57

selection on the dependent variable 57
selection on developmental phases 61
selection on a causal relationship 60
selection of critical cases 62
styles of reporting 136

tabulations (limits of) 130–134
target variables 79, 126
theories (use of) 76–77
theories (applications) 126–130
time series analysis 116, 123
triangulation 108

unique case 50

validity (types of) 36